RACE FOR THE EXITS

RACE FOR THE EXITS

The Unraveling of Japan's System
of Social Protection

LEONARD J. SCHOPPA

Cornell University Press
Ithaca and London

First published 2006 by Cornell University Press

Printed in the United States of America

Library of Congress Cataloging-in-Publication Data

Schoppa, Leonard J. (Leonard James), 1962–
    Race for the exits : the unraveling of Japan's system of social protection / Leonard J. Schoppa.
        p. cm.
Includes bibliographical references and index.
    ISBN-13: 978-0-8014-4433-3 (cloth : alk. paper)
    ISBN-10: 0-8014-4433-0 (cloth : alk. paper)
    1. Social security—Japan. 2. Economic security—Japan. 3. Human services—Japan. 4. Japan—Social conditions—1945– .
5. Japan—Economic conditions—1989– . 6. Japan—Social policy. 7. Japan—Economic policy—1989– . I. Title.
    HD7227.S37 2006
    362.952'09'051—dc22   2005025036

Cornell University Press strives to use environmentally responsible suppliers and materials to the fullest extent possible in the publishing of its books. Such materials include vegetable-based, low-VOC inks and acid-free papers that are recycled, totally chlorine-free, or partly composed of nonwood fibers. For further information, visit our website at www.cornellpress.cornell.edu.

Cloth printing   10 9 8 7 6 5 4 3 2 1

For Munakata Miyo

Contents

Figures and Tables

Preface

Because I grew up in Japan, that nation's social safety net—or its "system of social protection" as I call it in this book—has been something I've been observing for almost forty years. In the 1960s, when I first experienced life in Japan as the son of a missionary family in Hokkaidō, the safety net still had some very large holes in it. One family in my father's congregation was headed by a tailor. When the rapid expansion of the apparel industry destroyed his livelihood, his family was left to live in poverty with virtually no help from the state: no unemployment insurance, no pension, no government-subsidized retraining program. Life was hard for many farm families in the area as well, with some still relying on family members to plant rice by hand.

Japan has changed a great deal in the intervening years. By the time I returned to Japan in 1984 to work as an English teacher in Kumamoto, the social safety net was much more tightly woven. Agriculture was thoroughly mechanized and subsidized. When the local school board office sent me to visit a school in a farming area, my workmates told me to expect a sumptuous lunch. The district was among the wealthiest in the prefecture. Meanwhile the boys I had grown up with in Hokkaidō were by this time finishing college or training programs leading to secure salaried jobs. Most of the young men of this generation found "lifetime employment" jobs, with generous pension and health benefits. Even those hired by smaller firms were protected by state policies and economic structures that supplied their employers with stable financing and managed competition in order to prevent bankruptcies.

The girls I grew up with also found greater economic security than their parents had enjoyed, in most cases through husbands they met and married before turning twenty-five. Most are now "professional housewives" (*sengyō shufu*), as the Japanese refer to those who devote most of their time to caring for children and taking care of the home. They too are playing a distinct role in Japan's system of social protection. They provide unpaid care to children and other needy family members in order to allow their husbands to devote most of their waking hours to their employers.

The Japanese system of social protection that grew up between the 1960s and 1984 was in many ways well-suited to its time. It gave generations born in the postwar era a degree of economic security their parents could never have imagined. There were many fewer stories like that of the Hokkaidō tailor's family. A large proportion of the young women of this era *aspired* to be professional housewives, and rapidly expanding firms had a relatively easy time living up to their lifetime employment commitments, so these groups could accommodate the roles they were expected to play. Japan's economy certainly did not suffer, for it grew at rates that surpassed most of the advanced industrialized nations.

Another twenty years have now passed since I worked as an English teacher, and Japan is today a richer country than it was in 1984. Nevertheless, my most recent visits have brought into focus some serious strains in the system I just described—the "unraveling" that is the subject of this book. Many of the daughters of neighboring families I've met during recent stays in Japan are postponing marriage—in some cases because they are frustrated by the sacrifices they would have to make if they did. Others have gone to good colleges and found career jobs but have been forced to give it all up when they've married and had children. Both choices are leaving Japan with a declining supply of workers. Meanwhile the sons in these families have had to work much harder to find employment. Some work as freelancers (*furiitaa*) who are not covered by the lifetime employment system. Many Japanese firms are struggling to keep their heads above water under the weight of a system of social protection that burdens them with high costs and an aging, expensive workforce. This book explores why a nation that built a system of social protection that worked so well for the friends of my youth has failed to reform this system in the face of growing evidence that it is unraveling.

As suggested by these opening remarks, my writing of this book benefited first and foremost from my countless interactions with Japanese friends and families over the past four decades. Although few of them are official sources cited in footnotes, I have endeavored to write a book that is true to their experiences of "real life" in Japan. I thank in particular Munakata Miyo, to whom this book is dedicated. When I moved to Kumamoto in my first year out of college, she was the "Japanese mother" who reintroduced me to the country, and she has continued to be an inspiration to me in my life and work.

Many others, more than can be named here, have also assisted in the preparation of this book. In the early stages, I benefited from the opportunity to share ideas and draft chapters with Karen Cox, Steve Green, Müge Kökten, Arnd Plaage, Herman Schwartz, and David Waldner at the University of Virginia, as well as Mikanagi Yumiko, Ishida Hiroshi, Shirahase Sawako, and Brad Glosserman in Japan. I thank all those who gave generously of their time in interviews and conversations, but especially those who met with me several times, including Yashiro Naohiro, Kawamoto Akira, and Kawamoto Yūko.

As the argument began to take shape, I had the privilege of getting extensive feedback during paper presentations at International Christian University, hosted by William Steele; the University of Tokyo, hosted by Katō Junko; Sophia University, hosted by Nakano Kōichi; the University of Pennsylvania, hosted by Jennifer Amyx; the University of Michigan, hosted by John Campbell; Harvard University, hosted by Susan Pharr; MIT, hosted by Richard Samuels; Columbia University, hosted by Hugh Patrick; the Washington Japan Seminar, organized by Edward Lincoln; the University of Illinois, hosted by Nancy Abelmann; and Cornell University, hosted by Robert Weiner. At each place, my hosts and other faculty, students, and guests contributed ideas and raised questions that helped me improve the book.

The book would have been impossible to write without opportunities to spend time in Japan. A Fulbright Research Fellowship, administered and funded by the Japan-U.S. Educational Commission and the Council for International Educational Exchange, made possible the longest period of fieldwork, in 2000–2001. The faculty and staff at my host institutions that year, at the International Christian University Institute of Asian Cultural Studies and the University of Tokyo Institute for Social Science, were generous with their time and support for my work. I especially thank William Steele and Ishida Hiroshi. A short follow-up research visit was made possible with a grant from the Japan Foundation in December 2002. Additional research support for this project was provided by a Sesquicentennial Fellowship and summer research grants from the University of Virginia, a short-term travel grant from the Association for Asian Studies Northeast Asian Council, and a grant from Shiina Motoo's Policy Study Group in Japan.

Maria Farkas, Watanabe Shino, and David Moore each provided tireless research assistance at various stages of the project, as well as helpful comments on draft chapters. During the final year, I received invaluable feedback from four individuals who read the entire manuscript and offered comments and suggested improvements at a book conference funded by the Japan Foundation Center for Global Partnership: Mary Brinton, Edward Lincoln, Ayako Doi, and Kojō Yoshiko. Additional advice came from Ethan Scheiner and Yamawaki Takeshi, who read specific chapters closely and gave me useful feedback on those parts of the book. Frances Rosenbluth and the other reader for Cornell University Press provided suggestions that further improved the final draft. Roger Haydon lived up to his impressive reputation as an editor authors love to work with. Any errors that remain after all of this feedback are my own.

Finally, in a book about families and how they are protected and constrained by Japan's system of social protection, I would be remiss not to thank my own family— my wife Gabrielle and my daughters Melina and Isabelle. My own experiences of Japan during the last fifteen years have been enriched by sharing my time with them, which has given me a richer sense of how life is experienced there by women and girls.

LEONARD J. SCHOPPA

Charlottesville, Virginia

Conventions and Abbreviations

Throughout the text, Japanese names are written in Japanese order (family name—given name) with the exception of cases in which Japanese authors of English-language publications have listed their names with given name first. Macrons have been omitted in commonly used place names (e.g., Tokyo).

In the text and in notes, Japanese government ministries and agencies are referred to by their official English translations. Note that the names of many ministries and agencies changed on January 6, 2001, due to an extensive reorganization of central government units. In the case of ministries affected by these changes, I refer to the name that was in use at the time of the publication or event referred to in the text (e.g., the Ministry of Health and Welfare before 2001; Ministry of Health, Labor and Welfare after that date).

All translations are by the author unless otherwise noted.

DINK	double-income no kids
DPJ	Democratic Party of Japan
EEOL	Equal Employment Opportunity Law
EHI	Employee Health Insurance
EPS	Employee Pension System
FDI	foreign direct investment
FILP	Fiscal Investment and Loan Program
FSA	Financial Services Agency
IEA	International Energy Agency
JIL	Japan Institute of Labor
JFTC	Japan Fair Trade Commission
LDP	Liberal Democratic Party
LTCI	Long-term Care Insurance
METI	Ministry of Economy, Trade and Industry

MHLW   Ministry of Health, Labor and Welfare
MHW   Ministry of Health and Welfare
MIAC   Ministry of Internal Affairs and Communications
MITI   Ministry of International Trade and Industry
MOF   Ministry of Finance
MOL   Ministry of Labor
NCB   Nippon Credit Bank
NHI   National Health Insurance
NIPSSR National Institute of Population and Social Security Research
NPS   National Pension System
NTT   Nippon Telegraph and Telephone
OECD   Organisation for Economic Co-operation and Development
TEPCO   Tokyo Electric Power Company
TFB   Trust Fund Bureau (of MOF)

RACE FOR THE EXITS

Chapter 1

Exit, Voice, and Japan's Economic Problems

The setting and the topic of conversation could hardly have been more discordant. The restaurant in which we were dining, on the top floor of a ritzy hotel in central Tokyo, featured white linen tablecloths and black-tie waiters. The presentation of the gourmet Chinese food suggested that the chef had trained in France. Yet my host, Kōno Tarō, the son and grandson of Liberal Democratic Party (LDP) cabinet ministers and now an ambitious politician in his own right, was riffing on Japan's economic decline. "Japan is the last socialist country on the planet," he said, "and like the rest of the socialist countries is headed toward collapse." The fault, he continued, lay with his own political party, the LDP, which should actually be called "the Communist Party of Japan."[1]

Kōno is known for hyperbole, so it was tempting to dismiss his analogy as mere theatrics. Yet the more I thought about it, the more valid it seemed. Japan's poor economic performance in the period since 1990 is now well known. After growing economically by an average of 8.4 percent from 1950 through 1973 and 3.5 percent from 1975 through 1990—rates that placed Japan at the top of the growth charts for the industrialized world over both of these periods—Japan has grown by an average of just 1.01 percent from 1991 through 2003.[2] After recording just one year of negative growth over the first four decades of the postwar period (in 1974, following the oil shock), Japanese endured four years of negative real growth in rapid succession, in 1993, 1998, 1999, and 2002. Because of deflation, the nominal economy has grown even more slowly. In 1995, the nation's gross domestic product stood at ¥497 trillion. In 2003, it was exactly the same size: ¥497 trillion. These statistics were not nearly as dire as those experienced in the Soviet Union, but given Japan's record up until 1990, its performance over the past decade and a half ranks with the Soviet collapse as one of the great reversals of fortune of our age.

Less well known outside of Japan is another parallel between Japan's economic system and that of the old Soviet Union: the "socialist" way in which Japan's economic system made sure most Japanese shared in the nation's economic gains. Between 1963 and 1993, the income gap between those in the top and bottom quintiles of the nation's households shrank sharply, from a factor of 5.6 to 3.4.[3] Midway through this period, a famous study by the Organisation for Economic Cooperation and Development (OECD) declared that Japanese levels of income distribution were among the most equal in the industrialized world, just below those of Sweden and Norway.[4] By the 1980s, 90 percent of Japanese routinely told pollsters that they were members of the "middle class."

What was amazing about the Japanese version of socialism was that it was able to build such an effective safety net for society without massive government expenditures—unlike Sweden and Norway, and completely unlike the Soviet Union. Rather than redistributing income through government spending and providing care through public services, Japan built a system of social protection that relied largely on firms and families (especially women) to provide a safety net of income, benefits, and care.[5] Japan's secret was a system of regulations, taxes, and benefit rules that encouraged and enabled firms to offer "lifetime employment" to their core male workforce while encouraging women to care for children and other needy family members. These private actors were expected to help make sure all Japanese advanced economically together, like a convoy of ships moving ahead at a slow but steady pace, with the government providing a naval escort through its regulatory interventions.

Japan's system of "convoy capitalism," with its bank-centered financial system, cartels, and extensive regulations, all carefully managed by the state, has been known mostly for the role it played in facilitating the success of Japanese export industries and the rapid economic growth of the nation as a whole.[6] But this system was also designed to protect vulnerable members of Japanese society, including workers and their families, by keeping firms in business so they could keep their commitments to employees and business partners. Convoy capitalism, like the welfare state regimes of Europe, had productive *and* protective elements that were mutually reinforcing.[7]

This system worked quite well during Japan's high-growth years, producing a "miracle" combination of growth and equity. Yet by the 1990s, like the Soviet version of socialism, the system was in trouble. Not only did national growth slow abruptly but levels of equity declined as well. The income gap between the bottom and top quintiles of the nation's households widened from a factor of 3.4 in 1993 to 4.6 in 1998, reversing much of the progress made over the previous three decades.[8] Many Japanese still had the money to enjoy expensive meals at rooftop restaurants, but many others were struggling to get by. The number of homeless living in Tokyo's parks and other public spaces grew sharply, and high school graduates around the country struggled to find work in a terrible job market.[9] Describing the new inequality trend in Japan as the most rapidly emerging one in the industrialized world, economist Tachibanaki Toshiaki argued that Japan had become one of the most *unequal* nations in the OECD, right up there with the United States and Britain.[10]

Along with the troubling decline in growth and the rise in inequality came signs that it was taking growing sums of taxpayer money to keep the leaky convoy system

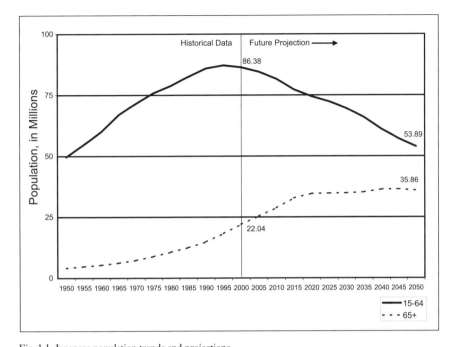

Fig. 1.1. Japanese population trends and projections
Source: Historical census data is from National Institute of Population and Social Security Research, *Population Statistics of Japan* (Tokyo, 2003), 13; projections beyond 2000 are based on the medium-case scenario reported in NIPSSR, *Population Projections for Japan: 2001–2050* (Tokyo, 2002), 12.

afloat. By 1998 it became clear that the banks could no longer carry out their assigned role in the system without taxpayer help. The government attempted to bail out financial institutions in ways that would allow them to continue protecting firms from pressure to restructure, but these bailouts only seemed to buy troubled banks and firms a few extra years. As insolvent firms desperately attempted to maintain cash flow without regard to profits, their excess production contributed to the phenomenon of deflation, which forced the government to ramp up public spending in a desperate attempt to keep the economy from sinking into a deflationary spiral.

By 2000, Japan's public expenditures had risen to almost 37 percent of GDP, up sharply from the level of 30 percent in 1990.[11] Because taxes are kept low to stimulate the economy, the nation is now adding about 7 percent of GDP to its public debt every year—a mountain of debt that had risen to 166 percent of GDP in 2003.[12] All of this is taking place as Japan's aging baby-boomer generation is just years away from retirement, a demographic jolt that is being made worse by the continuing drop in Japan's fertility rate. With the population of working-age adults expected to shrink by 16 percent in the next twenty-five years and another 22 percent by 2050 (see figure 1.1), Japan is entering a period of even slower growth and unstable government finances. Given this precarious situation, it is hard to imagine that just a decade ago Japan was seen as an economic juggernaut threatening the prosperity of the rest of the industrialized world.

What happened? With their system no longer producing growth and equity, why haven't the Japanese made needed reforms and created a new productive and protective system better suited to the new socioeconomic environment?

Kōno's answer is to blame it on the LDP, "the Communist Party of Japan." Blaming Japan's poor economic performance—its lackluster growth and growing inequality—on its politicians is certainly a popular pastime.[13] It has been almost as popular as blaming the failures on Japanese bureaucrats.[14] These simple explanations neglect to take the next step, however, and ask why Japan's politicians and bureaucrats have been so ineffectual. In the Soviet Union, it hardly seems surprising that Communist Party apparatchiks and bureaucratic *nomenklatura*, insulated from society by their firm grip on power, could steer the nation into such trouble. But Japan has a democratic system of government, with opportunities for those frustrated by the status quo to seek change through elections, social movements, campaign contributions, and free expression. Why haven't the Japanese people forced their politicians and bureaucrats to change course?

Firms and Women

This book seeks answers to this question by looking closely at the behavior of two groups that have had the greatest cause to be frustrated with the failing system of convoy capitalism: firms, especially those in export sectors; and women, especially young women eager to live a life in which they have the opportunity to enjoy both meaningful careers *and* the experience of raising children. It is axiomatic in much of the literature on globalization that firms in the traded goods sector—Toyota and Sony, for example, in the Japanese case—should be at the forefront of economic reform movements in their home countries. Because these firms must compete against rivals in other nations, their profits and survival depend on their ability to minimize costs associated with social programs and the protection of sheltered sectors of the economy.[15] While the Japanese system of convoy capitalism was long known for its ability to generate superior growth rates, it also imposed costs on firms. Employers faced restrictions on their ability to lay off workers during recessions, and they had to pay high prices (relative to what their overseas rivals paid) for electricity, financial services, construction, transportation, and retailing because these sectors were sheltered from market forces by extensive government rules and regulations.

For the first several decades after Japan's postwar recovery, the nation's export-oriented firms were able to thrive, despite these costs, because the same system of convoy capitalism protected *them*. International capital flows were strictly regulated, limiting the degree to which Japanese firms had to compete against foreign multinationals in the domestic market, and the government faced few restrictions on its ability to use regulations and trade barriers to protect these firms from international competition. By the early 1980s, however, capital was flowing freely in and out of Japan, most formal trade barriers had been negotiated away, and the government faced threats of trade sanctions whenever it attempted to use its regulatory authority to protect Japanese firms. As a result, firms that had been content to pay high prices in order to play their part in the convoy system, confident that the government would be able to manage competition so that they would not suffer, found that they were exposed. They were still expected to pay the high prices, but the government could no longer protect them from international competition, at least not to the degree it had previously. In this book I look at how these firms responded to their situation and how their responses fed into the policy process.

Women have received much less attention in the literature on economic and welfare state reform.[16] I have chosen to focus on this group, along with firms, because women were the other segment of Japanese society that was heavily constrained by the role they were expected to play in providing social protection under Japan's system of convoy capitalism. Women were expected to devote their primary energies to the care of children and other needy family members, such as frail mothers-in-law. To ensure they were available for this caregiving, and to give firms the flexibility they needed to keep core male workers on the payroll, female participation in the paid labor force was largely confined to part-time and temporary work. Tax policy encouraged women to quit work once they married and had children. Work rules and the limited availability of leave to take care of their children and childcare services made it hard for them to continue in full-time careers after they had children, even if they wanted to do so. Once they quit such jobs, the lifetime employment system, which provided few opportunities for mid-career job mobility, kept them from ever gaining access to the best jobs. Many Japanese women were content with this system, but a growing number began to grow frustrated with the strict assignment of gender roles and restricted job opportunities. In this book I look at how these women responded and how their response fed into the policy-making process.

The key to understanding why Japan has not acted more proactively to deal with the crisis of convoy capitalism is to recognize that these two affected groups, women and firms, were not restricted to a *political* response when they became frustrated with the system. Most studies of economic reform in Japan, reflecting the bias in the broader political science literature, have assumed that all of the action that matters takes place in the political arena. Thus T. J. Pempel argues, for example, that a "regime shift" is imminent in Japan because leading manufacturing firms are much more exposed to trade and tied to international business networks than they used to be. He rightly points out that this change in the business environment has made these firms frustrated with LDP policies that force them to pay high prices and fork over tax money to support sheltered sectors of the economy such as construction and agriculture.[17] He misses something, however, when he takes the next step of assuming that firms would necessarily express this frustration by splitting the social coalition that has backed the LDP for so many years and mobilizing for economic reforms. Faced with policies that have raised their production costs, these firms have frequently taken the option of *escaping* from the problem by relocating operations overseas. If they can "exit" from their problems in this way, why bother taking on powerful opponents of reform in the LDP?

Young Japanese career women, too, have had exit options that have reduced their propensity to mobilize in the political arena to challenge a system of social protection that relies on them, rather than public social services, to care for children. Few have exercised the most extreme exit option (leaving the country, marrying a foreigner, and working for a foreign firm), but a great many have exercised the "partial exit option" of giving up on one part of their work-family goals. Many women who began their working careers expressing a desire to work and have a family have opted out of the struggle to hold onto their careers after having a child, choosing to throw all of their energies into raising their children. A smaller but significant number have given up on marrying and having children. Whichever choice they make, they lose much of the motivation to mobilize for expanded childcare services and changes in benefits and work rules designed to make it easier for mothers to stay in the full-time labor force.

It is my argument that we cannot understand the pattern of Japan's response to the crisis of convoy capitalism without appreciating the complex ways in which these exit dynamics affect the policy process. The overall inadequacy of the response to this crisis, as well as the uneven and reactive character of the reforms that have been implemented, reflects the mix of reform-sapping and reform-inducing effects of exit on policy outcomes. On the one hand, the ability to exit from problems reduces the incentives affected groups have to campaign for improvements in the system. This can result in a perpetuation of failing status quo policies as the political process is left under the control of opponents of reform. On the other hand, when large numbers exit all at once, this uncoordinated individual behavior can create problems that force the government to respond. Thus the decision of many firms to move production operations overseas has created a "hollowing-out problem" (*kūdōka mondai*) that is receiving the attention of government elites. Likewise, the decision of increasing numbers of women to opt out of motherhood has led to a sharp fall in the fertility rate, to a record low of 1.29 in 2003, contributing to a debate over how Japan should respond to its "declining fertility problem" (*shōshika mondai*). The future of Japan's system of convoy capitalism is being determined by varying exit dynamics that have deprived reform movements of energy in most cases but propelled it forward in a few areas.

Exit and Voice

To understand where Japan is going, we need an analytical framework that can help us understand how exit dynamics interact with the political process to produce policy outcomes. The obvious place to start is with the work of Albert Hirschman, whose book *Exit, Voice, and Loyalty* remains one of the few works that genuinely bridges the fields of economics and political science.[18] Hirschman deserves this accolade because he realized that, for all of our attempts to divide the world into economic markets where organizations respond to uncoordinated individual decisions (exit) and political structures where organizations respond to mobilized demands from inside the group (voice), organizations in the real world are confronted by both response mechanisms. Corporations that manufacture automobiles, for example, are organized to respond to the uncoordinated individual decisions of millions of customers to buy or not to buy their products, but they may also be confronted periodically by a consumer movement, led by someone like Ralph Nader, that demands that they make better or safer products. Similarly, labor unions tend to be organized to respond to the mobilized demands of their members, changing course when they are confronted with noisy speeches, letters, petition drives, or campaigns to recall the union leadership. Yet, they are also frequently confronted by the problem of mass defections, or exit. Because all social organizations deal with both exit and voice, social scientists need to think carefully about how these response mechanisms differ and how they interact.

Hirschman provides us with two insights that are critical to understanding the impact of exit on the policy process in Japan. First, exit and voice represent two very distinct mechanisms that organizations respond to when there is dissatisfaction with their performance, each with the potential to spark a turnaround. Exit works quietly, as many individuals react to their dissatisfactions by changing their purchasing behavior, leaving their organization, or tying to escape from negative effects in some other way that involves uncoordinated individual action. The turnaround begins when managers, watching the bottom line, diagnose the problem, propose solutions, and put them into effect. Voice, naturally, involves a great deal more noise as those who are dissatisfied mobilize within the group—attend meetings, write letters, and build coalitions with like-minded individuals—to bring about changes in the group's way of doing things.

This insight suggests that complex social organizations such as states have the capacity to turn around their performance in response to exit, and not just in response to voice. Social scientists have long held that states have their own interests, such as security and national wealth, which shape foreign and economic policies.[19] The managers of the state, the bureaucrats and the top leaders, are in effect responsible for watching this bottom line in the same way that corporate executives watch profit trends. When large numbers of citizens exit from the negative effects of policy in ways that threaten the nation's wealth and security, these managers can be expected to intervene in the policy process in a top-down manner to put into effect reforms designed to return the nation to a richer and more secure path. This dynamic constitutes the upside of exit, its capacity to prompt a turnaround in the performance of states, such as reforms in a malfunctioning system of convoy capitalism.

Hirschman's second insight, in contrast, points to the downside of exit. He argues that in spite of the capacity of both exit and voice to spark improvements in performance, most social organizations are unable to respond with equal effectiveness to both mechanisms. The difficulty arises because the two response mechanisms are so different that social organizations inevitably have to structure themselves to respond primarily to one or the other. Corporations organize themselves to respond to exit by making sure executives receive timely information about what is happening to the bottom line and by empowering them to respond quickly. Democratic states, despite their interest in making sure managers are able to look after the bottom line of wealth and security, inevitably structure themselves primarily to respond to voice, the mobilized demands of social constituencies. This structure suits states fine as long as constituencies frustrated with the performance of their leaders respond by organizing social movements, voting for parties that favor reform, and campaigning for change. It doesn't work very well, however, when frustrated individuals start to exit.

This difficulty is aggravated, Hirschman argues, by the way exit opportunities affect the propensity of frustrated citizens to use voice. When disgruntled individuals have opportunities to escape from the problems created by a given policy, they are less likely to use voice to complain about it. Hirschman called this his hydraulic model: "Deterioration generates the pressure of discontent, which will be channeled into voice or exit; the more pressure escapes through exit, the less is available to foment voice."[20] Democratic states structured to respond to voice will be more likely to turn around in the face of a decline in performance when frustrated citizens with no way out begin communicating their concerns and working together to move the state in a new direction. When frustrated individuals begin opting for exit, states are not likely to respond effectively because exit will reduce the volume of complaining voices that states are listening for. Even if those choosing exit options do so in such numbers that their behavior begins to affect the wealth and prosperity of society, states will tend not to respond as effectively because their structures make them less responsive to this mechanism.

One of Hirschman's examples nicely illustrates how governments confronted by exit are unlikely to respond effectively. Public school systems, he pointed out, give parents dissatisfied with the performance of their schools two options: they can stay and use voice to try to improve their schools or they can exit by sending their children to private schools or by moving to another school district. Since public school systems are democratic structures organized to respond to parents' concerns expressed through the PTA, in school board elections, and in other forms of political mobilization, they tend not to respond very well when parents react to a decline in educational quality by *leaving*. The immediate effect of the departure of disgruntled parents is a decline in the volume of complaints that school leaders hear. Principals and school boards may actually find their lives more restful when the noisy complainers are gone. In time the decline in school enrollment may prompt a response, but because school systems have not traditionally been organized to respond to the exit mechanism, school officials are not likely to respond quickly or very effectively. What public schools are left with, Hirschman suggests, is the worst possible combination of exit and voice: enough exit to draw concerned

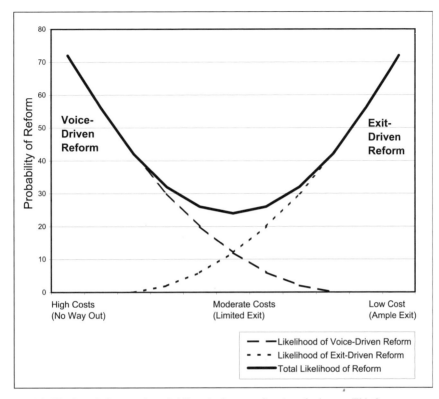

Fig. 1.2. Hirschman's framework: probability of reform as a function of exit costs. This figure assumes that dissatisfaction with the status quo and the costs of mobilizing in the political arena are constant.

parents out of the political debate over how to improve public schools but not enough to motivate needed changes through market forces.

The reason democratic structures such as public school systems are prone to this worst-of-both-worlds situation is because they make available exit options that are *moderately costly,* in the middle of the range of exit costs (see figure 1.2).[21] To take their children out of a public school, parents must either spend thousands of dollars a year on private tuition or uproot their families and move to another school district, in many cases one with much higher housing costs. Because these options may cost a lot, only some parents can afford to leave, and those who do leave tend to do so over a long period of time. Confronted with only a trickle of exit, school administrators accustomed to paying more attention to parent complaints than to enrollment trends are unlikely to respond by making improvements in the school's educational services. Since the immediate result of the departure of the school's most frustrated parents is a diminution of complaints, school officials in this situation are also unlikely to respond to the voice mechanism. With neither mechanism signaling the need for the school administration to change course, the school is likely to continue to spiral downward in its performance.

Hirschman's framework suggests that the performance of the organization would have been much better if the cost of exit was much higher (at the left end of the cost range shown in figure 1.2) or much lower (at the right end). If exit were close to costless, parents would respond to a decline in quality by moving their children quickly and in large numbers or by using the *threat* to pull their kids out of school to demand improvements. Faced with the prospect of seeing their schools rapidly depopulated, school system leaders would have no choice but to improve educational quality in order to win back their customers.[22] Alternatively, if exit were extremely costly, if parents had no choice but to put their children into a given public school, they would respond to a decline in performance by getting more involved in the PTA, calling the principal, and behaving in a determined way until the quality of education improved.

Hirschman's insights and this example show why it is critical to take into account what I call "exit dynamics" in order to understand the pattern of Japan's response to the decline in the performance of its system of convoy capitalism. Barriers to reform in the political system certainly matter, and so does the degree of discontent among those affected by public policies, but what Hirschman tells us is that, holding these factors constant, one can nevertheless get a wide variation in the responsiveness of the system depending on how costly it is to exit. If frustrated individuals have *no way out*, they will mobilize despite the barriers to political action, helping to push through reforms. If they can *escape at moderate cost*, they will be less likely to use voice to call for reform, depriving the voice mechanism of energy—and yet they won't exit quickly enough or in large enough numbers to prompt leaders to institute top-down reforms out of concern for the national interest. Exit will only propel reforms when frustrated individuals can *escape at little or no cost*, generating exit trends that are so pronounced that even distracted leaders will realize the need for action, diagnose the problem, and push through reforms.

Convoy Capitalism Confronts Shifting Exit Dynamics in Japan

The system of convoy capitalism that is the focus of this book is composed of a large number of policies and practices that for several decades fit together neatly in a way that generated economic growth and a remarkable degree of social protection. One of the best known is the practice of lifetime employment, encouraged by labor regulations that make it very difficult for firms to lay off regular employees. Another is the regulatory system that managed competition in a wide range of sheltered sectors, such as electricity and telecommunications, so that firms were able to operate in a business environment where they did not need to worry about sudden price swings that would push them into bankruptcy. A similar regulatory system for financial firms played a particularly critical role in protecting the convoy of banks from financial instability, giving the convoy system its name. The government restricted financial firms to a narrow range of services, set prices, and managed competition so that banks were guaranteed against the risk of bankruptcy themselves and so could afford to enter into long-term main bank arrangements with their borrowers. These policies worked together to provide Japanese firms with a secure and predictable business environment in which they could make long-term relational commitments to workers, suppliers, and distributors.[23]

Another set of policies encouraged women to serve as primary caregivers for their families. Tax and benefit rules subsidized "dependent" housewives by providing them with pensions to which they did not contribute themselves, tax credits, and other benefits that were so substantial they had a strong financial incentive not to boost their annual earnings above ¥1.5 million ($12,500) a year. The limited supply of childcare and eldercare services, and the complete absence of family leave, pushed many women to quit their jobs when they had children or when a family member needed care. Finally, work rules offered little protection to full-time working mothers who needed flexibility to care for their children or frail elderly relatives. In combination, these policies pushed and pulled women into fulfilling a vital role in the system of convoy capitalism: wives were to be available at all times to provide care to family members so that husbands and the state did not have to; and they were to serve as a flexible labor force so that firms could keep core male workers on the payroll when times were tough.

This entire system has come under pressure as a result of socioeconomic changes, in particular globalization and the changing aspirations of women. Firms have been increasingly frustrated by the high prices they have to pay for a variety of inputs, such as labor and electricity, at a time when many of them are less insulated from market pressures than they used to be. They have also begun to worry about the long-term implications of public debt, which has been mounting as the government has struggled to patch holes in the convoy system. Similarly, more and more women have become frustrated with being expected to focus most of their energies on caregiving.

These frustrations should be prompting Japanese citizens to engage in a national debate about how to update their system of production and social protection. How can the burden of caregiving be reallocated between husbands, wives, employers, and the state so that children and the elderly receive high-quality care while both women and men balance work and family life? How can social protection for individuals be maintained without requiring that Japanese firms and the taxpayers pay high prices and subsidies to declining sectors of the economy? If the Japanese were able to debate these questions and arrive at answers, the nation might well be on its way to solving its problems of public debt, lagging growth, rising inequality, and declining population.

Unfortunately, this is a debate the Japanese continue to avoid. The reason women and firms have not forced the country to engage in this debate is because both have found opportunities to escape from some of the most frustrating features of the system. Just as America's urban school systems have suffered as large numbers of parents have taken their children out of them rather than pressing them to improve, Japan is suffering because women and firms have found their own private exit strategies. The problem is that these exit strategies have by and large fallen in the moderate cost range that Hirschman's framework identifies as most problematic. They have consequently failed to spark either an exit- or voice-driven response, while adding to Japan's economic difficulties.

Escaping from high production costs by relocating to China and elsewhere overseas allows firms a way out, but this strategy takes many years and many yen to implement. Because it has taken so long for the extent of the trend to become visible and because the opportunity to exit has made firms less likely to speak up to identify the problems that are driving them overseas, it is only recently that some observers have begun to describe the foreign direct investment (FDI) trend as a "hollowing-out problem." The managers of the state have been trying to figure out what's wrong, but without the support of firms they are having difficulty diagnosing the problem and pushing through controversial reforms.

Similarly, women have found that their partial escapes from the system are not costless. The single and double-income, no-kids (DINK) lifestyles are second choices for most women, who continue to tell pollsters that they would ideally like to marry and have children. Only some of these women have been willing to give up forming families in order to continue in their careers, and they generally only come to this decision after many years of self-questioning. The declining fertility trend that has recently become a national obsession has therefore taken many years to emerge—with demographers predicting as recently as 1997 that the dip in fertility rates was only temporary. Because women opting not to marry and not to have children have made these decisions individually and silently, there has been no young women's movement to define the problem and advocate solutions. Instead, it has been left to bureaucrats to identify the "declining fertility problem," determine the reasons it has emerged, and advocate gender-role changes that some have now concluded are necessary before the trend can be reversed. Without more active support from young women, government officials have found it difficult to grasp the extent of social and policy change that is required, and they have found it even more difficult to accelerate social change.

While the main focus of this book is on these reasons for the slow pace of reform of the system of convoy capitalism, I do not argue that the system is intact—far from it. Key elements of the system have been subject to far-reaching reforms. The extensive liberalization of the financial services sector has weakened a vital pillar of the entire system. The Gold Plans of the 1990s, which sharply increased government spending on eldercare services, and the introduction of the ambitious Long-term Care Insurance (LTCI) program for frail elderly in 2000, combined to guarantee a hitherto unimaginable level of social service provision for senior citizens. Notably, these programs were specifically designed to relieve female family members of much of the burden that used to fall almost exclusively on their shoulders.

These exceptions to the pattern of stasis, I argue, can also be explained by the distinct exit dynamics that have produced very different responses by women and firms affected by these policies. In the case of financial services, firms frustrated by the limited availability and high cost of specific services frequently found that they could exit at little or no cost. All they had to do was book the transaction in London or Singapore or Chicago. The low cost of exit allowed firms to exit quickly and in large numbers, producing the hollowing out of specific financial service markets. The magnitude of the exit behavior and its causes were so obvious that it propelled reform, culminating in the "big bang" reforms adopted in 1996. With the Gold Plans and LTCI, it was women with no way out that helped propel reform. While young women could get around the problem of balancing careers with childcare by opting not to have children, older women who were expected to drop everything to care for frail family members could not easily opt out of having parents or in-laws, or of aging themselves. The inability to exit motivated women to form groups, lobby bureaucrats, and run for office, even winning the support of conservative men in the LDP.

These exceptions, unfortunately, do not signal that Japan's system of convoy capitalism is smoothly evolving toward something new and functional. On the contrary, the uneven patterns of reform driven by varying exit dynamics have helped make the system more dysfunctional than ever. The system is unraveling, and only when the problems of hollowing out, declining fertility, and perhaps the most threatening exit trend of all, capital flight, reach crisis levels will the Japanese be motivated to respond.

What's Ahead

Hirschman subtitled his book "Responses to Decline in Firms, Organizations, and States." Most of the examples in his book are drawn, however, from the first two categories, and his frequent references to "customers," "managers," and "members" seem to have discouraged other scholars from applying his insights to organizations as large and complex as states. Instead, most scholars who study economic and social policy have built their models on foundations laid by two other economists with aspirations to apply their discipline's tools to the study of politics: Anthony Downs and Mancur Olson. From Downs we have models that treat the policy-making process as a "political marketplace," with voters choosing parties and parties choosing policy in ways not dissimilar from the way customers buy goods and firms sell them; whereas from Olson, we have models that assume that concentrated costs and benefits cause political actors to organize and mobilize in the political arena.[24] In neither of these approaches, however, is there much room for voters and other political actors faced with a policy they don't like to *avoid its ef-*

fects rather than acting in the political marketplace. Ironically, these economists and the political scientists who have followed their lead seem to have forgotten that there is a market out there where individuals frequently have opportunities to exit instead of using voice.

Although this book is organized around the puzzle of Japan's poor economic performance, it also challenges the preeminence of Downs and Olson in political science by insisting that we take seriously Hirschman's insights about the "hydraulic" relationship between exit and voice. As I discuss in more detail in chapter 2, political economists studying the effects of globalization and scholars studying women's movements, reflecting the influence of Downs and Olson, tend to focus most of their attention on what is going on in the political arena. As globalization makes the costs of welfare states more salient and social change leads (some) women to grow frustrated with welfare policies organized around male breadwinners, they assume that women and firms will mobilize in the political arena in an effort to change policy. Even if they don't succeed at first because political institutions get in their way, when they get frustrated enough they will mobilize to change these institutions so that they can realize their goals. The assumption that frustrations lead to mobilization makes most of these scholars "optimistic"—if that is the right word given that many analysts of welfare states bemoan the pressures these policies face—that state structures will not remain out of conformance with socioeconomic conditions for long.

Hirschman's observation that individuals frequently have exit options and that their exercise of these options will tend to draw them *out* of the political arena should lead us to rethink those theories and arguments about globalization and women's movements that do not adequately take into account the hydraulic implications of exit. Although the empirical discussion in this book is focused primarily on Japan, chapter 2 makes it clear that if my application of Hirschman's logic to the areas of economic and social policy in Japan helps make sense of the slow and uneven pace of reform there, we should be asking similar questions about other nations. Maybe one reason the U.S., German, and Italian governments have been slow to expand public childcare systems is because career women in those nations too have exit options that take them out of the political process. Likewise, instead of focusing primarily on labor union power to explain why Germany has been slow to introduce more flexibility into its labor market, we should be asking whether the ability of German firms to relocate production to eastern Europe has reduced the vehemence with which they seek reform through the political process.

After drawing out the broader comparative implications of this study, I return the focus to Japan in chapter 3, detailing how the nation's system of convoy capitalism operated before it came under pressure, focusing on its productive and protective features. While much of the literature on Japanese political economy has emphasized the productive advantages of elements such as the main bank system, cross-shareholding, vertically integrated production networks, and government industrial policy, the emphasis in this chapter is on how all of these structures, to-gether with the fragmented system of social insurance and the reliance on women as primary caregivers, also contributed to social protection under the socioeco-nomic conditions of the high growth years.

Yet these conditions inevitably changed. Chapter 4 looks at how socioeconomic changes since 1980, in particular the economic changes captured by the term "globalization" and changes in young women's role aspirations, have caused women and firms to become increasingly frustrated with the system of convoy cap-italism. Although some have responded by mobilizing in the political arena, I argue that the predominant response has been slow, quiet exit through foreign direct in-vestment by firms and declining fertility and departure from the full-time work-force by women.

The next three chapters make up the heart of the book, the exploration of how the uncoordinated exit decisions of Japanese firms and women have affected the policy process. In chapter 5, I describe how long it took for the decisions of firms to exit via FDI to be seen as a hollowing-out problem. When the trend first began, it was actually applauded by bureaucrats, who developed policies to encourage Japa-nese firms to relocate production overseas in hopes this would appease critics of Japanese-style capitalism in the United States, Europe, and Southeast Asia. Even after Japan entered its "long decade" of stagnation, now stretching to fifteen years, Japanese officials hesitated to call FDI a problem. Not surprisingly, this hesitation has blunted exit-driven policy change in Japan. In chapter 6, I examine a series of case studies of labor market reforms, electricity-market reforms, and public-sector reforms. In none of these areas, I argue, did the state respond vigorously out of concern for hollowing out—in large part because the trend emerged slowly and was hard to interpret. Yet the slow departure of Japanese corporations provided enough of a relief valve that it sapped the energy that firms might have devoted to demand-ing economic reforms in the political arena. Without more support from this con-stituency, Japanese officials found it difficult to convince the Liberal Democratic Party to tackle these structural reforms.

Chapter 7 spotlights the features of the system of convoy capitalism that affect women, in particular those affecting their ability to combine work with child rear-ing. I examine how the declining fertility trend has affected the policy process, fo-cusing on the complications that have made it difficult for government officials to grasp the significance of the problem, diagnose causes, and formulate a response. I also examine how the ability to exit affected the women's movement and its role in this policy debate. Finally, I focus on the limited reforms that have and have not been implemented in this area, including childcare leave (as leave to care for one's own children is called in Japan), expanded childcare services, tax and benefit re-forms, and reforms in employment regulations.

In the penultimate chapter I examine the two exceptional cases of far-reaching reform, those in the financial services sector and those expanding services for the frail elderly. I examine the effects of exit dynamics on the reform processes in these sectors and then summarize the lessons from the comparison across cases in this book. Chapter 9 returns to the big question with which we began: Why haven't the Japanese people forced their politicians and bureaucrats to change course? Can we expect them to get the message anytime soon? And is there a way for Japan to reform its system before it faces a true "race for the exits" crisis?

Chapter 2

Taking Exit and Voice Seriously

As befits a topic of such importance to the contemporary world, scholars and policymakers have been engaged in a lively debate about the degree to which globalization, declining fertility, and aging threaten the mechanisms through which advanced industrialized nations provide social protection for their citizens. Some tell us we are doomed to see laboriously constructed social programs cut back and dismantled, with the whole world converging on the U.S. model of unfettered capitalism, while others tell us we can expect a diversity of systems—including systems with generous social protection—to survive. Who's right? What are the implications of these debates for Japan? And what are the implications of this study for these debates?

What I find when I review this literature is that most works focus on "the political marketplace" to the neglect of the economic marketplace that operates alongside it. Global economic changes, demographic shifts, and value changes are seen as drivers of new patterns of political mobilization, typically a realignment of political forces for and against policies that provide social protection. This pattern of realignment is then seen as the driver of systematic policy change.

This literature has not completely neglected the role of exit in the economic marketplace. Scholars who study globalization place a great deal of stress on the role of greater capital mobility (or capital exit) as a factor reshaping social and economic policy. Similarly, some scholars who study family policy have stressed the role of falling fertility rates (another type of exit) as a motivator of policy change. What is notable about this work, however, is that all of it expects the economic and political processes to operate separately, but in tandem, to reshape policy. Capital mobility is expected to *work with* the mobilization of traded goods firms in the political system to push governments to scale back social protection. Falling fertility rates are expected to *work with* the mobilization of women in the political arena to push governments toward adopting more gender-neutral social policies.

If Hirschman is right, however, we can't count on political and economic forces working neatly with each other. Limited exit opportunities, he argued, are likely to draw the most concerned actors out of the political process without generating enough pressure to force leaders to respond. Only when the volume of exit becomes very large and creates obvious problems should we expect a policy response. In this chapter I trace the implications of these insights for the existing literature, questioning the assumptions that underlie various models and proposing that taking exit seriously can help account for some of the gaps between what these models predict and the pattern of policy change actually observed. Particular attention is given to scholarly work that has applied these models to the Japanese case.

Globalization and the Political Marketplace

The literature on how globalization is challenging state efforts to cushion market forces through trade protection, regulation, and redistribution includes an extensive focus on how global economic forces are supposedly driving domestic actors to mobilize for and against economic reform in the political arena. One of the most influential strands of this literature is exemplified by Jeffry Frieden and Ronald Rogowski's chapter in the edited volume *Internationalization and Domestic Politics.*[1] Frieden and Rogowski argue that a decline in the costs of international economic transactions has increased the costs of domestic policies that shelter segments of the economy from global market forces. In particular, local producers that are trying to export goods and services based on a nation's competitive advantage are likely to feel increasingly burdened by policies that protect uncompetitive local manufacturers (raising the cost of inputs), regulate labor markets (raising the cost of labor), and "manage" financial markets (raising the cost of capital). These internationally oriented producers, they posit, will be driven everywhere to mobilize in favor of reforming such policies, taking on the interests that seek to maintain levels of protection. Frieden and Rogowski's argument has been echoed in recent works that have focused more specifically on the effects of globalization on welfare state programs in the advanced industrialized nations. Here too studies have described how the trend toward more intense global competition has led workers and employers in exposed sectors of various societies to promote welfare retrenchment out of fear that growing public expenditures on welfare state programs (and consequent high tax and social insurance obligations) will price them out of world markets.[2]

Most of the literature has been careful, however, not to predict convergence on a single neoliberal model due to these dynamics in the political marketplace. What most authors describe is a tendency toward *political realignment* around issues of economic reform, with the actual outcome of the policy debate depending heavily on the structure of existing policies and political institutions. Paul Pierson, for example, emphasizes that the outcomes of welfare reform debates in the advanced industrialized nations have reflected the distinct coalitions of interests built up around existing welfare regimes. In many European states, especially those with social democratic or Christian Democratic welfare regimes, employers as well as public and private sector workers have developed a stake in maintaining existing levels and forms of social provision. Even employers have consequently been slow to mobilize in favor of welfare retrenchment or labor market reforms.[3]

Broader institutions of national political economies have also been implicated in this literature. Where political authority is centralized and trade unions are weak, Geoffrey Garrett and Peter Lange argue, we can expect more reform. Where "veto points" are numerous, unions powerful, and electoral systems overrepresent voters associated with internationally uncompetitive sectors, the faction opposing economic reform is likely to prevail.[4] Garrett and Lange admit, however, that institutions themselves are subject to change. Consequently, they expect globalization will in some circumstances sweep away institutional barriers to economic reform—a pattern exemplified by the way in which British prime minister Margaret Thatcher worked first to destroy union power before pushing ahead with her neoliberal reform agenda.[5]

As this last caveat on the possibility of institutional change suggests, the literature on globalization and political markets at times verges on the schizophrenic. When reform happens, it is because globalization is driving "exposed" interests to dismantle programs that provide social protection and plowing through institutional barriers when they get in the way. When it does not, it is because institutions and coalitions built up around existing programs are strong enough to deflect pressures to reform. The models provide little a priori basis for predicting which institutions and coalitions will oppose the globalization wave. With a focus on macrocoalitions and institutions, most are also poorly designed to explain variation within nations in the degree to which programs that provide social protection are subject to far-reaching reform.

Given the scattered predictions of the literature on globalization and political markets, it should come as no surprise that scholars seeking to apply insights from these works to the Japanese case have produced conclusions that are all over the map. Frances Rosenbluth, in a contribution to the volume that presented many of these ideas, argues that globalization has tipped the political balance against defenders of the illiberal status quo in Japan. She sees the 1994 reforms in Japan's parliamentary lower house as having been driven by the desire of the traded goods sector to change political rules that were stacked in favor of vested interests. Regulatory reforms in finance and retail in the wake of this reform, she argues, shows that globalization is giving the traded goods sector an advantage in the continuing political battle.[6]

Steven Vogel, in contrast, has built on the same literature and gone in the opposite direction, emphasizing how the structure of interest intermediation in Japan is not at all suited to the emergence of reformist voices. Those who might be expected to lead the reformist bloc (internationally competitive firms, their workers, consumers, and reformist politicians), he argues, are all locked in business partnerships, parties, and interest groups with beneficiaries of current policies. As a consequence, much of the reform talk in Japan has been little more than empty rhetoric. With little change so far in the structure of interest intermediation, he expects illiberal policies to persist despite globalization.[7]

While these two perspectives at least have the virtue of making clear statements about where Japan is supposedly going, T. J. Pempel's book *Regime Shift* manages to reflect all of the schizophrenic qualities of the broader literature in a single volume. Globalization, he argues, has motivated the internationally oriented firms and private sector unions with employment concentrated in these sectors to advocate liberalization more forcefully. At the same time, it has caused the beneficiaries of the status quo (the uncompetitive sectors, firms, and groups) to rally to preserve a system that benefits them. The result, according to Pempel, is growing stress in the Liberal Democratic Party's support coalition that was for many years home to both competitive and uncompetitive business interests. Nevertheless, he is unsure how quickly these globalization-generated forces will produce genuine realignment and reform. He describes how proreform forces have yet to coalesce, and in his conclusion, he imagines three scenarios that encompass the full range of possibilities: from rapid realignment to a continuation of the current "muddied mix" for many years.[8]

Clearly, something connected to globalization is roiling Japanese politics and challenging established social and economic policies. Scholars who study the Japanese political economy have had a difficult time getting a handle on what is happening, however, because they have made the mistake of assuming social actors will respond to tensions between the existing policy regime and the changing international economic environment primarily by mobilizing in the political arena. Like those writing more broadly about how globalization is affecting political economies, and like Downs and Olson who first inspired political scientists to think of politics as "markets," they have neglected to consider how *varying* exit dynamics in the parallel *economic* marketplace affect politics and policy.

Globalization and the Economic Marketplace

I emphasized *varying* in the previous sentence because the globalization literature has actually reserved a place for one phenomenon of the economic marketplace in stories about how globalization is reshaping social and economic policy—but has seen it as a uniform force driving economic reform everywhere. Capital mobility, many argue, has constrained the options available to states that would otherwise like to preserve or expand programs providing social protection. If they raise taxes too high in order to fund generous welfare programs, capital will flee to low-cost locales. If they maintain public service monopolies or economic regulations that buffer sectors of the economy from market forces but push up prices in the process, firms will relocate to other nations that allow them to purchase labor, energy, and services at lower prices. If they try to fight unemployment by lowering interest rates, capital will force a quick reversal when it flees to other locations that offer higher returns. In the classic statement of this genre, capital mobility produces a "race to the bottom."

All of those who write in this tradition argue that exit and the threat of exit by holders of mobile capital reinforce the power of those seeking liberalization in political markets.[9] As Robert Keohane and Helen Milner write, "Owners of capital who can 'exit' can use the threat of exit to magnify their political influence, or 'voice.'"[10] Robert Bates and Donald Lien take specific issue with Hirschman, insisting that he gets it wrong when he suggests that those who cannot or will not exit are more likely to exercise voice. Holders of mobile assets, they insist, will have more political influence because the state needs to be able to tax them in order to pursue the national interest.[11] Although all these authors cite Hirschman, their interpretations are based on a much more simplistic reading of his argument than the one I offered in chapter 1. Bates and Lien base their claim on a formal model that assumes the only alternative to Hirschman's "no exit" situation is one where mobile asset holders have ample exit opportunities such that their departure creates immediate and obvious problems that force the state to respond.[12] They neglect to consider that exit costs span a continuum that includes Hirschman's problematic middle range, where exit is not sufficient to cause immediate and clear problems but is sufficient to sap voice.

Not all scholars writing about capital mobility see it as an irresistible force that is destined to propel all societies down to the neoliberal bottom. Geoffrey Garrett, for example, points to states that have resisted economic and welfare state reform in an era of capital mobility as evidence that some states are better structured than others to resist the demands of mobile asset holders. Yet even he treats mobile capital as a challenge, describing it as a source of pressure that states must resist if they wish to avoid dismantling systems of social protection.[13] Like the authors who see mobile capital as an irresistible force, Garrett does not seem to have considered the possibility that, by providing an outlet for firms upset by high costs at home, capital mobility might actually *sap* the strength of reform movements in cases where the volume of departing capital does not reach the level where it threatens a crisis of capital flight.

This oversight has been shared by analysts who have written about how capital mobility is reshaping Japan's political economy. Henry Laurence, in his book *Money Rules,* offers a careful reflection on how the liberalization of international capital movements has influenced financial market regulation in Japan and Britain.[14] Even he, however, buys into the idea that exit cuts only in the neoliberal direction. In both Japan and Britain, he argues, the liberalization of international capital flows provided domestic consumers of financial services who were dissatisfied with the menu and prices of services available at home with opportunities to shop for what they wanted abroad. Their ability to get around domestic regulations gave them the leverage to demand financial market reforms at home. At the same time, by showing domestic financial service providers that they were destined to lose business if certain regulations remained in place, exit helped convert previously staunch defenders of the old regulatory regime into advocates of reform.

While Laurence is careful to limit his claims to financial regulations, others have made more sweeping claims about how capital mobility is reshaping the political economy of Japan. Pempel, for example, argues in his book *Regime Shift* that the liberalization of capital controls, by allowing firms to rapidly expand FDI and raise capital in foreign financial markets, has "contributed fundamentally to the conservative regime's fragmentation and loss of cohesion."[15] He thus suggests that increased capital mobility has helped turn Japan's internationally oriented firms into vocal advocates of liberalization across the range of economic issues, although he doesn't explain why or offer any evidence to support this link. More recently, Pempel has backpedaled on this point, recognizing in a 1999 article that capital mobility has reshaped Japanese corporate practices while leaving the nation's political structure largely untouched. Like others in the broader globalization literature, however, he continues to insist that capital mobility poses a *challenge* to the regime, explaining away the apparent delay in policy reform by blaming it on the "institutional stickiness" of Japanese politics.[16]

The literature on the Japanese political economy, therefore, shares with more general works the tendency to assume that globalization has unleashed a political and economic dynamic in which exit and voice work in tandem to "challenge," if not overwhelm, the varieties of capitalism that have been erected in advanced industrialized societies since World War II, in particular those like Japan's and continental Europe's that have attempted to protect citizens from the brunt of market forces. Neither in the general literature nor in Japan-specific studies do we see any consideration of the possibility that capital liberalization, by giving firms a way around costly domestic policies, has actually diminished political mobilization in favor of reform in certain issue areas.

Globalization and an Approach That Takes Exit and Voice Seriously

It is time to think more carefully about how the possibility of exit facilitated by capital mobility combines with voice to shape the economic reform process. In this section, I draw on Hirschman's insights to develop a more complex model that does not assume exit and voice always work in tandem. I specify the conditions under which capital mobility is likely to *add to* pressures for reform arising from the fall in the cost of trade, while also identifying conditions under which the exit opportunities provided by capital liberalization are likely to *subtract from* reform pressure. At each step in the development of the model, I also spell out its implications for Japan, specifying what pattern of reforms we should expect to see there if my argument is correct.

The starting point for my model is the same as Frieden and Rogowski's. Like them, I expect the steady decline we have seen in the costs of trade to have increased tensions between "traded" and "sheltered" sectors of the economy. With the range of industries exposed to global competition growing every year due to the falling costs of trade, and with those previously exposed facing tougher competition for the same reason, there is likely to be in every advanced industrialized country a growing coalition of businesses that have reason to be frustrated with policies that raise the price of labor, the cost of taxes and social insurance, and the cost of inputs from sheltered sectors. Because of the rapid elimination of formal trade barriers, the growing scrutiny of informal barriers, and the appreciation of the yen, the frustrations should be at least as strong in Japan as in other OECD countries. Other things being equal, these frustrations should propel firms in traded sectors to mobilize in the political arena in favor of labor market reform, the liberalization of sheltered markets, and welfare state retrenchment.

Where I part company with this conventional wisdom is in the assumption that exit opportunities afforded by capital liberalization are likely to uniformly reinforce this pressure. Capital mobility does not necessarily produce exit-driven pressure for across-the-board economic liberalization, especially in countries with ample domestic savings, low inflation rates, and strong currencies (like Japan and Germany). Hirschman tells us that exit is likely to prompt managers to respond when it takes place in sufficient volume to generate clear problems in the bottom line. Capital liberalization opens the door for exit behavior to create such problems in two distinct ways. When either of these causal mechanisms is operating, exit will indeed work in tandem with voice to accelerate economic reform.

The first causal mechanism is the phenomenon of capital flight. One need only read the headlines during a period like the Asian financial crisis to get a sense of how uncontrolled capital outflows can transform economies and societies. Faced with capital flight and the threat of financial collapse, Thailand, Korea, and Indonesia were all forced to adopt a broad set of reforms: not just macroeconomic adjustments to address payments imbalances but also changes in policies that had protected domestic financial systems from foreign competition, labor market regulations, and government procurement. Even advanced industrialized nations such as Great Britain, Australia, and New Zealand have been forced to adopt neoliberal reforms when international capital has judged their balance of payments positions to be unsustainable and threatened to take flight. These are the episodes featured in works predicting a global "race to the bottom" driven by capital mobility.

Careful consideration of how markets constrain policy in this way, however, tells us that this causal mechanism is likely to come into play only under certain conditions: when states face an imminent risk of defaulting on their sovereign debt or when inflation and currency devaluation threaten to deprive bondholders of the expected rate of return on their investments. Layna Mosley argues that because the chance that an advanced industrialized nation will default on its sovereign debt is virtually nil, the range of policies actually scrutinized by markets in these societies is very narrow. Capital is likely to leave and thus drive up real long-term interest rates only if inflation is rising, currency values are falling, or if markets judge government deficits and debts to have reached a level where inflation is likely in the near future. Short of these points, she finds, market participants have little interest in how states spend their money or regulate the domestic economy. She finds, furthermore, that market participants have extremely short time horizons of just one to three years. Even macroeconomic policies that are unsustainable over the long term, she suggests, will not generate a market backlash as long as policies do not threaten to ignite inflation in the short term.[17]

Mosley also reminds us that the punishment generated by capital "exit," higher real long-term interest rates, cannot dismantle systems of social protection on its own. It has to generate voices calling for cuts in public expenditures on welfare programs, the privatization of public corporations, the liberalization of regulated markets, or other neoliberal reforms. When interest rate increases are modest, voices calling for potentially painful reforms of these types may be slow to emerge. When capital is genuinely spooked, however, we can be quite sure voices calling for these types of reform will follow. Businesses hurt by sharply rising real interest rates and middle-class voters with variable interest-rate mortgages will be at the front of a long line of groups complaining about the pain of higher interest rates. If the falling cost of trade has already generated calls for neoliberal reforms from exposed sectors of the economy, these voices are likely to amplify those calling for relief from the pain caused by capital exit. Finally, we can expect state officials, especially those working in finance ministries, to articulate a vigorous case for neoliberal reforms to stanch the outflow of capital. The threat posed by capital flight in cases like this are well understood by economic officials in all advanced economies, so their expert advice is likely to add to the pressure on politicians to adopt reform policies. For all of these reasons, in this scenario exit and voice are indeed likely to work in tandem in favor of a broad range of economic reforms.

While the reality and threat of capital flight have driven countries ranging from Indonesia and Korea to Brazil and France to adopt reforms, we should not assume that all countries are always subject to this type of pressure just because low barriers to international capital flows *allow* capital to flee if it chooses to do so. Contemporary Japan has no barriers to capital outflows, but because the nation has not suffered from high inflation rates or a falling currency (two of the indexes markets watch most closely), there have been virtually no worries about the risks of a capital flight crisis. In the period since the mid-1970s, Japanese inflation rates have been consistently below those in other OECD nations. Between 1981 and 1995, its currency appreciated more than any other nation's currency. And in 2004, after many years of current-account surpluses, Japan had foreign reserves of $777 billion, equivalent to 20 percent of its GDP.[18] The sum was more than enough to deter investors who might hope to make money by shorting the yen and trying to drive down the value of the currency. Japanese have tended to worry much more about the adjustment costs associated with currency appreciation than about the risks of devaluation.

Japan's performance on the other two dimensions of interest to capital markets has been much less impressive, especially since 1990. Since the collapse of the bubble, the Japanese government has run annual budget deficits, sometimes as great at 10 percent of GDP, and by 2003 it had accumulated gross public debts equal to 166 percent of GDP. This record clearly raises questions about the long-term sustainability of Japan's economic policies: when the debt reaches a point where markets demand an interest rate premium to cover the risk that the government will default, they will force the government to turn to inflation as its only way out. We can expect capital markets *at that point* to serve as a powerful driver of broad neoliberal reforms, but the focus of the markets on a one-to-three-year time frame means this future possibility has not yet constrained Japanese policy. With neither inflation nor currency devaluation serving as a source of worry for investors with money in Japan, the pressure of capital flight has failed to serve as a motivator of across-the-board liberalization in the way it has in some nations.

To understand how globalization is driving economic reform in Japan, therefore, we need to turn to the other mechanism through which capital mobility constrains economic policy: by providing a means for getting around high domestic costs. Even when no net outflows (and consequently no interest-rate effects) are involved, capital liberalization creates opportunities for firms frustrated with the high costs of domestic labor, taxes, and inputs to get around these costs. Manufacturing firms can escape from virtually the entire range of costs by relocating production operations overseas through foreign direct investment. A subset of these costs can be circumvented without even having to go to the trouble of setting up extensive operations abroad. Firms can frequently get around specific high domestic costs by importing goods, outsourcing services, or booking transactions in overseas markets.

While every country with low barriers to international capital flows, including Japan, is subject to this causal mechanism, Hirschman's insights tell us we should not expect these opportunities for exit to produce uniform pressures for reform. Whether exit adds to or subtracts from reform pressures will depend on how cheaply firms can get around specific domestic costs. If they can escape from high domestic regulatory costs at virtually no cost, the volume of exit is likely to be so substantial (and the threats of exit so credible) that it will transform regulatory politics and accelerate economic reform through a process of regulatory arbitrage. On the other hand, if the costs of getting around high domestic prices are moderate, the volume of exit is likely to be smaller and will emerge more slowly. In this case, it will not be sufficient to accelerate reform via the exit mechanism, but the opportunity to escape will be great enough to reduce political pressure for reform.

The first of these processes, that of economic reform driven by regulatory arbitrage, is extensively discussed in the existing literature.[19] Henry Laurence explicates the causal process through which it has propelled financial market liberalization.

First, consumers of financial services (large borrowers and institutional investors) *threaten* to exit, using their enhanced leverage to force financial authorities to authorize cheaper and more varied products. Second, if their threats don't change policy, they go ahead and take their business abroad, creating such a loss in business for domestic providers of financial services that these previous beneficiaries of regulatory protection go to the authorities and ask for the policy changes needed to allow them to win back the lost business. And third, financial authorities themselves become concerned that the outflow of financial transactions is causing a hollowing out of domestic money markets and move to implement regulatory changes designed to bring the business back.[20]

Unfortunately, the existing literature has largely neglected the other possibility suggested by Hirschman's logic: that exit opportunities can deflate political pressure for reform without generating sufficient market pressure to bring about reform through that mechanism. Hirschman warns us that this outcome is likely when both exit *and* voice are options, but where both are costly. In cases like this, those with the greatest concerns about the high cost of a regulated good or service will be the first to exit, since they will be the ones who are willing to pay the costs of escaping to another jurisdiction. This exit will take some business away from domestic providers, but if the cost of exit is high, only a few will leave and providers will have little incentive to mobilize to remove regulations or implement other reforms that will deprive them of the rents they can earn on the remaining captive domestic customers. The situation with costly exit will actually be worse, Hirschman argues, than one where society has no exit option, because in the latter case those most concerned will mobilize to try to improve the situation.

What Hirschman's logic suggests is that globalization actually *reduces* the likelihood that states will liberalize their economies when firms' only way around high costs of labor, taxes, and specific inputs is to move their production operations overseas or to escape in some other costly way. In Japan's case, for example, it suggests that the ability of high-volume electricity users to get around high domestic prices by relocating abroad (or building their own self-generating capacity in Japan) is likely to have *reduced* the likelihood that consumer interests would prevail in the political marketplace. Those most concerned about high prices will leave, rather than investing resources in a long-shot campaign to liberalize electricity markets. But because exiting in these ways is so costly, the number of consumers leaving is small enough that Japanese utilities do not ask for liberalization in order to win them back. Limited exit is unlikely to bring consumer or producer interests around to the point where they raise their voices in support of reform. Neither is it likely to generate concerns about a hollowing out of the electricity market on the part of government officials.

In summary, taking exit and voice seriously leads us to recognize that globalization is unlikely to produce economic reform everywhere or in all sectors. In a situation in which capital is prone to flee, threatening to raise real long-term interest rates unless states adopt a package of neoliberal reforms, there is the potential for far-reaching and broad changes in systems of social protection. In places where capital mobility merely creates a conduit for a variety of international transactions, however, we should expect a much more issue-specific pattern of reform. More concretely, we should expect rapid liberalization in areas where the cost of conducting transactions abroad has fallen to near zero, whereas we should expect much less reform in areas where firms have to move entire operations overseas at high cost in order to secure cheaper, less-regulated inputs.

Changing Gender Role Expectations and the Political Marketplace

The other major challenge to national systems of production and social protection examined in this book is the one posed by changing gender role expectations on the part of women. As women across the industrialized world have expanded their role expectations to encompass opportunities to work as paid employees, they have run headlong into socioeconomic structures that were built on the assumption that men would be the primary breadwinners.[21] Social insurance systems in many countries privilege full-time, regular employees, under the assumption that by covering these workers, mostly male heads of household, they are covering women and children as dependents. Programs designed to protect labor rights similarly tend to privilege prime-age male workers by squeezing out women, young, and older workers when recessions reduce the number of jobs available. Compounding this gender bias are childcare and eldercare programs with limited benefits; work rules that, in many countries, provide only limited time off from work for those with young children or dependent elderly relatives; and biases on the part of husbands and their employers that limit the time husbands devote to caregiving and household chores. All of these deficiencies pressure women to give up full-time, regular employment when their care "duties" exceed what they can provide.

As a consequence of these gender biases, women in many advanced industrialized societies face unprotected risks when they choose to have children. While men are generally protected against the risk of losing their jobs and becoming disabled, women frequently enjoy only modest protection from the risk that, after giving up career employment, they will suddenly have to support themselves and their children because their husbands have divorced them. In most countries, couples with children also must accept a reduction in income, since the need to care for them tends to reduce full-time employment opportunities and associated benefits for at least one spouse, usually the wife.

The gap between the new needs for social protection arising from changing gender role expectations and the levels and types of protection provided under established policy has driven women in many societies to mobilize in the "political marketplace" for changes in social policy designed to provide them with protection suited to their preferred life course. This trend has been thoroughly analyzed in the extensive literature focusing on women's movements in the advanced industrialized nations. Joyce Gelb, for example, describes how women in Sweden campaigned in the 1960s for expanded high-quality, state-provided childcare that would make it possible for them to continue working after having children, while women in the United States fought for laws protecting them from employment discrimination. In both cases, women hoped that by enhancing their ability to work and hold on to jobs, they would improve their economic security.[22]

While emphasizing the common trend toward reforms addressing the concerns of women in most advanced industrialized nations, this literature has also emphasized cross-national differences in the goals of women's movements and in the degree to which they have succeeded in transforming policies and norms that limit their economic security and constrain their ability to make their own choices about how to combine work and family. Recent works on the gender implications of social policy regimes, for example, contrast the way "liberal" welfare states such as the United States and Canada protect women by securing "gender neutral" employment rights with the way the Swedish welfare state protects women by providing them with the social services and work rules they need because they are women: childcare centers, childcare leave, and part-time work with full-time benefits. Each of these models, they emphasize, is in turn distinct from those found in Germany, Italy, and other continental European countries where the social programs are designed to protect women by reinforcing the breadwinner role of men.[23]

Scholars who have sought to explain this cross-national variation have tended to focus on differences in societal organizations and political institutions, much like their counterparts studying the effects of globalization. Gelb, for example, emphasizes how Swedish women's successful campaign to expand public childcare services grew out the "political opportunity structures" provided by powerful unions, the Social Democratic Party, and sympathetic bureaucrats—whereas different structures led women in the United States to focus on equal opportunity employment rights.[24] Julia O'Connor, Ann Shola Orloff, and Sheila Shaver similarly point to differences in political opportunity structures, as well as ideologies, in explaining differences between Australia, Canada, Great Britain, and the United States.[25]

In much the same way, scholars who have analyzed the women's movement in Japan have stressed the inhospitable political opportunity structures and ideological climate facing efforts to change the system. Susan Pharr describes how women's efforts to protest their working conditions have been constrained by a political culture that has restricted the range of demands they can make and the tactics they can employ.[26] Frank Upham stresses the hostility of the Japanese bureaucracy and the legal regime.[27] Finally, Mikanagi Yumiko points to the ways in which the long-dominant Liberal Democratic Party—which has few female legislators and many traditional conservatives among its leadership—has watered down reform initiatives such as the 1985 Equal Employment Opportunity Law.[28]

While this extensive cross-national and Japan-specific literature on women's movements has identified some important political variables affecting how societies are modifying their systems of social protection to reflect the changing role expectations of women, the explanations do not adequately account for the forces that shape the varying goals of women's movements and motivate women to join them. It is harder to accept, for example, that women in Scandinavia chose to campaign for public childcare services while those in the United States chose to prioritize employment rights legislation primarily because the political opportunity structures controlling access to the policymaking process in those states differ. Likewise, since women in all the advanced industrialized nations have grown frustrated with social structures that assign rigid gender roles, it is hard to accept that women in some nations (such as Japan) have hesitated to challenge these structures as aggressively mainly because they face a hostile political environment. Something closer to the life experiences of these women must be shaping their preferences and their propensity to mobilize in the political arena.

Approaches centered on the goals of women's movements and the barriers they face also have difficulty accounting for the decisions of some male-dominated states to embrace progressive social policies that aim to relieve women's care-giving burdens and bring them into the workforce, such as those seen in Sweden in the 1930s and France in the 1960s.[29] Theories aimed at explaining the cross-national pattern of reforms in breadwinner-based systems of social protection should be able to account for top-down reform processes dominated by male bureaucrats and policy experts.

These weaknesses in explanations centered on the political marketplace can only be addressed by reflecting on how the preferences of various actors involved in the policy process are affected by women's individual, uncoordinated *exit* options in the "economic marketplace." Hirschman's approach reminds us that we should not assume that women, faced with a system of social protection that doesn't fit their work and family aspirations, will simply choose between political action and no action. They may seek to escape the effects of the offensive policy regime through one of several exit strategies.

In extreme cases, some women may choose emigration if they feel other societies provide them with better opportunities. Others may marry foreign men or go to work for foreign multinationals. Finally, some women who would ideally prefer to work full time *and* have children may choose to give up one or the other part of their ideal life course. These final strategies do not constitute complete exit since they involve submitting to the forced choice imposed by the established regime, but they do constitute a partial exit. Giving up on marriage and children in order to pursue career opportunities can allow women to assure their economic security through the income and benefits associated with full-time work and to avoid the unpaid care-giving burdens associated with marriage (eldercare for in-laws) and motherhood (childcare). A woman who makes this exit choice can at least avoid these burdens, dependencies, and risks, even if she is forced to sacrifice marriage and the experience of parenting a child. Conversely, a woman who exits her career in favor of marriage to a partner who has breadwinner job security can at least rely on these indirect sources of social protection even as she sacrifices the autonomy that she might have enjoyed had she been able to sustain her career.[30] Partial exit opportunities give these women fallback options they would lack if they faced poverty and immediate exposure to the risks of the marketplace as their only alternative to political inaction. Our theories linking women's movements to policy change need to take account of the fact that some women have these fallback options in the economic marketplace.

Changing Gender Role Expectations and the Economic Marketplace

Two strands of literature, in the fields of demography and labor economics, look at the implications of women's actions in the economic marketplace. Both strands, however, fall into the trap we observed in the globalization literature on the effects of mobile capital. They assume that exit and voice work separately but *in tandem* with the women's movement in the political arena to *accelerate* the pace of change in social policy.

The first of these literatures looks at what happens when large numbers of women start choosing the exit option that involves reducing the number of children they bear. If enough women in a given nation respond this way, the result is an abrupt fall in that nation's fertility rate. Demographers and some analysts of family policy have noted that unusually low fertility rates have played an important role in motivating family policy innovation in some countries. In France, for example, fertility rates persistently lower than England's and Germany's led to a broad-based pronatal movement. The leading pronatal group, with over thirty-five thousand members during World War I, published posters depicting a shrinking French military facing a growing German one and urging the government to implement a strongly pronatal family policy.[31] In Sweden, Alva and Gunnar Myrdal published an influential book pointing to the nation's "population problems" and urging changes in family policy, in this case easier access to birth control along with expanded social benefits, designed to increase "voluntary parenthood."[32] In each case, governments responded to these pleas by setting up study commissions charged with recommending policy responses. Family policy changes were then implemented. Historical examples like this suggest that if women opt out of motherhood in sufficient numbers in response to policies and social norms that give working mothers little support, this uncoordinated "economic" behavior can work in tandem with social movements in the political arena to bring about policy changes that respond to their needs.

The second strand of literature focuses on what happens when many women choose to withhold their labor from the labor market in order to devote their energies to the care of their children. Labor market economists tell us that under tight labor market conditions, such behavior creates pressure on employers to offer higher wages, improved work conditions, and enhanced benefits (such as subsidized childcare) in order to bring women into the workforce.[33] It can also lead them to become advocates, alongside women's organizations, of expanded public childcare centers, childcare leave benefits, and other changes in the system of social protection designed to make it easier for women with children to enter the paid workforce.

Economists such as Yashiro Naohiro have applied insights from demographics and labor economics to the Japanese case in arguing that the government *should* respond to the continuing birth dearth and the looming labor shortage by making it easier for women to combine full-time work with child rearing.[34] Government reports such as the Ministry of Health and Welfare's 1998 white paper on *Thinking about a Society with Fewer Children* have echoed these recommendations.[35] Ito Peng, in her recent work on welfare state restructuring in Japan, argues that concerns about demography and a future labor shortage actually have played an important role in propelling reform forward over the past fifteen years.[36]

In both the cross-national and Japan-specific literatures, however, the operative assumption has been that women's actions in the economic marketplace—having fewer children, withdrawing from the workforce—cumulate in ways that reinforce their demands in the political arena. No one seems to have considered the possibility that women who have exited from careers or families may subsequently be less interested in reforming systems in ways that make it easier for the next generation to "have it all."

Changing Gender Roles and an Approach That Takes Exit and Voice Seriously

How exactly should we expect women's exit decisions to affect the public policy process? Anne Gauthier, who has written on a range of cases in which demographic concerns have influenced family policy over the past century, nevertheless cautions that we should not assume that low fertility rates automatically produce policy change. For one thing, the link between population and military power that motivated early French pronatalism—and similar movements in prewar Japan and Germany—has largely disappeared in a postwar environment where population is no longer the critical ingredient guaranteeing military superiority. While the French have subsequently shifted their concerns about population to economics (the need for workers), the linkage here is more complex. On the one hand, a shrinking workforce threatens to retard economic growth and make it difficult for governments to finance social programs for the elderly. On the other hand, a shrinking population promises long-term ecological benefits, and even the aging societies we can expect in the interim may not be as great a problem as some warn because the elderly make important contributions to the economy.[37] Gautier sums up the postwar debate as follows: "The population question is therefore a complex one, and no unanimity has been reached among scholars. . . . This disagreement has led most governments to be very careful in their interpretation of the new demographic situation."[38]

Gauthier points to two additional complications that have stood between fertility trends and a policy response in many countries. First, perceptions in many societies that decisions about whether to have children should be a private concern keep governments from adopting explicitly pronatal policies. These concerns have been especially pronounced, Gauthier reports, in nations such as Germany and Italy that adopted aggressively pronatal policies before and during World War II on explicitly militarist grounds.[39] The Japanese policy debate has been similarly influenced by the legacy of that nation's prewar pronatalism. Second, family policy change has been slowed by concerns about the high costs of reforms and uncertainty about the benefits: the number of additional births that societies can expect in return for these expenditures.[40]

Disagreements about how to interpret labor market trends, cultural attitudes, and cost-benefit analysis have also stood in the way of policy responses to labor shortages that have been aggravated when women with children take themselves out of the workforce. Like the decision to have children, a woman's decision about whether to continue working after having children has been considered a private one in democratic societies, leaving governments hesitant to aggressively pull these women into the workforce. In many societies, cultural attitudes that view the breadwinner father with a stay-at-home mother as the ideal family structure have stood in the way of policies that would draw these women into the workplace. Finally, some societies have balked at the high costs of providing the childcare leave, childcare, and employment conditions needed to draw women with children into the full-time workforce.[41]

All of this reminds us that women's decisions to exit by not having children or leaving the work force, though holding the *potential* to motivate policy change by creating a variety of economic problems, must nevertheless be communicated through the political process. Policymakers must be convinced that women's exit decisions—the resulting fertility decline or labor shortage—constitute a "problem" that can be solved in ways that are cost-effective and do not violate anyone's privacy rights. When women's exit decisions are the primary factor motivating a policy response, policymakers (in many cases male bureaucrats and politicians) must overcome these thresholds on their own: defining the problem, proposing solutions, and mobilizing political support for change. We should expect these tasks, in all societies, to constitute a significant barrier to a policy response. Policymakers should have a much easier time shepherding policies through the legislative process when they are assisted by an active women's movement that helps them define the problem, proposes solutions, defends these ideas against those who question the legitimacy of government intervention, and puts its political muscle behind the initiatives.

The relationship between women's exit decisions and their propensity to mobilize for political action is thus critical. Studies of family policy up to this point, including Gauthier's, have treated women's movements and demographic problems/labor market shortages as two distinct inputs into the policy process. What if they are connected?

Hirschman's insights suggest that we cannot count on exit to work only in favor of policy change. Exit opportunities are likely to draw out of the process those women most motivated to change policy to make it easier to combine career with family: the young women with ticking biological clocks who strongly wish to continue their careers but also would like to have children. These women should be the leading candidates for rejuvenating women's movements in societies that continue to make it difficult for women to achieve this dual goal. Those women who partially exit from this dilemma by giving up one part of their goal or the other, however, are likely to be much less interested in changing society after this decision is made. Those who choose to give up careers are unlikely to be interested in expanding day-care centers they will never use themselves. Likewise, those who choose to give up families are unlikely to be any more interested in daycare than their stay-at-home sisters.

Of course, if *all* young women had relatively easy exit options of this kind (if they could provide adequately for their economic needs without too much loss of autonomy by choosing to be full-time housewife-mothers or careerists without children), the exit "problems" created by such a broad-based change in behavior might be large enough to generate a policy response on their own. A plunging fertility rate and acute labor shortage would likely motivate policymakers to do everything they could to reverse these trends even without a women's movement. We should expect family policy to respond to mass exit of this kind in the same way economic policy responds to large-scale capital flight.

At the other extreme, in a situation in which most women find exit to be impossible or prohibitively expensive, we should also expect a policy response—in this case driven by a political movement motivated by women with no way out. Women who find it economically necessary to work and who already have children, for example, are likely to be at the forefront of political mobilization to make their balancing act easier to sustain. And even career women who opt not to have children are likely to face greater difficulty turning their backs on their elderly mothers and fathers when their parents suddenly need home care. The greater difficulty in "exiting" from this latter challenge should produce more vigorous political mobilization to address the need for eldercare support than to address the shortage of childcare for children.

In contrast, political mobilization is likely to be least intensive when women have *limited* exit options. Exit will in this case draw out those most motivated to change society without producing the plunging fertility rate or labor shortage necessary to prompt policymakers to initiate reforms on their own. A minority of women who originally hoped to have children will give up on that plan. Another subgroup will give up on careers and leave the full-time workforce. Neither of these groups of women will mobilize to bring about the far-reaching changes needed to bring a career-and-family life course within reach of the next generation.

Applying Hirschman's insights to the Japanese cases suggests we should see variation across issue areas (childcare versus eldercare) and across time in the ways in which exit and voice interact to generate pressure for change. In Japan, the ability of women to opt out of being a wife and mother was limited for many years by social pressures and employment discrimination that forced most women to give up careers. Some who wanted badly enough to have a career and were willing to give up marriage and children, however, *were* able to pursue careers. As these opportunities opened to more women without children in the 1980s, Japan was left with a classic limited exit situation. The exit-voice approach employed here suggests that this situation should have produced little policy change because the nation should have seen neither the political mobilization nor a steep enough fall in fertility rates necessary to propel social policy changes.

Whether trying to explain economic reform policies or to explicate the process leading to varying family policies across the advanced industrialized nations, political scientists have tended to focus on the political marketplace to explain policy outcomes. If economic reform is proceeding rapidly in response to globalization, it is because changes in the global economy are driving societies and political systems to realign in ways that accelerate liberalization, privatization, and retrenchment in social programs. If economic reform isn't happening, that is attributed to barriers in the political system. Similarly, where progressive family policies have been adopted, these have been widely attributed to political opportunity structures that have facilitated the efforts of women's groups to shift social policy away from the male-breadwinner approach. Where societies have stubbornly resisted moving away from this model, the blame has been put on hostile political opportunity structures.

These studies are not completely off base. Some political systems *are* more hostile to the representation of women than others. Globalization *has* created incentives for business groups to take a hard look at the costs of welfare state programs. Where I find fault with these conventional political science models and the way they have been represented in recent works on Japan's social and economic policy is with their assumption that citizens and firms that are frustrated with policy can only respond by mobilizing (or not mobilizing) in the political arena. If it is true, as Hirschman argues, that frustrated individuals frequently have exit options, and policy outcomes are affected by the exit choices citizens make, models that neglect these dynamics are liable to misinterpret what is going on. Perhaps the slow pace of economic reform or family policy reform that is being attributed to hostile political structures is also (or instead) a result of what I have called "limited exit dynamics," in which the most frustrated are drawn out of the political process by the availability of uncoordinated, individual coping strategies in the economic marketplace. Or perhaps the inverse it true: the fast pace of economic or family policy reform that is being credited to an amicable political structure is also (or instead) a result of exit dynamics I have labeled "no way out" or "ample exit."

Unfortunately, analysts who *have* focused on the impact of uncoordinated individual behaviors on economic and social policy—including those who have examined the effects of capital flight, declining fertility rates, and labor shortages—have only considered the role these phenomena can play in *accelerating* policy change. Ironically, many of these works have cited Hirschman without appreciating the implications of his observations about how limited exit can work against a timely or effective response to the voice mechanism. What has been missing is a recognition that exit dynamics can *vary* in ways that have systematic implications for the way policy is made.

In this book I focus on Japan's struggle to adapt its system of convoy capitalism not only because the nation's difficulties pose an interesting puzzle—Why haven't the Japanese people forced their politicians and bureaucrats to change course?—but also because taking a close look at reforms across a number of domains in a single country gives us an opportunity to explore the impact of varying exit dynamics. As summarized in the first part of this chapter, capital mobility has created opportunities for firms to get around the costs of various domestic regulations, but at different costs. Financial regulations can sometimes be skirted at virtually no cost by booking transactions overseas. In contrast, firms seeking to avoid high electricity costs must relocate entire production operations overseas (or build their own generating capacity), in either case at great cost. Similarly, in the second half of the chapter I described how Japanese women at various stages of their lives face quite different opportunities to exit from family care responsibilities: young women can opt out of having children; middle-aged women with aging frail relatives have not been able to opt out of having parents.

In all of these cases, the women and firms frustrated with these various components of convoy capitalism have had to confront the same political structure. Over the entire time period examined in this book, with the exception of 1993–94, the political system has been dominated by the heavily male, heavily clientelistic Liberal Democratic Party. While Japan adopted electoral reforms in 1994, these had only begun to change political behavior by the first years of the twenty-first century.[42] If the outcomes of reforms across these sectors vary according to their exit dynamics, despite the similar political structure, we will have strong evidence that political science theories need to be modified to take account of this factor. Not only those who study Japan but also those who study Germany and Italy and the United States will be on notice that they need to take exit and voice, and their interactions, seriously.

Chapter 3

Productive and Protective Elements of Convoy Capitalism

In 1980, Japan devoted just 10 percent of its GDP to public and mandatory private programs designed to protect the nation's citizens from risks inherent in modern society: the risk they would lose their jobs, that they would outlive their savings in old age, or that they would require expensive medical care due to illness. This level of expenditures placed Japan at the very bottom of the G7, lower even than the United States, which devoted 14 percent of its GDP to social expenditure in that year. Japan's expenditures were much less than those devoted to these purposes by welfare states in Europe, whose shares ranged from 18 percent (Britain and Italy) to 30 percent (Sweden).[1]

And yet Japan managed to provide for its needy citizens quite well. Visitors from the United States and Europe were quick to note the absence of pockets of poverty in Japan of the type seen in blighted urban neighborhoods and depressed rural areas of their own countries; homelessness was virtually unheard of; the distribution of income was among the most equal in the world; and with access to medical care under national health insurance, the nation's citizens enjoyed the longest life expectancies in the world. As commentator Nakagawa Yatsuhiro declared in 1978, Japan was a "welfare super-power."[2]

The secret behind Japan's ability to provide such a high level of social protection with so little government outlay, Nakagawa argued, lay in the "amazing efficiency of the Japanese people."[3] Indeed, looking at Japan in the 1980s, one could not help but be impressed with what the nation had achieved in the years since its defeat in World War II. Not only Nakagawa but also American observers like Ezra Vogel in his book *Japan as Number One* stressed that Japan's economic achievements were not limited to its rapid economic growth rate. What was even more impressive was that Japan had achieved such rapid growth while spreading the benefits quite widely, and that it was able to provide this protection in ways that actually made the society more productive.[4] These themes were to be repeated in dozens of books extolling the Japanese economic miracle during the remainder of that decade.[5]

Reading these glowing accounts twenty-five years later, after Japan has been through fifteen years of economic stagnation and after the income gap between rich and poor has begun to widen, one cannot help but wonder whether it was all a mirage. Were we right to call Japan a "welfare superpower" in those years? What happened to the vaunted "efficiency of the Japanese people" that allowed it to protect citizens while spending much less than the amount required for this purpose in other advanced societies? And what happened to the vaunted synergies between production and protection that were supposed to operate under the Japanese model of capitalism?

What Japan achieved by the 1980s *was* real. Most Japanese enjoyed meaningful protection from threats to their ability to provide for their own needs, and the Japanese came up with a formula for providing this protection at a bargain price and in a way that made the society more productive. But these achievements were contingent on the existing socioeconomic conditions.

Japan was able to offer generous protection at a low cost because, up through the 1980s, the nation's firms and women were willing and able to carry a significant share of the load for "free." When women stayed home from work to care for elderly relatives and when firms chose not to lay off workers during recessions, these actions helped provide income and care for the needy without the expenditure of a single yen by the state. The same held true when the government kept agricultural markets closed to imports (raising the incomes of farmers who otherwise would have been much poorer) and helped make sure banks and large industrial firms avoided bankruptcy by managing competition through the use of regulations. Although these "secrets" made it possible for Japan to provide social protection on the cheap, they also defined the limits of this arrangement. When women and firms were faced with circumstances that made them less able or willing to carry their share of the load, and when globalization imposed limits on the government's ability to keep the convoy moving steadily ahead, the system was no longer able to provide protection at a bargain price.

Likewise, the Japanese version of capitalism for many years provided protection in ways that facilitated production. Lifetime employment, while protecting workers from the risk of unemployment, encouraged firms to invest in training and human capital. It also encouraged workers to cooperate with efforts to incorporate labor-saving technology into the workplace, secure that they would share in the productivity gains firms enjoyed as a result. The main bank system, with deep and reliable credit lines, allowed firms to extend increasingly generous social benefits to workers in good times and keep them on the payroll in slow times, but it also provided extensive capital for investment in long-term growth along with a mechanism for monitoring management and assuring that this capital was being put to good use. Finally, convoy regulatory protection by bureaucrats relieved firms of the risk that "excess competition" would drive them out of business, once again encouraging them to make long-term commitments to workers even as they invested heavily for growth. These synergies also depended on socioeconomic conditions that constrained exit by firms and women and encouraged the use of voice.

The Limited Direct Role of the Japanese State in Providing Social Protection

The Japanese state's role in protecting citizen welfare has been hard to classify, given the standard "liberal-residual," "conservative-corporatist," and "social democratic" categories. Gøsta Esping-Andersen, whose categorization scheme is the most widely cited, originally classified the Japanese welfare regime as lying near the "liberal-residual" model on some dimensions while being located near the "conservative-corporatist" model on others.[6] More recently he classified it as a "hybrid" still in the process of finding its home.[7] John C. Campbell, a leading scholar of the Japanese welfare state, points to the generous provision of health care and pensions for the elderly and argues that Japan's welfare regime resembles to some degree those found in the social-democratic Scandinavian countries.[8] Müge Kökten, in contrast, emphasizes Japan's meager spending on employment-related social policies, describing its efforts in this area as even more residual than those in Britain and the United States.[9]

The difficulty categorizing Japan's system of social protection grows out of its extreme dualism. By the 1980s, public employees and core workers employed by large firms enjoyed job protections and social benefits comparable to those of workers in Germany and in other corporatist systems in Europe. But these workers made up barely a third of the workforce. Those employed by small firms, those working on a part-time or temporary basis for larger firms, as well as self-employed farmers and shopkeepers, were all excluded from the most generous social benefits. These groups of workers enjoyed few job protections and were covered by programs that offered much lower benefits. Rather than directly providing all citizens, or even all workers, with generous social protection, the Japanese state had come to play what was mostly an indirect role: propping up large firms so that they could retain their core male employees and continue extending generous social benefits to their workers, while offering regulatory and trade protection to those employed in small firms and on farms.

The extent of this dualism is suggested by Toshimitsu Shinkawa and T. J. Pempel's description of benefits typically provided to core workers in large firms:

Many Japanese firms spend considerable sums to create, if not cradle-to-grave socialism, at least its hiring-to-retirement equivalent. They provide subsidized housing, housing allowances, and/or down-payment loans for new homes; transportation allowances; medical facilities for employees and their families; in-plant canteens, barber shops, nurseries, and discount shopping centers; organized company vacation spots at ski centers or hot springs; child care allowances and often on-site nurseries; as well as company picnics, athletic clubs, marriage brokerage facilities, cultural clubs and libraries. In addition, the best programs provide generous insurance schemes and retirement plans.[10]

The authors report that in the 1980s occupational welfare programs such as these typically added 21 percent to the wage bills of firms employing over five thousand workers.[11] Smaller firms, in contrast, could not afford to give their workers social benefits of these types, so these workers had to rely on the much more limited benefits provided directly by the state in its "residual" programs.

The Pension System

The gap between the benefits available to core workers in large firms and those available to the rest is best illustrated by the structure of the pension system, the most expensive element in Japan's system of social protection. Japan's pension system first began to take shape early in the twentieth century during an era when firms saw retirement allowances primarily as a way to control employees. Large firms began offering them to skilled workers to keep valued employees during the labor shortages of the World War I economic boom, but workers enjoyed no "rights" to these promised occupational benefits. This allowed firms to reduce or withhold allowances from those who quit to work for a rival company or otherwise challenged management.

Employees' rights to their retirement allowances were guaranteed by the state, ironically, only after "social bureaucrats" in the Home Ministry took the initiative in the mid-1930s in place of labor unions, which had been repressed with the help of the Peace Preservation Law. Pressed by the business community to limit their costs, however, Home Ministry officials agreed to limit the provisions of the Retirement Fund Law of 1936 to firms with over fifty employees—drawing the first of many lines that would enshrine dualism in the nation's retirement benefit system.[12] A similar cutoff based on a firm's size limited the range of employees covered by the new state-run Employee Pension System (EPS: Rōdōsha Nenkin) created in 1941 as the Pacific War got under way. Desperate to gain access to the funds that workers and firms were obliged to contribute to this scheme in order to buy munitions and fund the war effort, state officials implemented this program over the objections of the business community.[13] What workers gained in exchange for their contributions was little more than a nominal promise of future benefits. Nevertheless, the EPS, together with the Retirement Fund Law, became key building blocks in the complex retirement benefit system that took shape after the war.

Amid the hyperinflation of the postwar Occupation, the EPS quickly broke down, but a new system with the same English name (Kōsei Nenkin in Japanese) was established in 1954, this time covering regular full-time workers in firms with over five employees.[14] Confronting labor shortages once again in the 1950s, larger firms also reestablished systems that provided defined-benefit retirement allowances payable on termination of employment after a qualifying period. The final important piece of the postwar system fell into place in 1959 when the government created a separate pension program, the National Pension System (NPS: Kokumin Nenkin), to cover farmers, the self-employed, and other irregular workers.[15]

Years of economic growth in the succeeding decades, combined with activism by enterprise unions that were happy to trade loyalty to the firm for increased retirement benefits and by politicians who were eager to win votes by expanding pension benefits, had by the early 1980s created a set of programs that promised extremely generous benefits—at least to those retiring after many years as public employees or as employees of large firms. By 1997, the average recently retired male covered by the EPS was receiving ¥198,900 a month—a sum he could start to draw at the age of sixty. In addition, if married, his household could count on another ¥65,000 "basic pension" once his wife reached the age of sixty-five, even if she had never worked and never made contributions to the pension system. Such a couple could therefore expect to receive a total of ¥263,900 ($2,199 at an exchange rate of $1 = ¥120). Public employees covered by similar second-tier pension programs received equally generous benefits. Thirty-nine million workers (of sixty-five million in the employed workforce) were covered by these pension systems in 1998.[16]

These monthly benefits, however, were just part of what many of these workers could draw at retirement. Most public workers and many employees of large firms could also draw a supplemental pension and/or a lump sum retirement allowance from one or more Pension Funds (Kōsei Nenkin Kikin) providing defined-benefit retirement payments. The lump sum payments were often substantial, typically set to equal thirty-five to forty-five months of wages. The average male college graduate entitled to a PF retirement allowance in 1998 received a payment of ¥28.7 million (or $239,000).[17] In that year, twenty-three million workers were covered by pension funds promising benefits of this type.[18]

These generous pension programs, however, covered a little more than one-third of the Japanese workforce.[19] The rest—including the self-employed and farmers, as well as those working irregularly—had to rely on coverage under the NPS. In 1998, the NPS was the sole pension program covering twenty million households, promising each program participant a flat "basic pension" of ¥66,625 starting at age sixty-five (compared to sixty for the EPS). An elderly couple, both of whom had paid into the program for forty years, could thus expect to receive a pension of ¥133,250 (or $1,110)—about half the benefits received by an employee covered by the EPS with a nonworking spouse.

Two groups of citizens faced particularly dire financial risks under the rules governing this segmented pension system: workers changing jobs or leaving the workforce before qualifying for the more generous pension programs; and women divorced by employee-husbands. Rules specified that employees contributing to the EPS for less than twenty-five years were not eligible for any benefits under this program. Pension Funds generally allowed workers to claim limited benefits based on shorter periods of work, but they too penalized voluntary early departures relative to those with long careers. Many employees thus faced the possibility that they could fall from a very privileged position as beneficiaries of the EPS and Pension Funds to one where they would have little beyond the meager basic pension provided under the NPS.

In practice, most of those denied benefits under the generous pension programs have been women whose family "responsibilities" have forced them to leave full-time work prior to the conclusion of the vesting period. There have also been male workers who have lost pension fund benefits when their firms have gone bankrupt before they put in the required number of years. Those unable to find regular employment after this experience have sometimes lost EPS benefits as well. By linking pension benefits so closely to employment by a specific employer and allowing benefits to be so unequal, the program has generated pressure on the government to assume an important indirect role in assuring that male breadwinners, at least, are not deprived of their "just rewards" by bankruptcy or layoffs.

The wives of breadwinners, in contrast, were not viewed as entitled to the same indirect guarantee. As just noted, many have lost eligibility for their own EPS benefits and full Pension Fund benefits when pushed out of the full-time workforce after marriage, childbirth, or the need to care for a dependent elderly relative. Others have lost eligibility during economic downturns that have forced firms to restructure—typically by laying off female workers first. These inequities grew out of the Japanese social insurance system's emphasis on households. Protecting the incomes of male breadwinners was viewed as more important because it was assumed that all or most women would be members of households headed by such a breadwinner.

This assumption paid little heed, however, to the possibility that at least some women might feel trapped by economic dependence on their husbands. Pension rules guaranteed that this dependence would continue even after their husbands retired. The rules specified that the divorced spouse of an EPS breadwinner had no claim on her husband's second-tier pension benefits or the retirement allowance provided by Pension Funds. The many married women who were ineligible for the EPS on their own (typically because they never worked or worked only part-time after they married) thus risked being left with nothing but the basic pension provided under the NPS if they were left by, or chose to leave, their husbands.

Japan's pension system reflected the essential features of convoy capitalism that took shape during the nation's high-growth years. It promised that the convoy would move steadily forward, offering generous protection to most citizens, as long as male breadwinners remained employed by their firms and as long as most citizens belonged to households headed by a breadwinner. By binding the company and family together, the system encouraged workers and family members to view their enterprise as a team effort. Employees put in long hours to help their firms thrive while wives took on all the work of the home so their husbands could devote all their energy to their companies. The system thus aimed to provide meaningful social protection for most citizens in a way that also stimulated the productivity of the society.

Health Insurance and Eldercare

Japan's system of social insurance covering health care costs also took root in the prewar period under the leadership of "social bureaucrats." As in the case of pensions, state involvement in health insurance began with an effort to provide just a segment of the population (public employees and workers employed by large companies) with reliable coverage. The Health Insurance Law of 1922 mandated coverage only for those employed in large-scale manufacturing and mining operations. The broader public was not provided with an opportunity to enroll in these programs until 1938, again during the war, when the state encouraged trade associations as well as cities, towns, and villages to establish health insurance associations.[20]

After the war, coverage continued to vary depending on the employment status of breadwinners. Large companies provided workers and their families with Employee Health Insurance (EHI: Kenkō Hoken), but most farmers and self-employed workers, as well as those working for very small companies, remained without coverage until 1961 when the government required all citizens not covered by an employee plan to enroll in a community-based plan funded through the new, separate National Health Insurance system (NHI: Kokumin Kenkō Hoken). A third piece was added to this mélange in 1972 with the establishment of a program providing "free" health care to those over seventy.[21]

Although the system was subject to a number of reform initiatives in the years that followed, the dualistic structure did not change. By the 1980s, employees covered by EHI enjoyed generous benefits, with low co-payments (10% for the primary insured and 20% for family members) and access to company health facilities including leisure resorts and spas. Those covered by NHI, on the other hand, had to pay higher co-payments (30%) and had more limited benefits. As in the case of pensions, therefore, the quality of health insurance available to citizens depended on their employment and household status.

The system providing health insurance and care services for the elderly deserves particular attention here because when the health of an elderly person declines to the point where he or she requires constant care, this can disrupt the lives of other family members. The free health care program initiated in 1972 (later modified to require modest co-payments) provided quite generous coverage of the cost of hospitalizing elderly citizens. It did little, however, to expand the range of eldercare facilities and services available to ease the burden on those responsible for looking after elderly relatives. As late as 1982, Japan had just one hundred thousand nursing home beds.[22] These facilities gave priority to elderly people with limited means and no relatives, leaving families with means to compete for the limited number of beds available in intermediate care facilities. Daycare centers for the elderly were virtually unheard of. Home health services typically provided just one half-day visit a week.[23]

Given the limited services available, the eldercare system in place in the 1980s required, in effect, that a family member (usually a daughter or daughter-in-law) be available to provide much of the care herself. Such labor-intensive care frequently made it impossible for these women, and sometimes men, to remain in the paid workforce. Unfortunately, the risk that one might have to leave work for this reason was not covered by the system of social protection in place during the 1980s. Those needed at home to care for elderly relatives were almost always forced to quit their jobs because the state did not mandate (much less subsidize) leave benefits, and few firms provided them on their own initiative. Those forced to quit work for this reason, often forced into premature retirement, received no compensation other than the limited benefits provided under unemployment insurance.

This situation has improved somewhat as a result of reforms adopted during the 1990s (discussed in chapter 8), but up through the 1980s the health and eldercare system in Japan reflected once again the essential features of convoy capitalism. The most generous benefits were provided through employment-related programs, subsidized heavily by firms. The government would limit the costs of providing coverage for the rest of the citizenry by keeping the benefits available under these residual programs modest and by restricting the supply of facilities and services. Once again, it would rely on families to fill in gaps—in this case by asking women to care for their elderly relatives at home. By linking social benefits to work, the health care system (like the pension system) encouraged dedication to the employer and stimulated production. By relying on women to fill in the gaps in care services, the program again reinforced mutual aid within families as another component of the convoy.

Other State Social Benefit Programs

Although the description of Japan's social benefit programs in the areas of pensions, health, and eldercare has stressed the dualism and gaps in social protection, these areas, in fact, are those where the state has devoted the most resources. Japan's public and mandatory private social expenditures as a share of its GDP, in comparison to similar figures for other leading OECD nations (figure 3.1), shows that pensions and health expenditures account for the bulk of Japan's social expenditures. These categories of spending account for the largest shares of GDP in the other nations shown as well, but the other nations' total social expenditures are higher primarily because they spend significantly more on other categories of benefits: unemployment insurance, worker retraining, public housing, child allowances, welfare payments to alleviate poverty, and social services. It is in these areas that Japan's system of convoy capitalism has differed dramatically from the systems of social protection operating in other nations.

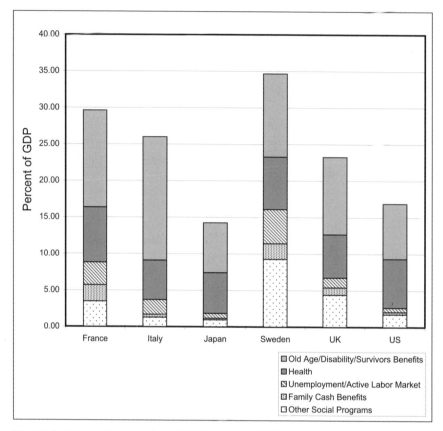

Fig. 3.1. Social expenditure in selected OECD nations in 1995: public and mandatory private social expenditures
Source: OECD social expenditure data, calculated based on the System of National Accounts, 1968.

The spending gap is particularly prominent in employment-related social programs. In 1995, Japan spent just 0.66 percent of its GDP in these areas, compared to 4.70 percent in Sweden, 3.10 percent in France, and 1.34 percent in the United Kingdom.[24] Some would dismiss this gap as reflecting nothing more than the difference in unemployment rates across these nations. Japan's unemployment spending, however, has been persistently lower than one would expect given its unemployment rate, based on the relationship found in OECD nations.[25] It is widely recognized, moreover, that Japan's unemployment rate does not fully reflect the size of the nation's employment problem. To be counted as unemployed, a worker must be without a job, be actively seeking work, and ready to work immediately if a job becomes available. This definition takes out of the "unemployed" category a large group of "discouraged workers" who would like to work but believe they have no prospects of finding a job. A 1998 survey revealed that 4.1 million people fit this category, far more than the 2.5 million listed as "unemployed" at the time.[26] Another large group of workers remain on a payroll but are "redundant" in that they are not adding to their firm's production levels. One study estimated that Japan had 4 million redundant workers in 1994.[27]

Japan's employment-related social programs address only a small part of the nation's broader employment problem defined by these numbers. The bulk of its expenditures go to its program of unemployment insurance, but the duration of benefits provided is much shorter than in most Western European systems.[28] In the late 1990s, the longest one could receive benefits under the Japanese system was 270 days, and most unemployed qualified for just 90 to 180 days of benefits if they qualified for any at all.[29] The government, moreover, spent very little on retraining programs. A middle-aged breadwinner asked to retire early from a well-paid job could derive very little help from this set of policies. The employment system's emphasis on hiring young workers and giving them seniority wages meant middle-aged unemployed workers had little prospect of finding a decent job quickly. And yet such a worker was faced with losing benefits after just half a year and could not even count on help with retraining. Japan's unemployed young people, whose number has been growing since the mid-1990s as large numbers of high school graduates and even some college graduates have had difficulty finding full-time jobs, are also poorly served. Not having contributed to the insurance program, unemployed youth qualify for no cash benefits. Only recently has the state begun to assist them in obtaining job skills.

Instead of being designed to help these types of unemployed workers into new jobs, the unemployment insurance system that developed over several decades of strong economic growth was designed to ease certain groups of workers *out* of the labor force: older workers forced to retire early could get some help; women leaving the workforce to get married or have children could also claim a few months of benefits. Although it helped some irregular workers, such as those in the construction trades, get through periods between jobs, it offered little to those needing help in getting into a new line of work.

Even more than in the pension and health care areas, this system counted on firms and families to fill in the gaps. Because it served middle-aged breadwinners so poorly, it relied on firms to keep these workers on their payrolls, even when they were redundant. Firms also took on the obligation to retrain and find new work for their core employees. Likewise, because the state served unemployed youth not at all, it counted on families to support these youths at home (a category of young people known derisively as "parasite singles") and to pay the private tuition they might need to obtain postsecondary training in occupational skills.

Another area of social spending where Japan ranks low relative to other OECD nations is in "family cash benefits" (see figure 3.1 above). This category of social programs includes child allowances for families with young children, designed to help them offset the added costs and lost wages associated with child rearing; and additional means-tested payments to poor families with children. Japan spent just 0.21 percent of its GDP on these programs in 1995, compared to 2.23 in France, 2.13 in Sweden, and 1.00 in Britain.[30]

Japan's program of child allowances was established much later than the social programs discussed thus far, with the first payments not made until 1973. Initially aimed at helping large families (only those with three or more children under fifteen received an allowance), the program has been modified a number of times to broaden the number of families receiving the benefit. In each case, however, benefit levels and means-testing have been adjusted in order to keep the program small. Japan's expenditure on allowances per child under fifteen has risen 175 percent since 1973, but this increase is well below the rate of growth in per capita GDP (274%) and far below the increase in per capita spending on the elderly (1,081%).[31] In 1996, before the recent round of reforms discussed in chapter 7, the program provided for a payment of ¥5,000 per month for each child three years old or younger, with benefits limited to families in the lower 60 percent of income. A qualifying family could therefore expect a total of ¥180,000 ($1,500) to help offset the large expense of raising a child.[32]

A number of other programs provide support specifically targeted toward poor families. First, the child maintenance allowance (*jidō fuyō teate*) for mothers or other relatives who are raising children without a father provides monthly stipends of ¥47,370 ($400) to two-child families of this type. Another program of public assistance (seikatsu hogo) is designed to offer enough additional aid to poor households to keep their income above the poverty line. A single mother raising two children alone in a high-cost area like Tokyo thus might qualify for another ¥163,000 a month in public assistance, enough to bring her family income above ¥200,000 a month ($1,667).[33]

Although the latter sum sounds relatively generous, in practice few families with children qualify for public assistance. Before receiving this help from the state, families are required to exhaust their savings, draw on support from their extended families (grandparents, aunts), and make every effort to collect child support from the father. The local officials who administer these programs are notorious for their harassment of mothers seeking aid. As a result, many divorced and unwed mothers left with the responsibility of raising their children without help from fathers depend heavily on their own parents.[34] Many ask their mothers to provide childcare so they can work outside the home to support their children, drawing only the child maintenance allowance from the state.[35] In 1997, just 52,000 fatherless households drew public assistance while 650,000 received the less generous child maintenance allowance. Fatherless households constituted just 8.3 percent of the households on public assistance. Instead, the bulk of this aid went to "households with elderly people" (44%) and "households of people with disease, injuries, and disabilities" (41%).[36]

Closely related to public assistance in most advanced industrialized nations is the system designed to assure that all families have access to adequate housing facilities. In the decades immediately following the war, the Japanese government constructed extensive public housing projects, building 7.5 percent of new dwelling units in the 1950s and 14 percent in the 1960s. As per capita incomes rose, however, it constructed fewer new units. Those that remain are mostly of poor quality in comparison with accommodations available on the private market. In 1997, just 4.3 percent of new dwelling units and 6.7 percent of the housing stock were units that were built as public housing owned and rented by local governments (*kōei*) or as rented units managed by public foundations (*kōdan* or *kōsha*).[37] Most of the lower-rent *kōei* units, in particular, housed older citizens who had lived there for many years.[38] The generation that is currently leaving home and entering society thus gets little help from the state in securing the living space needed to raise a family.

Finally, let us consider social services that aid families by providing children with care and education. Clearly, couples that choose to have children face additional demands on their time. Young children need constant care, and educating a child so that he or she has the social and technical skills needed to thrive in the modern economy requires a substantial investment of time by parents and schools. The Japanese state, like those in other advanced industrialized nations, plays a major role in providing children with a public education—a role it took on in the late nineteenth century when it required all boys and girls to attend elementary school. Since the 1950s, it has also provided subsidized childcare centers (*hoikuen*) to assist working families. Nevertheless, this is another area where Japan's system of social protection has relied heavily on the family, and especially women, to provide care and education beyond that provided by the state.

Public schooling in Japan starts at age six and continues through age eighteen. The state also operates a national university system that offers a high quality higher education at a subsidized price. Access to the best public high schools and colleges is restricted, however, to those passing very competitive entrance examinations—forcing parents who want their children to survive the notorious "examination hell" to devote extensive time and resources to their children's education. Schools have irregular schedules, with early dismissal at around noon at least once a week for elementary school children. PTA meetings are scheduled in the afternoons, rather than in the evening, under the assumption that a parent is at home during the day. After-school care is available, but only until 6 p.m. in most areas and only up until the third grade. Those whose work obligations make it difficult to be there at these times have difficulty finding supplemental care services on the private market because such services are simply not available in most areas. As a result, career women typically have to rely on their families (usually their mothers or mothers-in-law) to juggle the school calendar and supervise homework.

Parents face not only a time burden but also a significant financial burden in order to provide the supplemental "cramming" necessitated by the nation's exam-oriented school system. Approximately 37 percent of public elementary school children and 76 percent of public junior high school children attended *juku*, or private cram schools, in 2000. The Ministry of Education estimated that the average parent sending a child through twelve years of *public* schooling would spend ¥4.6 million ($38,000) on fees, school supplies, private tutoring, and cram schools. Parents that added, as is common, three years of private kindergarten (for ages three to five) at the front end and upgraded, as is also common, to a private high school at the upper end would need to spend ¥7.2 million ($60,000).[39] For financially strapped families, these are imposing sums.

The greatest challenges facing dual-career parents who wish to continue working after having children, however, come in the period immediately after children are born. Up until 1992, employers were not obliged to provide childcare leave privileges to women (or men) beyond the six weeks prenatal and eight weeks postpartum maternity leave required under the Labor Standards Act. Public employees were frequently entitled to additional weeks of unpaid leave, but only the largest and most progressive firms provided this type of benefit.[40] Because childcare for children eight weeks old was in short supply in most areas (and frequently unavailable except at a very steep price on the private market), most women without a relative willing to care for a small child had to quit their jobs.

Finding enough childcare centers to allow women to continue in their careers was a challenge not only for parents of newborns but of older children as well. The government, as noted above, has provided heavily subsidized childcare for several decades, but this care was not designed to allow women to work the kind of hours widely expected of salaried workers in Japan. Most childcare centers closed between 5 and 6 p.m., a pick-up time few commuting working mothers (or fathers) could make. Even after reforms extended hours in more locations, almost all centers closed at 7 p.m. or earlier.[41]

In urban areas, waiting lists were another problem—especially for parents with very young children. In 1989, childcare centers accepted just sixty-four thousand infants during the first twelve months after their birth and another fifty-five thousand toddlers during the year after their first birthdays—in a nation where annual birth cohorts at the time numbered about 1.2 million.[42] The amount of childcare available in Japan in the 1990s, in fact, was among the lowest in the OECD nations, with just 15 percent of children under three and 35 percent of children aged three to six in daycare facilities.[43] Those figures compared to rates of 40 to 60 percent of children under three enrolled in daycare in the Nordic countries, Canada, and the United States, and to rates close to 80 percent for children from age three to mandatory school age in most European nations.[44] Not surprisingly, the limited number of slots in childcare centers created shortages in many areas, especially in fast-growing cities and suburbs. In several urban jurisdictions, thousands of young children were waiting for spots in childcare centers, leaving parents to choose between quitting their jobs, imposing on relatives, or settling for costly and potentially unsafe "baby hotels."[45]

The childcare shortage was also a problem for women seeking to reenter the workforce after leaving employment to care for their infants. Many women in urban areas reported that they were trapped in a Catch-22 situation. Employers would not consider them for jobs unless they had lined up childcare, while childcare centers would not jump them ahead on the waiting lists until they had a job. And the childcare problem was not the only one hampering the efforts of women to restart careers. Whereas most women who leave the workforce temporarily in the United States and Europe have opportunities to reenter their line of work at a later date, most career jobs in Japan are closed to those who wish to reenter the workforce at an "advanced" age (such as thirty-five).[46] Many job notices listed age as a condition of employment, typically ruling out applicants over thirty-four. Because this type of age discrimination was not precluded by any government legislation but was instead a core feature of the nation's employment system, most women who reentered the workforce ended up having to settle for part-time and temporary jobs at a fraction of the pay and benefits they could earn were they on the career track.[47]

The deficiencies of Japan's convoy system of social protection were arguably the most striking in this area. As we will see in chapter 7, the Japanese government addressed some of these gaps to a limited degree during the 1990s, but the system in place at the start of the decade clearly did little to protect families, and in particular women wishing to continue their careers, from the risk that having children would foreclose that option. In fact, the difficulties faced by working mothers were such that this was not so much a "risk" as a virtual certainty—unless women had support, once again, from their extended family.

This description of the Japanese state's *direct* role in providing social protection has emphasized the limited nature of its commitment and consequent heavy reliance on employers and family members. No state, of course, assumes complete responsibility for providing social protection on its own. Everywhere, societies seek to balance the role of the state, markets, and families in protecting individuals from the risks inherent in capitalism.[48] Repeated references to how the Japanese state's direct commitment compares to those in other societies have made it clear, however, that the balance struck in Japan was extreme in its reliance on firms and families. Key elements of the safety net that are a state responsibility in most other societies—such as the system protecting workers from the risk of unemployment; the system protecting families from the poverty that tends to follow when women raise children without fathers; and the system that eases the efforts of dual-career families to balance family and work responsibilities—were under Japan's convoy system a responsibility of firms and families.

Japan's Generous Informal System of Social Protection

That this convoy system was nevertheless able to protect most citizens from poverty, unemployment, and abandonment in old age is testimony to the ability and willingness of Japanese firms and families to carry a disproportionate share of the load and to the state's indirect role in keeping the convoy going. Though Japan's system was extreme in its reliance on firms and families, these two private institutions were able to carry the load they were asked to bear—and by doing so were able to provide Japanese households with an unprecedented (for Japan) and rarely matched (abroad) level of economic security. This success was contingent, however, on the willingness of these groups to continue bearing their load even as the socioeconomic environment changed—and on the ability of the state to sustain its indirect, supporting role.

Lifetime Employment

The system's success in protecting households from the risk of unemployment can be seen in the very low unemployment rate the nation has maintained over the past several decades. Japan's unemployment rate remained very low throughout the period, never exceeding 3 percent prior to 1995 and staying below 2.5 percent in all but a few years (figure 3.2). Forbearance by Japanese employers had much to do with this achievement. In the period immediately following the first oil crisis in 1973, Japan's capacity utilization rate fell sharply as factories were idled by the sudden drop in demand. Yet Japanese employers refrained from laying off workers, and the unemployment rate rose only slightly from 1.3 percent in 1973 to 2.2 percent in 1978. Again, following the second oil crisis in 1979 and the collapse of the bubble economy in 1990, capacity utilization fell without an immediate, corresponding increase in the unemployment rate.

The well-known Japanese practice of "lifetime employment"—the commitment of large Japanese employers not to lay off core workers when the economy stumbles—is captured in statistics in figure 3.2. Though sometimes assumed to apply to most Japanese workers, this commitment has always been limited to full-time, permanent employees in the public sector and in large private firms. Over time, however, the commitment has been extended to a larger and larger segment of the workforce. In 1980, 46 percent of workers in large firms (five thousand or more employees) in the forty to forty-four-year-old cohort had never changed jobs, while by 1994, this figure had risen to 77 percent.[49] Though women were largely excluded from this practice, most were indirect beneficiaries of the job security afforded to their husbands, fathers, and sons—albeit dependent beneficiaries.

Firms' ability and willingness to extend this guarantee was contingent on several positive conditions that characterized Japan's high growth period. First, throughout the period up to the 1990s, Japan's labor force (and in particular its employee labor force, as distinct from the workforce engaged in farming and self-employment) was expanding at a rapid rate. Second, with the exception of a few years after each of the oil crises, the Japanese economy grew steadily at rates that averaged nearly 10 percent a year up to 1973 and 4 percent a year after that. Most firms expanded rapidly during this period in order to meet rising demand, and to do so they hired a larger cohort of young workers with every passing year. This

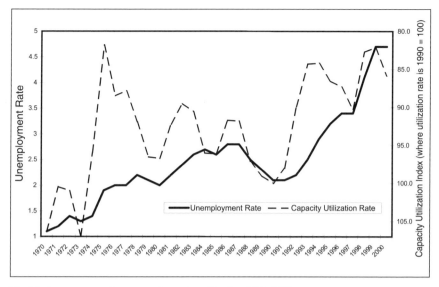

Fig. 3.2. Japanese unemployment and capacity utilization, 1970–2000
Source: Adapted from Bank of Japan, *Comparative Economic and Financial Statistics: Japan and Other Major Countries,* 1997; updated with data from the *Japan Statistical Yearbook,* 2002.

combination of beneficent conditions made it relatively cheap and easy for Japanese firms to sustain the lifetime employment deal. Because this bargain came with a system of "seniority wages" under which young workers were paid below-market wages in their early years in exchange for the promise that they would be paid steadily rising wages as they aged, Japanese firms were able to save money on their wage bill as long as their workforce was heavy with young workers. For most firms, this savings more than justified the cost of living up to their obligation during the rare slow years when they had surplus workers.

Inevitably, there were some firms that found themselves in industries with no long-term growth potential such as coal mining, textiles, and aluminum. Others, such as Tōyō Kōgyō, the maker of Mazda automobiles, in the 1970s and a number of petrochemical firms in the 1980s, experienced temporary but severe downturns in demand that left them with more workers than they could afford to pay. As long as such firms were in a minority, however, it was relatively easy for their network of related firms—their *keiretsu,* the former family holding companies that were dissolved after the war and reorganized around banks—to come to their aid.

Keiretsu and Main Banks

The keiretsu and the main banks were, in fact, key elements of Japan's convoy system of social protection. Though most literature on Japan's political economy has focused on the role these institutions played in helping firms invest heavily, expand their market share, and keep out competition from newcomers, these institutions also played a vital role in helping firms live up to their lifetime employment commitments.[50] Under the system of Japanese-style capitalism that developed by the 1970s, most of the nation's firms were enmeshed in networks of cross-shareholding where firms committed to holding for the long term a block of stock from many of the firms with which they did business: banks held shares in the firms to which they made loans; insurance firms held shares in the companies they supplied with insurance; manufacturers held shares in their suppliers; and firms with a common history (such as a common lineage linked to prewar *zaibatsu* family-organized conglomerates such as Sumitomo, Mitsui, and Mitsubishi) held stakes in one another. In most cases the individual blocks of stock were small, but the sum of all stable holdings added up to over half of all shares in the case of most major Japanese firms.[51]

These cross-shareholdings cemented multifaceted long-term relationships based on reciprocal obligations and trust among Japanese firms. Subcontractors involved in these networks knew their customers would not desert them the moment a new, low-cost supplier became available. Borrowers knew that their banks would not abandon them when they needed capital the most. The latter concern was the particular responsibility of "main banks" in the Japanese system. Main banks typically supplied firms with 20–30 percent of a borrower's credit but assumed responsibility for the borrower as a "lender of last resort"—reassuring other lenders that they would keep their clients supplied with fresh credit if conditions deteriorated, thus discouraging them from withdrawing their own credit lines at the first sign of trouble.

This assumption of risk by main banks was important in protecting capital, of course, but it also protected labor. The cushion afforded by main banks often allowed firms to avoid having to lay off workers in a hurry to meet creditor demands for restructuring, a frequent feature of business life in the Anglo-American countries. Firms, instead, had opportunities to work with creditors over an extended period of time to identify management problems, improve productivity, and (in some cases) reorient the firm toward pursuing new growth opportunities.

The role of these institutions in saving Tōyō Kōgyō in the late 1970s illustrates their importance in Japan's system of social protection.[52] Mazda had experienced a particularly sharp drop in purchases of its vehicles in the aftermath of the 1973–74 oil crisis because Mazda engines were less fuel-efficient than those of Toyota and Nissan. Sales were down 31 percent, and the firm faced dim prospects of recovering market share in the face of continuing high gasoline prices. Mazda salesmen were growing increasingly frustrated with the firm's failure to address this and other management failures and were starting to desert the firm in droves.

The company was saved and layoffs were avoided in large part because its network of "relational contracts" (as Ronald Dore terms it) came through.[53] Sumitomo Bank, its leading creditor and main bank, assumed responsibility for coordinating with all other creditors to assure that the firm would have the financing to get through several bad years. Its "virtual guarantee" of all of Tōyō Kōgyō's debts went a long way toward keeping credit flowing to the struggling company. Other members of the Sumitomo Group (e.g., Sumitomo Fire and Marine Insurance) committed to purchasing nothing but Mazdas for their fleets. The enterprise union worked with the company to help it overcome cash-flow problems by delaying bonus payments. It also agreed to a novel arrangement under which the au-tomaker's employees "volunteered" to take turns being posted to outlying areas of Japan as salesmen in Mazda dealerships (replacing the salesmen who had deserted the company). Finally, the firm's network of suppliers agreed to accept across-the-board reductions in prices.

The system, under which so many parties agreed to sacrifice some current in-come in order to assure the long-term viability of a relational partner, worked to so-cialize risk in much the way state-run social insurance systems do. Only in this case the system was entirely private. As a result of all of these commitments, Mazda was able to improve its productivity dramatically, expand its market share once again, and reemerge as a viable automobile company. It froze hiring for several years, but it did not lay off any workers. Dore's *Flexible Rigidities* argues that the pattern seen in the Mazda case was one that characterized broad swaths of the Japanese econ-omy, reflecting what he describes as a culture imbued with the view that "caring is a duty" and also good business for everyone in the long run.[54]

The Government's Role in Sustaining the Convoy

The government's role in sustaining the convoy remained invisible most of the time during the high- growth years. Only on a few occasions did the government need to intervene overtly to arrange bailouts of troubled financial firms. When industrial firms in a specific sector like steel or petrochemicals encountered difficulties, the government was usually able to help them get through periods of declining demand by nudging competing firms to form recession cartels to share the pain of cutting back production and keep prices stable. Although some sectors like agriculture re-ceived large public subsidies, inefficient sectors received much more support through less visible trade and regulatory protections that limited competition. That the government's role was largely informal and did not draw extensively on public revenues, however, does not mean it was not important. The convoy could not sur-vive without it.

The most important form of support, the policy that gave Japan's version of capitalism its name, was the government's "convoy" approach to regulating finan-cial institutions.[55] The system of financial regulation begun under the postwar oc-cupation and further developed by the Ministry of Finance (MOF) during the 1950s enforced, first, a rigid segmentation of financial services. Banks were pre-vented from underwriting and dealing in securities, making this line of activity the exclusive province of securities firms. Banks were further segmented into several categories: city banks were in charge of making short-term loans (usually less than three years) to large corporations; long-term credit banks were responsible for making longer-term infrastructure loans to sectors like the electric utilities, steel, and petrochemicals; and regional banks, savings banks, and credit cooperatives collected deposits that were routed through the "call market" to the city banks.[56] Neither banks nor securities firms could sell insurance products.[57]

Second, MOF maintained strict control over deposit and loan interest rates, authority it used to keep credit markets suppressed: interest rates were kept artificially low, creating a situation in which there was always a greater demand for loans than there was a supply of funds. Banks could not compete to attract depositors by raising interest rates on deposits; to gain access to funds they had to borrow from the Bank of Japan or expand their branch network with MOF permission. Likewise, because interest rates on loans were also low and fixed, banks made profits by spending as little as possible on credit evaluation and by making loans in the largest possible increments, a practice of "over-loaning" that left them dependent on government support whenever their heavily indebted borrowers encountered unexpected difficulties. Securities firms too were dependent on MOF protection because the government policy of encouraging indirect financing (bank loans) by keeping interest rates low left them with an uphill fight in their struggle for business.

MOF's extensive regulatory control over these aspects of the financial industry and its willingness to use its discretionary power to prod financial institutions to follow its "administrative guidance" made it possible for the ministry to sustain convoys of firms in each financial service sector without a single bankruptcy among major firms for almost fifty years. Until Hokkaidō Takushoku Bank and Yamaichi Securities failed in 1998, not a single large or medium-sized bank had failed since 1950. Yamaichi Securities had come close to bankruptcy in 1965, but it was rescued and returned to profitability. Tōtō Bank and Heiwa Sōgo Bank came close to insolvency in 1978 and 1990, but the MOF arranged for them to be absorbed by Mitsui Bank and Sumitomo Bank, respectively.[58]

The importance of this record for the entire system of convoy capitalism cannot be underestimated. Because banks knew the Ministry of Finance stood ready to stand behind them as a "final guarantor, or bail-out institution of last resort," they were willing to take on the risk of serving as main banks responsible for monitoring the firms they served as leading suppliers of credit.[59] Because other lenders knew the main bank was ready and able to back up borrowers, with MOF support, they too were willing to keep firms supplied with credit so that borrowers could live up to their lifetime employment commitments. Because MOF and banks backed up the system of lifetime employment for their husbands, women did not need to maintain second careers for the family as insurance against the risk that spouses would lose their jobs—leaving the women free to take care of children and elderly relatives. And because firms and women took on all of these responsibilities, the government did not need to develop generous unemployment insurance or retraining programs, expansive childcare provision, or publicly funded leave benefits.

The government's system of financial regulation, however, was simply the most important piece in a broader network of government policies that sustained convoy capitalism. Also very important were the government's restrictions on levels of market competition in broad swaths of the economy. The financial sector was simply the most important example of this approach: banks, securities firms, and insurance firms all operated in a severely restricted environment in which the products they could offer and the prices that they could charge (e.g., interest rates, commission rates) were strictly regulated. The regulations were rigged, moreover, so that even the weakest performers could make a profit. The strongest—such as the largest city banks—were able to make superprofits.

This same approach was applied to the telecommunications, transportation, and utilities sectors. Key suppliers of these services, such as Nippon Telegraph and Telephone (NTT), Japan Airlines, and the electric utilities, were given national or regional monopolies so that they were effectively insulated from most market pressure. Even in segments of these markets where some competition was allowed, such as in trucking and taxi service, licensing rules were used to manage supply so that it would not exceed demand. In other words, the government made sure that new entries would not undermine stable prices or risk driving established players into bankruptcy.

While many nations regulated these service sectors until the deregulation wave began sweeping the advanced industrialized nations after the rise of Thatcher and Reagan, Japan continued to manage supply and demand even as it began "deregulating" telecommunications, finance, and other sectors starting in the early 1980s. As Steve Vogel describes, its approach to deregulation in the financial and telecommunications sectors was carefully calibrated by bureaucrats to assure that established players were not threatened and that newcomers to these sectors gained market share only slowly.[60]

Japan was also distinct in the degree to which its supply–demand balancing style of regulation extended to sectors that operated much more freely in other nations. Most notorious was the nation's system of regulating retail stores under the Large Store Law that was in place from 1974 until 1998, and which existed in another form before that. For most of this period, the bureaucrats who oversaw this regulatory regime allowed incumbent retailers organized in local chambers of commerce to veto proposed large store expansion plans in their areas. Until the government accepted liberalizing reforms under foreign pressure in 1990, existing retailers were able to force large store chains to put up with lengthy delays and accept major reductions in floor space and operating hours as conditions for opening in their area. In this way, the government assured that small retailers would be cushioned from market competition, preserving this sector as a "labor sponge" that would absorb those displaced from other lines of work.[61]

Construction was another "labor sponge" sector that enjoyed protection from market competition under government policy. The Japanese government directed very large sums of public revenue toward public works, and all of this was put out to bid under rules that essentially guaranteed that construction firms of all sizes would get profitable pieces of the pie. Rather than putting projects up for open bidding, the government chose to designate a small number of companies (usually ten) to bid on projects. Frequently, the same group of firms would be asked to bid on a series of projects. This structure made it easy for the firms concerned, organized into cartels known as *dangō*, to work out among themselves bid-rigging deals under which they would each have a turn winning inflated bids. The structure also encouraged large contractors to include many smaller subcontractors in their bids to make sure potential spoilers were content not to challenge the cartel.[62]

Although most analysts have emphasized the corrupt side of the system of bid-rigging, its role in sustaining Japan's system of social protection also needs to be stressed. As Brian Woodall notes, the *dangō* provided, in effect, a "mutual insurance system for firms in a volatile industry."[63] Not only firms, but construction workers too, benefited from a system that kept five hundred thousand construction firms in business, employing an estimated 9.6 percent of the workforce.[64] The bulk of public works projects, moreover, were built in rural areas of Japan where structural shifts in the economy were squeezing workers in the primary sectors of agriculture, fishing, and forestry. By providing these workers with a way of supplementing their income in the off-season or after other industries became uncompetitive, the "public works state" protected them from market forces as effectively as the more formal welfare state programs developed in Europe.

The Japanese state also went further than other advanced industrialized nations in its efforts to manage supply and demand in segments of manufacturing, especially in the intermediate goods sectors that Mark Tilton calls the "basic materials industries."[65] These are sectors requiring large asset-specific investments and high utilization rates to maintain competitiveness: sectors such as petroleum refining, petrochemicals, cement, integrated steel mills, flat glass, paper, soda ash, and aluminum. Chalmers Johnson has described how the government used licensing rules, favorable credit and tax policies, and other direct forms of intervention in the 1950s and 1960s to coordinate and encourage investment in these targeted sectors.[66] Tilton updated the story by showing how the Ministry of International Trade and Industry (MITI) went on to use more informal means, such as a lax antitrust policy, to help firms in these industries survive economic downturns in the 1970s and 1980s. During the particularly difficult period after the oil shocks, MITI secured formal "recession cartel" exemptions from the Anti-Monopoly Law for most of these sectors, allowing them to coordinate capacity cutbacks in order to keep prices from falling and to share the pain of structural adjustment. MITI also used informal administrative guidance to assist firms in organizing cartels, supplying them with information needed to police cartels and pressuring the Japan Fair Trade Commission (JFTC) to turn a blind eye on cartelistic practices.

Most of the focus in the academic literature on these policies has been on the role they have played in excluding foreign competition. Indeed, Japanese firms were major beneficiaries at the expense of more efficient foreign competitors. This should not lead us to neglect, however, the role these policies played in sustaining Japan's system of social protection. Most of the basic materials firms discussed by Tilton were large firms employing thousands of lifetime employees. Absent the kind of protection they received, these firms would have been forced to violate that commitment and lay off large numbers of workers. The cushion they were provided allowed those in the greatest difficulty (firms in the aluminum, steel, and cement sectors) to shrink their workforces gradually through attrition, early retirement, and transfers. No firms in these industries had to lay off prime-age workers, nor were they pushed into bankruptcy.[67]

As Japan entered the 1990s, virtually the entire service sector of the economy as well as much of the intermediate goods segment of manufacturing was sheltered from market competition entirely or to a significant degree. To this could be added farmers, fisherman, and forestry workers, many of whom benefited from price supports and trade protection that provided them with more income than they would have received in a free market. The set of policies providing this protection, like the government's support for the financial industry convoy, played a critical role in allowing large firms to live up to their lifetime employment guarantees. It also obviated the need for more generous unemployment insurance and retraining programs by creating comfortable enough conditions, even for small retailers and construction firms, that they were generally able to survive downturns in the economy and add workers displaced from other segments of the economy to their payrolls.

While the two elements of the government's support system discussed above were the most important in *enabling* firms to assume a significant portion of the burden of providing social protection, a final set of regulations, those governing the labor market, helped assure that they would do so. These regulations have been interpreted by the courts such that firms have been judged to be in violation of the "doctrine of abusive dismissal" if they lay off regular full-time employees under anything short of the most dire conditions. Firms must be facing "a compelling and unavoidable necessity" (such as imminent bankruptcy) before they are allowed to carry out such dismissals. Before they can do so, they are expected to have eliminated overtime work, suspended new hiring, farmed out workers to related companies, and fired temporary and part-time workers. They are also expected to abide by "reasonable standards applied fairly" when selecting persons to be dismissed.[68] In practice, these expectations have been so restrictive that large employers have uniformly avoided outright dismissals of workers, preferring instead to negotiate gradual workforce reductions with their unions, relying mostly on attrition and early retirement incentives, along with transfers and out-placements. The difficulty firms have laying off workers has reinforced their support for (and dependence on) the web of informal government help described above.

Government Policy Sustaining Traditional Gender Roles

The Japanese government, in fashioning regulatory and other policies designed to help firms live up to the obligations they bore in the convoy system of social protection, was often quite explicit about what it was doing. The Japanese-style firm (*nihongata kigyō*) was a critical component of what Noguchi Yukio has called the "1940 System," so it was only natural that the government would do everything it could to help assure that firms could carry out their assigned role as both the engine of growth and the provider of social protection.[69] In contrast, the government policies that guided women into traditional gender roles were less the product of conscious design than of benign neglect. The policies had grown up in an era when most career employees were men and most women prioritized family over work, and they ended up reinforcing these patterns. Nevertheless, these policies played a critical part in encouraging women to serve as vital "shock absorbers," entering the workforce as temporary workers when labor markets were tight and leaving when economic conditions deteriorated or when their children or elderly relatives needed care. Without women acting as shock absorbers, the convoy would have ground to a halt long ago.

Policies encouraged women to play this role, first, through gaps in the formal system of social protection. By not requiring firms to provide childcare or eldercare leave benefits and by providing inadequate childcare and eldercare services, policies encouraged women to give up full-time, regular jobs whenever family members needed care. Similarly, by saddling mothers with the responsibility of guiding their children through an examination-centered education system that could destroy their life chances at a very young age, the education system severely constrained mothers' ability to go back to full-time work even after their children were older. This passive encouragement of traditional roles was supplemented, however, by a number of more active policies.

The first of these can be found in the government's labor market regulations. For many years, Japanese labor standards were explicitly designed to provide female workers with extra protection. Firms were constrained in the number of overtime hours they could ask women to work (just 150 a year for women, while allowing 350 for men) and in their ability to assign them to night shifts. Such standards reflected, but also reinforced, societal expectations that women, unlike men, would subordinate work responsibilities to their family obligations.[70] At the same time, until women won a number of legal cases in the early 1980s, employers faced few sanctions for discriminating against women in retirement and lay-off policies. The law was even weaker in its prohibitions against discrimination in training, benefits, and promotion. This combination gave firms a green light to treat male and female workers differently, and firms obliged by routinely requiring women to quit work when they married or had children, firing female workers first when they faced difficult economic circumstances, and refusing to promote women to positions of responsibility.[71]

The policy changed in form, but less in substance, with court victories and the adoption of the Equal Employment Opportunity Law (EEOL) and related legislation in 1985. This legislation relaxed overtime and night-shift protections for women in professional and managerial positions. At the same time, it barred firms from discriminating against women in retirement policies, layoffs, and benefits, and called on them to "strive" to treat women equally in recruitment, hiring, placement, and promotion.[72] This package did little to improve the treatment of women in the workplace, however. Firms were now expected to pay, promote, and retire women equally with men when they were in the same job category, but they could also ask them to work night shifts and long hours of overtime—expectations few women with children could meet given limited childcare and inadequate support at home. At the same time, the lack of enforcement provisions to make sure that firms did their best to recruit and place women equally meant that firms were free to design separate job categories in order to perpetuate gender-based tracking. Most firms responded by simply creating one set of job classifications designed mostly for men (with better pay, promotions, and benefits in return for complete dedication to the job) and another for women. Consequently, the majority of female employees were channeled into jobs with much lower levels of pay and fewer benefits than those held by men.[73]

The other set of policies that worked to constrain female employment were tax and benefit rules that encouraged women to work part-time. In 1998, the wife of a salaried employee who kept her own earnings below ¥1.03 million ($8,583) avoided having to pay any income tax, earned credit toward a basic pension without making her own contributions, qualified her husband for a dependent-spouse income tax break, and earned her family spousal bonuses and benefits such as subsidized housing through her husband's work. Once her earnings crossed thresholds near this level of income, however, she suddenly had to start paying income tax on her earnings; she had to begin making pension contributions; her husband lost his income tax deduction; and the family frequently lost spousal bonuses (an average of ¥180,000 a year at large corporations) as well as housing benefits.[74] A woman in this position could thus except to pay a major penalty for increasing her earnings. Ōsawa Machiko has estimated that a spouse who increased her pay from ¥1 million to ¥1.5 million would earn virtually no additional disposable income for the 50 percent increase in hours worked.[75]

Not surprisingly, many women reported adjusting their hours in order to keep them below these critical thresholds. The majority of married women thus chose to work part-time, giving up the job protections and benefits that come with full-time, regular employment.[76] Because many were on one-year contracts, they could be dismissed much more easily by their employers. Those who worked fewer than twenty-two hours a week were not covered by unemployment insurance. Such workers generally did not qualify for retirement allowances, nor did they earn credit toward a more generous employee pension.[77] Incentives to work part-time combined with regulations that tolerated discriminatory gender-based tracking to keep female wages lower in Japan than in any other advanced industrialized nation. In the mid-1990s, Japanese women aged forty to fifty-five were paid at a rate that was about half that of men the same age—compared to the United States where the pay rate for women in the same age group is about 80 percent that of men.[78]

To imply that this pattern was entirely the result of government policy, of course, would be a gross overstatement. Many Japanese women have chosen to be full-time housewives or to work only very limited hours because this is the lifestyle they prefer. In response to a 1997 poll asking unmarried young women how they would like to combine family and work, 21 percent reported they hoped to be a full-time housewife. Another 34 percent reported they hoped to leave work for some time after having children, and then return to work.[79] Iwao Sumiko explains why so many Japanese women aspire to be full-time housewives:

> A full-time housewife can enjoy a certain amount of financial affluence from her husband's income as well as a generous amount of time to do with as she pleases when her husband is not around. She can take pleasure in building human relationships—without, like her husband, having to do everything superiors command—and she can derive a sense of fulfillment from cultural pursuits and numerous other activities.[80]

Although women are more ambivalent than they used to be about identifying themselves as housewives, or *shufu*, Robin LeBlanc argues that the identity retains enough appeal that "the politically salient cleavages by which housewives themselves argue they should be classified are their gendered roles as caretakers."[81]

This identity is in turn the product of social structures and norms beyond those that are formalized in government policy. Japanese women themselves are immersed in social networks, such as those surrounding the kindergartens their children attend, that help socialize them to take on the role of "education mothers" (*kyōiku mama*).[82] As they go about the chores involved in caring for children and elderly relatives, every day they confront "cultural ideals" that demand a selfless devotion to caregiving, with relatives as well as strangers chiding them with disapproving looks whenever they stray from the ideal by, for example, dropping their infant off at a childcare center.[83] Finally, there are the habits of their husbands and employers that assume it is the role of women to do the bulk of childcare and almost all housework. These attitudes are reflected in housework surveys that show that the average Japanese husband spent just 2.5 hours a week on household chores, compared to 33.5 hours for his wife, in 1994. The imbalance was almost as large for households in which the wife worked long hours outside the home: husbands devoted 3.1 hours a week to chores and wives 26.6 when wives worked more than 49 hours outside the home![84] Surveys show that Japanese husbands similarly skimp on childcare, with the average Japanese father of a child under six spending just ten minutes a day helping with childcare on weekdays.[85] Time constraints are therefore a major force driving Japanese women to forgo full-time work.

However one assigns weight between government policy and broader societal structures and norms, the importance of the resulting gender-related employment pattern for the maintenance of Japan's system of convoy capitalism cannot be underestimated. Firms would have found it impossible to live up to their lifetime employment commitments to their core, mostly male, workers, and they would have found it difficult to pay them seniority wages with generous benefits, were it not for the availability of a low-paid, much more easily dismissed female workforce.[86] Equally important, these policies relieved the state of the burden of having to provide extensive social services by assuring women would be available to take primary responsibility for caregiving whenever family members were in need. While the ability of women to choose their own life course was clearly constrained, this system of differentiated gender roles nevertheless made possible the "miracle" combination of low government spending, high growth, and high social protection summarized at the start of this chapter.

Socioeconomic Conditions That Made the System Work Symbiotically

The various pieces of convoy capitalism fit together very well—as long as they were situated in the specific socioeconomic context that characterized the high-growth era. During this period, production and protection did not come at the expense of each other but were provided symbiotically: the more protection, the more production, and vice versa. By providing job security and social insurance through firms, the system was able to give workers unprecedented levels of economic security, while at the same time motivating them to work harder and to work with management to secure the long-term viability of the firm. By relying on families (women) to provide most care for children, the elderly, and other needy citizens, the system was able to provide these groups, again, with unprecedented levels of care, while also making families (men) more productive cogs in the system. Finally, by concentrating its own role on *informal* protection of a type that needed the "reciprocal consent" of affected businesses and state officials, the government was able to assure that its interventions would uphold the convoy system of social protection, but in ways that were "market-conforming" and thus consistent with increased productivity.

The catch was that all of these elements of symbiosis in the system of convoy capitalism depended on socioeconomic conditions that were in place at the time and would not (in fact, could not) last forever. The very success of the system, in particular its success in generating wealth for firms and families, created exit options that were to undermine the effectiveness of social dynamics that depended on the *unavailability* of exit options and the tendency of such conditions to motivate concerned parties to make full use of voice to improve organizational performance. The challenges to the system that emerged once limited exit options opened up are the stories to be told in succeeding chapters. In the final section of this chapter, I focus on the ways in which the unavailability of exit options served as a necessary condition facilitating the symbiotic operation of convoy capitalism during the high-growth era.

Let's start with the role of unavailable exit options in driving the state to make only "market-conforming" interventions able to win "reciprocal consent." Richard Samuels, who coined this phrase, has eloquently described how reciprocal consent worked.[87] Comparing the way the Japanese state intervened in energy markets during the postwar period to the way European states behaved, Samuels gives the Japanese state credit for getting out of the way of market transitions, in particular from a primary dependence on coal to the extensive use of oil. In Europe, he notes, most states nationalized energy industries such as coal mining operations, electricity firms, and oil companies before, during, or immediately after World War II. In contrast, the Japanese state left energy industries in private hands, in coal, oil, and even in the electricity sector. It did so, he argues, not so much because it wanted to but because it was forced to. State officials on several occasions proposed nationalizing energy industries, but in each case they were rebuffed by private energy firms and their political allies.

The market structure bequeathed by this battle over ownership, Samuels argues, guaranteed that the state's interventions in energy markets would be much more market-conforming than they would have been had the state taken an ownership stake in coal, oil, and electricity. Whenever the state attempted to slow the transition out of coal, for example, it was constrained by firms operating in the market. Steel and electricity firms, the largest users of coal, resisted efforts to saddle them with the costs of purchasing expensive domestic coal. Similarly, coal firms resisted efforts to force them to use subsidies to keep mines open, realizing before the state did that coal was a dying industry. The result of the standoff over an appropriate response was a complex set of policies that ended up heavily subsidizing coal mining firms so they could buy out workers, close mines, and diversify out of coal. The need to come up with policies that could win the "reciprocal consent" of state officials and the various industries concerned, Samuels argues, enabled private firms to use state policy to achieve market ends.[88]

The role of user firms in Samuels's narrative deserves particular scrutiny because it is their interests that are subject to change once exit through foreign investment becomes easier. In the debate over whether to save the coal industry, Samuels describes users as having played a critical role, especially in the late 1960s and early 1970s when the move out of coal accelerated:

> The steel industry refused to purchase additional domestic coal, claiming that its growth was slowing, that new steel-making technologies had reduced its need for coke, that foreign suppliers were pressing for long-term sales contracts, and that the strengthening of the yen had made overseas coal even cheaper. It refused to make further sacrifices for the sake of national policy

and in fact resolved to reduce domestic coal purchases unless it received full reimbursement.[89]

Samuels goes on to describe the critical role played by Nippon Steel president In-ayama Yoshihiro, who headed the Coal Industry Advisory Council during the early 1970s. In this capacity he helped broker a deal under which coal production targets were dropped to twenty million tons, a target that was not revised upward even after the 1973 oil crisis pushed up the price of oil.

The position of user firms is critical because they are the ones, even more than the private firms in the industry seeking protection, that have an interest in making sure the state doesn't get in the way of market transitions. Samuels correctly em-phasizes the role of the user firms (especially steel) in keeping coal policy market-conforming, but he does not do enough to reflect on the conditions that drove steel firms to invest political capital in a fight to shrink the coal industry. At various points, he emphasizes that steel was sensitive to domestic costs because, as an ex-port industry, it competed head-to-head with foreign steel firms for overseas mar-kets. Also critical, however, was that the Japanese steel industry lacked the opportu-nity to shift production abroad to get around domestic costs. In 1970, the Japanese steel industry was still entirely domestic. All of Japanese firms' integrated steel mills were in Japan. For much of the period before 1970, steel firms would have had difficulty moving abroad, even if they wanted to, because of strict government lim-its on capital exports. In succeeding years, these firms went on to make major in-vestments in Korea, China, Brazil, and the United States, but in 1970 steel execu-tives were stuck with Japanese production. Coal was a major element of the industry's cost structure, so it had no choice but to intervene in the political process to assure that it was not saddled with the costs of supporting an uncompetitive coal industry.

Samuels argues that the reciprocal consent dynamics he identifies in the coal in-dustry and other energy sectors was what made Japanese economic policy market-conforming, at least during the period he studied:

> The Japanese state is a market-conforming player not because it is strong enough to control by other means, nor because it is smart enough to appreci-ate the efficiency of the market, but because in the development of commerce and industry powerful and stable private actors emerged who established en-during alliances with politicians and bureaucrats.[90]

I agree that private actors played a critical role in keeping policy market-conforming during this era, but suggest that user firms in particular were moti-vated to play this important role by their constrained position in the market. Be-cause they had few opportunities to exit via foreign investment during this era, they were forced to intervene in the political process to assure that policy did not delay market transitions too long or at too great a cost. In making this case, user firms frequently had to fight against the LDP's tendency to coddle declining industries, but their motivation was strong enough that it drove them to expend the political capital necessary to limit the LDP's interventions.

We turn next to the role of unavailable exit opportunities in keeping the family's role in the system of social protection symbiotic. The exit option that was largely unavailable to women during the high-growth years was, of course, the option of choosing not to marry and not to have children. Of the cohort of women born in 1950, just 4.9 percent remained childless at the end of their childbearing years.[91]

A number of economic and social factors helped bring about this record rate of fertility during the high-growth years. First, rapid socioeconomic growth provided push-and-pull factors that led most women to marry and form their own families. Rising incomes across generations meant that prospective husbands' incomes, even in their early working years, were often similar to or higher than those of their own fathers. Consequently, most women could expect to enjoy a higher standard of living soon, if not immediately, after leaving to set up their own household. The families of young people of this generation, moreover, tended to have small homes and limited incomes, making it difficult for them to board unmarried daughters or sons after they reached marriageable age. Finally, men and women of this generation were pushed and pulled out of their parents' households by the large-scale migration that took place between the countryside and the city. Families tended to be in the countryside while the best-paying jobs were in the city.

Adding to the pressure to marry and have children were social norms that prescribed "good wife, wise mother" as the appropriate life aspiration for young women. When asked what they thought of the statement "men should be out working; women should be in the home," 85 percent of the public agreed.[92] Women were expected to marry young, and once married they were expected to have two or more children. Those who formed families were then expected to devote themselves totally to the care of their children and, later, their elderly relatives. As Susan Orpett Long writes, "The Japanese cultural ideal of nurturance [carried] the expectation that caregiving is a totalizing experience. Nurturing children, husband, and elderly parents has been considered a women's major role. Other obligations and desires should not be allowed to interfere with caregiving obligations."[93]

This confluence of economic incentives and norms that channeled the vast majority of women into the role of full-time mothers obviously helped sustain, on the cheap, the protective side of convoy capitalism. During the high-growth years, however, it also "fit" the productive side. During this period, the economy had plenty of workers: young male workers born in the immediate postwar baby boom were entering the workforce in record numbers, supplemented by middle-aged men from the countryside looking for jobs in the city. Even Japanese feminists such as Maeda Masako have recognized that there was an element of "efficiency" in that era in a system that directed men into the paid workforce and encouraged women to become full-time housewives:

There were plenty of young male workers and there was no need for women to work so it made sense for Japan to rely on full-time housewives to provide unpaid childcare and eldercare in a 'Japanese-style welfare society.' That way it could avoid the social costs associated with northern European-style welfare and social insurance programs, and consequently could grow more quickly.[94]

The Japanese system of convoy capitalism was indeed a wonder to behold. It was able to provide most citizens with unprecedented economic security: care for those who needed it, job security for workers, and a safety net that bought time for firms to restructure their operations. And it was able to do all of this without compromising economic growth. As recently as 1994, Ronald Dore was still able to write effusively about the "x-efficiency" of the Japanese system, its ability to avoid the "equality-efficiency trade off" and propel society forward toward higher technical and productive achievement.[95]

In this chapter I have described how that system worked. The role of the state in providing social protection was kept deliberately small, with a primary focus on providing pensions and health care insurance for the elderly. Government aid to the unemployed, single mothers, and children remained minimal in comparison with social provision in European welfare states, leaving the task of providing for these groups primarily in the hands of firms and women. Employers were not alone, however, in their efforts to live up to the lifetime employment commitments that were at the heart of the Japanese social contract. Banks and elaborate "relational networks" gave firms the economic security they needed to provide security for their employees, and the state stood ready to back up these networks by guaranteeing banks against failure and other regulatory interventions. Likewise, women were channeled into their prescribed roles through policies that tolerated gender discrimination in the workplace and through tax and benefit policies that discouraged full-time work and subsidized full-time housewives.

What enabled a system that provided so much economic security to avoid the usual efficiency loss were a number of socioeconomic conditions that kept the enterprise market-conforming. In particular, the absence of exit opportunities for firms and women led them to take up vital roles that kept the system productive even as it was being protective. Firms such as those in the steel industry that were exposed to competition but lacked the ability to relocate production abroad to escape high domestic costs helped make sure government economic interventions did not delay market transitions too long. Likewise, the constraints on young women's ability to avoid marriage and family led them to play their assigned protective, productive, and reproductive roles in the system in ways that fit well with the demographic and labor market conditions of the day.

The set of structures and policies that made up convoy capitalism credited with making Japan a "welfare superpower" remained in place in the 1990s. The govern-

ment continued to back up the banks that continued to back up firms who continued to back up their core male workforce, and women continued to back up the
whole system by going along with policies that encouraged them to be full-time
housewives. But the socioeconomic conditions that had helped make sure the entire
enterprise ran symbiotically began to change. Firms and women now had exit options. The next chapter explores what happened when they began to exercise those
options.

Chapter 4

The Race for the Exits Begins

The Japanese system of convoy capitalism was well adapted to the socioeconomic conditions that were in place through 1980. The system worked because up to this point women and firms were willing and able to carry a hefty share of the load involved in providing society with care and income protection. Firms were willing and able to do their part, in turn, because up through the 1970s the government faced few constraints on its ability to use trade protection and regulations to protect the convoy and keep it moving steadily ahead. Women too were willing to focus their efforts on caregiving because social norms encouraged them to accept this role and because demographic conditions had yet to create labor shortages that would open up career opportunities and raise their wages. Neither women nor firms had significant incentives or opportunities to exit from their prescribed roles in the system of convoy capitalism.

Starting around 1980, however, the socioeconomic circumstances that fit Japan's system of social protection so well began to change. Faced with growing foreign pressure to open its markets and eliminate its informal regulatory powers, the government was forced to begin exposing the convoy system to increasingly volatile market forces. Formal trade barriers were slashed, capital flows were liberalized, the yen was allowed to float up in value, and regulated segments of the economy were exposed to competition for the first time. These initial steps toward liberalization, though limited to what Japan had to do to forestall foreign pressure, fundamentally changed the environment in which firms operated. They now faced much greater competitive pressure *and* they had greater opportunities to exit.

Women too faced a new set of incentives while at the same time acquiring new exit options. A tighter labor market during the 1980s began to open up career options for women just as a new generation of young women began to seek more out of life than the devoted housewife role prescribed under the traditional family system. Meanwhile, young women found their families were now often wealthy enough to subsidize them while they pursued higher education, explored work opportunities, and considered who and whether to marry. The opportunity cost of marrying and starting a family rose even as the cost of staying out of marriage fell. These social changes too inevitably affected the Japanese system of convoy capitalism.

In this chapter I tell the story of how these changes affected Japan's women and firms. Ideally, these groups, which bore such a heavy burden under the established system of social protection, would have mobilized in the political arena to transform the system to fit the new socioeconomic circumstances: to make it more suited to shifting gender roles and a globalized world economy. Instead, they exited. Firms that had produced exclusively at home began moving more and more of their productive operations abroad, and women who would have preferred both to have a family *and* a career opted out of one or the other, giving up on marriage and children or settling for the life of a housewife with occasional part-time work.

Globalization Alters the Environment Facing Japanese Firms

Prior to the late 1960s, Japanese firms operated in a domestic economy that was hermetically sealed from international financial markets though strict regulations of international capital flows and an exchange rate that was immovably fixed at $1= ¥360. Manufactured goods moved across borders (indeed, Japanese goods exports as a share of its economy were larger in 1970 than in 2000), but capital flows in and out of Japan and currency speculation were virtually nonexistent. Japanese firms that wanted to import technology or finance operations by importing capital had to secure the permission of state officials who granted approval only when projects were deemed to be in the national interest. Firms found it even more difficult to export capital in order to finance foreign direct investment. Worried about the nation's chronic balance of payments difficulties, officials authorized the use of scarce capital to finance overseas investment only when the venture promised to secure raw materials that were unavailable domestically and needed to supply Japanese industry.[1]

This environment began to loosen up slightly by the end of the 1960s. Japan had agreed to liberalize foreign exchange controls and capital movements under the terms of its admission as a full member of the Organisation for Economic Co-operation and Development in 1964, and it soon faced pressure to live up to these commitments.[2] By 1967, Japan had legalized inward investment in select sectors such as sake brewing and corn flakes and was promising to gradually expand the list of approved sectors.[3] At the same time, the nation's success in overcoming its hard currency constraints by achieving a string of trade surpluses led government officials to take a more relaxed attitude toward outward investment. In 1971 alone, they authorized foreign investment projects valued at $858 million, compared to an average of just $179 million a year between 1951 and 1970.[4] Nevertheless, government officials remained worried enough about the potentially destabilizing effects of capital movements that they retained strict controls on short-term capital flows.

These restrictions too began to crumble, however, after the yen-dollar exchange rate came unglued in 1971. In the second of his famous "Nixon shocks," President Richard Nixon unilaterally closed the gold window, ending the Bretton Woods system under which all major currencies were linked at a fixed rate to the U.S. dollar, which was in turn pegged to gold at a fixed $35 per ounce. He also imposed a 10 percent surcharge on U.S. imports, effectively devaluing the dollar by that amount.[5] This sudden shift in the value of the yen created unbearable pressures on financial authorities, who responded by relaxing controls on short-term capital flows so that investors could protect themselves from currency risks. The increase in the value of the yen from $1 = ¥360 in 1971 to ¥272 in 1973 also generated an increased interest in longer-term foreign investment on the part of Japanese firms, which could now buy much more with their money. In 1973 alone, government officials approved foreign investment projects worth $3.5 billion—a 400 percent increase over the 1971 figure.[6]

The 1973–74 oil shocks put a temporary crimp in Japanese firms' expansion plans, but their effects on global financial markets simply accelerated the trend toward globalization. The huge sums of dollars amassed by the OPEC countries after they sharply raised oil prices had to be invested somewhere, so global capital markets—including an expanded Eurodollar market outside U.S. regulatory control—emerged to undertake this task. This unregulated market provided international capital with a wedge that it used to whittle away at financial controls around the world. By 1980, Japanese firms dissatisfied with the prices charged for financial services in Tokyo could raise capital in dollars or yen in the Euro markets at a fraction of the cost. Facing an outflow of financial business, Japanese authorities agreed to the further liberalization of Japanese financial markets in the yen-dollar talks that were concluded in 1984.[7]

Capital controls were not the only barriers to international transactions that fell by the wayside over this period. Average Japanese tariffs on nonagricultural products were steadily lowered, to the point where they were on par with those of the United States and Europe by the conclusion of the Tokyo Round in 1978.[8] As Japanese trade surpluses with the world and with the United States surged in the early 1980s, nontariff barriers faced increased scrutiny as well. Quotas protecting Japanese farm sectors, regulations protecting small retail firms, and collusive practices that closed foreign firms out of the bidding process for public works contracts were among the many trade barriers that became the subject of heated criticism by U.S. officials. By the end of the 1980s, the United States was charging that the Japanese economic structure as a whole constituted a barrier to trade, and set about trying to breach these barriers through "aggressive unilateral" demands, backed up by the controversial Super 301 provision of U.S. trade law.[9]

These political demands for liberalization from the United States were supplemented by market pressures growing out of the earlier decision of the United

States to open up its own regulated service sectors to competitive forces. Starting in the mid-1970s, the United States had begun rewriting regulations that shielded sectors such as transportation, energy, and telecommunications from competitive pressures. Firms such as AT&T that had been regulated monopolies were forced to compete with upstart firms like Sprint and MCI, while heavily regulated industries such as the airlines that had been able to avoid price competition were forced to adapt to a new free-wheeling environment where firms were free to charge what they wanted. By the 1980s, these regulatory policies had helped produce huge productivity and cost advantages for the U.S. airline, trucking, shipping, and telecommunications firms that survived the shakeout.[10] Japanese service firms that had to compete in these sectors—as well as Japanese manufacturers forced to procure domestic services at relatively high prices—faced adjustment difficulties as a result.

The net effect of these changes, captured by the phrase "globalization," was to dramatically increase the volatility of the business environment facing Japanese firms and to make it increasingly costly for them to live up to their obligations under the convoy system of social protection. For firms facing import competition at home and competition from foreign producers in export markets, the volatility of exchange rates was a particular challenge. Particularly difficult to accommodate were the sudden spikes in the value of the yen from ¥360 to ¥272 from 1971 to 1973, from ¥296 to ¥210 from 1976 to 1978, from ¥238 to ¥128 from 1985 to 1988, and finally from ¥126 to ¥94 from 1992 to 1995.[11] These spikes were difficult to accommodate, first, because they took place so rapidly. Firms had difficulty adjusting when they had to go from dealing with more orders than they could handle at an undervalued exchange rate (such as ¥238 in 1985) to a sudden drop in orders after their export prices rose sharply due to the rapid revaluation of the yen. The fact that the Japanese yen increased in value more than any other currency over this period made their adjustment burden even heavier.[12]

Japanese traded goods firms faced particular difficulties when exchange rate shifts magnified the premium they were already paying for certain services because of the productivity gap between their Japanese suppliers and the deregulated, more productive firms supplying their foreign competitors. By the mid-1990s, the price gaps between what Japanese firms had to pay for key inputs and what their counterparts in the United States and Europe had to pay were immense. The high cost structure facing Japanese firms that had to pay more than their American, German, and Asian counterparts for almost all inputs is summarized in table 4.1. Firms operating in these overseas locations, for example, had to pay an average of just 41 percent of what Japanese firms were charged for railway cargo; 35 percent for long distance telephone services; 86 percent for issuing bonds; and 62 percent for industrial power.

The difficulty Japanese firms had adjusting to rising costs and increased volatility was also a product of export surges from newly industrialized countries. Japan itself had caused headaches for managers in Europe and North America with its own surging exports of automobiles, steel, and electronics in the 1970s. By the

TABLE 4.1.
Japan's high cost structure

	Japan	United States	Germany	Korea	China	Singapore	Non-Japan Average
Energy							
Petroleum products	100	67	117	152	54	53	89
Industrial power	100	77	81	44	71	38	62
Transport							
Railway cargo	100	61	67	24	10	—	41
Port transport	100	90	—	47	—	53	63
International airfreight	100	55	73	98	36	80	68
Telecom							
Local call	100	97	115	52	14	29	61
Long-distance call	100	48	65	23	5	—	35
Finance							
Bond-issuing cost	100	86	—	—	—	—	86
Land							
Plant site	100	71	62	54	—	—	62
Office rental	100	55	52	56	135	70	74

Source: Adapted from Ministry of International Trade and Industry, Industrial Planning Bureau, *Action Plan for Economic Structure Reform* (Tokyo: MITI, 1998), 4.

1980s, however, Japan was starting to face pressure from the next generation of up-starts: Taiwan, Korea, and Southeast Asian "Tigers," later followed by China. Each of these nations was able to ride the wave of globalization, rapidly expanding production by importing capital and using it to purchase technology, plants, and equipment off the shelf. As these investments came on line, Japan faced growing competition "from below," from increasingly sophisticated producers in East Asia with much lower labor, land, and energy costs, even as the rise in the value of the yen and the growing productivity gap in services presented them with tougher competition from North American and European firms.

Much of what I have described will no doubt be familiar to readers of the literature on globalization, for in the years since 1971 all economies have had to adjust to more volatile financial and currency markets, new import competition, and the U.S. challenge in services. Japanese firms faced a particularly difficult burden of adjustment, however, because of the system of social protection in which they were embedded. When firms in the United States and Britain (post-Thatcher) faced new competition, they were much freer than their Japanese counterparts to respond by laying off workers, cutting wages, closing uncompetitive plants and operations, and shifting sources of supplies. When firms on the European continent faced these challenges, they frequently found ways to off-load some of the costs onto the welfare state: German manufacturers were able to shift excess employees onto the pension rolls, for example, while redundant Swedish workers were provided with state-funded retraining. In contrast, Japanese firms had to adjust while somehow living up to their commitments not to lay off workers, not to cut ties to established suppliers, to continue providing extensive employment-related benefits, to find new jobs for redundant employees, and to assist other firms that were part of their network. Moreover, they were asked to continue living up to their commitments even as the government was being forced to give up more and more of the policy levers it used to protect the convoy system.[13]

The Japanese firms that faced the greatest challenge as a result of all of these developments were its large manufacturing firms making traded goods, companies that included Nippon Steel, Sumitomo Chemical, Sony, Toshiba, Toyota, and Nissan. Each time these firms cut costs and improved productivity in order to compete at a higher value of the yen, they were hit with another round of yen appreciation that threatened their competitiveness. By the mid-1980s, these firms had enough experience struggling to maintain their competitiveness in the more volatile, less insulated business climate of the globalization era to sense that the system of convoy capitalism needed to be reformed. They needed more flexible labor markets, fewer responsibilities for providing social benefits, and deregulation to lower the prices they had to pay for energy, transport, and telecommunications. In particular, the constant ratcheting up of the value of the yen was a measure of the degree to which their interests were diverging from those of fellow Japanese businesses in the protected, domestically oriented sectors.[14] The yen seemed fated to continue rising until it reached a level where Japan's most efficient makers of traded goods could not compete—unless sheltered sectors were somehow forced to face market competition and absorb imports themselves.

The pathologies of the old system of convoy capitalism became even clearer to these firms, of course, in the aftermath of the bubble economy (1986–90). One reason stock and land prices rose as high as they did was because the banks that were financing the investments were protected from the risk of bankruptcy by the Ministry of Finance. Also implicated was the system's reliance on informal monitoring by main banks and bureaucrats, in place of monitoring by markets with access to accurate financial reports. Finally, the fact that some of most spectacular crashes of the bubble era involved firms and sectors with close ties to the LDP (e.g., the *jūsen* debacle involving the failure of financial firms with ties to LDP-affiliated agricultural cooperatives) was yet another sign of the price the Japanese economy paid for a system of social protection that relied so heavily on informal regulatory protection.

So how did firms such as Sony and Toyota respond? They could have mobilized in the political arena to demand far-reaching reforms in the system of convoy capitalism to make it more suited to the new globalized era. These were, after all, the largest and richest firms in Japan, with millions of employee-voters. They had access to prime ministers, political funds they could allocate as they wished, and good relations with labor unions. The political system, dominated as it was by the Liberal Democratic Party, which had close ties to sheltered sectors of the economy, did not exactly *invite* a major economic reform initiative, but they could have tried to transform the system to make far-reaching economic reforms possible. In addition to these political options, however, firms also had alternative ways of dealing with their situation through markets—more ways than ever before, in fact, because of the very phenomenon that was causing them such headaches.

Japanese Women Confront New Opportunities and Incentives

Return visitors to Japan who have been absent for some years often remark that nothing has changed so much as Japan's young women. Twenty-five years ago, the mothers of those who are now coming of age aspired above all to be full-time housewives (*sengyō shufu*). Most were content with a high school education or, if they continued beyond that point, with two years at a junior college majoring in early childhood education or home economics. In 1975, just 13.5 percent of eighteen-year-old women attended four-year colleges, compared to 41 percent of men, and less than half of women aged twenty-five to twenty-nine were in the labor force. The degree to which the "good wife, wise mother" ethic pushed this cohort of women to concentrate their energies on their roles as wives and mothers can be seen in two statistics: of women born in 1950 whose period of fertility spanned the years 1965 to 1990, 95 percent married and 90 percent had at least one child—figures suggesting that, given inevitable fertility problems among women and their partners, almost all women of this cohort who could have children did have children.[15] As late as 1985, single women approaching twenty-five were still being warned that they had better hurry and find a husband if they wanted to avoid becoming "Christmas cakes"—desserts that lose most of their value after the twenty-fifth of December.[16]

Young Japanese women today are very different. The proportion of unmarried women aspiring to be full-time housewives has fallen sharply, from 34 percent in 1987 to 19 percent in 2002 (see figure 4.1). In contrast, the proportion hoping in some way to combine work outside the home with child rearing (maintaining their careers after having children or hoping to return to work after leaving the labor force temporarily to raise children) has grown from 50 percent to 66 percent. The rising aspirations of women can also be seen in the recent sharp spike in the proportion of eighteen-year-old women attending four-year colleges (figure 4.2). This share rose from around 13 percent in the 1980s to 34.4 percent in 2003—at a time when college attendance among young men was rising only slightly from the low 40s to 47 percent. There is a parallel rise in the proportion of young women aged twenty-five to twenty-nine in the labor force, now up to 73.4 percent (figure 4.2).

These are only the most basic indicators of the changing aspirations of young Japanese women. Government statistics show that over 130,000 women—more than twice the number of men—leave the country to study abroad each year, typically to study English in the United States, Britain, or Australia.[17] Foreign study and foreign travel, pastimes that were the exclusive preserve of wealthy women

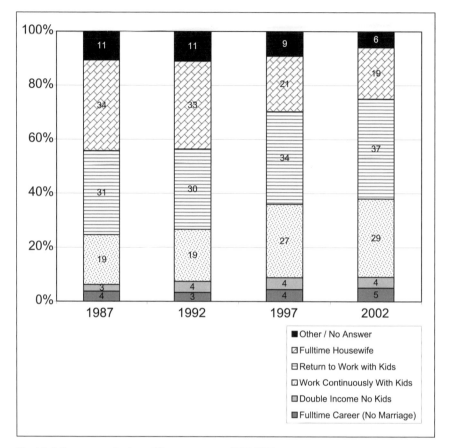

Fig. 4.1. Life-course aspirations of Japanese women, 1987–2002
Source: Based on data from National Institute of Population and Social Security Research, *Dai-12–kai shushō dōkō kihon chōsa: Dokushinsha chōsa no kekka gaiyō*, 2004, 16. The NIPSSR surveyed unmarried women aged 25–34 and asked them which life course they would "ideally" like to pursue.

twenty years ago, are now virtually a rite of passage for middle-class Japanese women. In 2003, almost three million women between the ages of twenty and thirty-nine traveled overseas.[18] Young women today are much more inclined to report that they hope to marry for love than their mothers did, many of whom met their husbands through introductions by intermediaries (*miai*).[19]

This "gender revolution" has had its most profound effects on young women, but it has not left their mothers' generation untouched. In fact, young women's discontents with traditional marriage and family norms reflect their perceptions of how their mothers feel about their own marriages and lives. The recent sharp rise in divorces by women whose children have left home is symptomatic of broader discontents among women of this generation with marriages in which they are valued

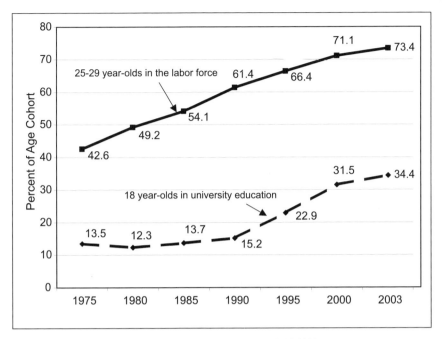

Fig. 4.2. Educational and career aspirations of Japanese women, 1975–2003
Sources: Based on data from the Ministry of Education, Culture, Sport, Science and Technology and the Ministry of Health, Labor and Welfare.

primarily for their unpaid work as cooks, housekeepers, and caregivers. That their dissatisfaction exceeds levels in other nations is suggested by the pattern of Japanese women's responses to a survey question that asked them to characterize their level of satisfaction with their "family life" (figure 4.3). Just 46 percent of Japanese women were satisfied, a proportion about 20 percentage points lower than in Britain, the United States, Sweden, and Thailand. Another survey, focused specifically on women's feelings about child rearing, found an even greater contrast. While 72 percent of U.S. mothers and 54 percent of Koreans said they found child rearing to be a "pleasure," just 23 percent of Japanese mothers said so.[20]

The shift in Japanese women's aspirations and their discontents with what they can achieve under the current system is perhaps best expressed by journalist Fuke Shigeko: "The era has ended when women will be satisfied just with being the section chief's wife. . . . Today's women, filled with desires and ambition, are no longer satisfied with either of the choices 'company' or 'marriage.' "[21] As suggested by the survey data in figure 4.1, most Japanese women want both, along with the leisure to enjoy life as individuals in ways that are not captured by their roles as workers, wives, or mothers.

These changes in Japanese gender-role aspirations are the product of broader,

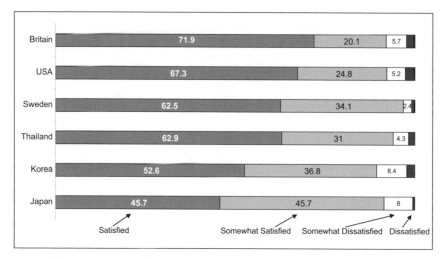

Fig. 4.3. Women's contentment with family life
Source: Adapted from Ministry of Health and Welfare, *Kōsei hakusho—Heisei 10–nen-han*, 1998, 5.

deeper socioeconomic and cultural processes that have been going on for some time and that are likely to push society in this direction for many more years. Economists emphasize in particular the role of shifting labor markets in changing women's aspirations and opportunities.[22] As long as Japan had a steady flow of young male school-leavers and migrants from rural areas to supply its urban labor markets, there were few incentives for firms to open up career opportunities to women or for women to seek work. Many career options were closed completely to Japanese women until the 1980s; even when work opportunities were available, they tended to pay much less than jobs open to men. In 1975, employed thirty- to thirty-four-year-old women earned just 64 percent of the wages of men of that age.[23] The work open to women during these years was frequently work behind the counter at the family store or in the fields of the family farm. In 1950, 30 percent of women worked in family businesses of these kinds, compared to just 10 percent who worked as employees. As late as 1962, family workers made up the majority of working women.[24]

By the 1980s, however, the flow of new male school-leavers and rural workers into urban labor markets had slowed significantly—just as demand for labor was pushed up by the rapid growth of the bubble economy. The result was a growing labor shortage that soon had Japanese business managers scouring the world for workers. The foreign workers they recruited were able to fill many dirty, dangerous, and difficult jobs, but they could not fill the skilled white-collar jobs that constituted the bulk of new employment growth during the decade. Managers thus began turning to female college graduates to fill positions that would never have been open to them before. By 1998, this cohort of female workers was in the thirty- to thirty-four-year-old age group and was earning significantly more than in the past, almost 78 percent of male earnings.[25] These higher wages naturally drew more women to focus on career opportunities and adjust their educational plans and aspirations accordingly.

In shaping women's attitudes toward marriage and having children, the nature of the new jobs was just as important as the higher rate of pay women could expect to earn. Whereas women who worked on the farm or in family businesses could expect to balance their work and child-rearing responsibilities, the new jobs demanded that women commute to urban job centers and work long days away from home.[26] Absent new social institutions, norms, and policies that would socialize the work of raising children, the shift in labor markets produced a sharp increase in the opportunity cost of marriage and motherhood.

The causes of the shift in women's aspirations, however, are certainly much more complex than the pull of labor markets. Some sociologists emphasize that shifting income differentials across generations constitute another important driver of this social change.[27] As noted in the previous chapter, men and women who reached maturity in the early 1970s faced decisions about marriage and careers at a time when the rapid economic growth of the preceding two decades made setting up their own households look attractive compared to the option of continuing their single lives at home with their parents.

The equivalent calculus today is quite different. The parents of today's young men and women are the wealthiest generation ever in Japan. Many pinched and saved and bought relatively spacious homes (most of which are now closer to job centers in the large urban areas), with room to accommodate their adult children while they remain unmarried. The breadwinners in these homes are typically in their peak earning years when their children are in their twenties and thirties, allowing them to subsidize their children so they can afford a rich single life. Young singles are thus able to use their paychecks to pay for foreign travel, luxury goods, and frequent dinners out on the town while paying nothing for their room and board and letting their mothers take care of cooking and cleaning. Yamada Masahiro, who popularized this account of generational change, calls these young people "parasite singles."[28] He emphasizes how the ability of young singles today to take advantage of parental subsidies—combined with the stagnant wage growth most young people can expect in today's slow-growth economy—is what accounts for the changing values of the new generation of women and men.[29] They can afford to wait for the ideal mate, holding out, as one woman put it, "until and unless I find a man with a high income who will help with the household chores, is good-looking and who would never cheat on me."[30]

Though we can certainly attribute some of the changing aspirations of Japanese young women to increasing work opportunities and the effects of shifting intergenerational income differentials, anthropologists who study the attitudes of young Japanese women describe their rising career and life aspirations as being part of a deeper cultural shift driven by exposure to norms that began transforming gender roles and relations in Western Europe and North America several decades earlier. Japanese women today do not simply want more career opportunities and better pay, they want more romantic marriages that are rooted in more equal partnerships. They want husbands who will do housework and help take care of the children. Unlike their mothers, they do not want to devote themselves entirely to the care of others, but want to travel and shop and live for themselves.

Karen Kelsky argues that Japanese women's aspirations, in particular those of upper-middle-class "cosmopolitans," have been powerfully influenced by what she calls the "global Imaginary," made up of media images flowing freely across borders in the form of movies, television shows, and the Internet, combined with the experiences available through foreign tourism.[31] Through these images and experiences, cosmopolitan Japanese women have been able to glimpse what they perceive to be the greater "sensitivity" of Western men, to sample what they describe to be more sexually adventurous and romantic relationships, and even to work in foreign settings where women are given greater responsibilities and opportunities. This foreign "mirror" has allowed them to reflect more critically on the social norms and structures that constrain their opportunities at home and has led them to challenge this system by celebrating their foreign encounters in travelogues, novels, manga (comic books), and movies.

While Kelsky's "cosmopolitan women" continue to push the envelope defining acceptable behavior for Japanese women, broader cultural norms have shifted too in ways that have changed the incentives facing young women. As noted above, a few years ago women as young as twenty-five faced incredible pressure to marry from friends and family. Those attitudes were reflected in survey data showing that in 1972, 80 percent of women and 84 percent of men agreed with the statement "women had better marry." By 1997, those figures had fallen to 68 percent and 74 percent, respectively.[32] Even more striking was the shift in attitudes toward women working outside the home. Whereas 83 percent of men and women had agreed with the statement "the external world is for men and the domestic world is for women" in 1972, by 2004 the proportion had fallen to 45.2 percent.[33] These attitude shifts meant women coming of age in the 1990s faced lower social sanctions— fewer disapproving looks from strangers, less nagging from family members—if they chose to work, and somewhat less stigmatization if they chose to remain single. These broader cultural changes thus supplemented the forces that were changing young women themselves, making them less comfortable with public policies and workplace rules that continued to push women with children out of careers.

This women's "revolution," as well as the deeper economic, social, and cultural currents that helped produce it, are of course not restricted to Japan. As in the case of globalization, however, the Japanese revolution in women's attitudes and aspirations has caused particularly severe adjustment problems because of the degree to which it flies in the face of the established system of social protection that depends so heavily on women willingly taking upon themselves a disproportionate share of care-giving work. Women who embarked on careers in the bubble years and enjoyed rising wages in their career-track jobs in the 1990s discovered when they wanted to marry and have children that the system was not set up to accommodate their hopes and desires. They were still expected to give up their careers when children came along or when aging relatives needed care.

The growing frustrations of young Japanese women with these constraints meant something would have to give. Either women would give voice to their discontents and attempt to change public policies, work practices, and their housework-challenged male partners, or they would find ways to navigate around the challenges they faced as best they could, through uncoordinated, individual exit strategies.

Firms Turn to Exit

We will examine women's responses in the next section, but first we return to the story of how Sony and Toyota and other firms responded to their own changing environment. Faced with rising costs of doing business in Japan, chief executives of internationally oriented firms occasionally spoke out in favor of far-reaching changes in the established convoy system. In the early 1990s, for example, Sony chairman Morita Akio called for Japan to move away from its version of capitalism toward the American model, with less emphasis on stability for the "stakeholders" (including employees) and more emphasis on profits.[34] Morita's comments sparked a flurry of media reports mulling over the implications of his remarks. Such episodes were newsworthy, however, precisely because they were so rare. Most business leaders avoided criticizing the lifetime employment system, the keiretsu system, or other core features of convoy capitalism. Instead, they quietly and individually began moving a growing segment of their business overseas where these rules didn't apply.

The broadest measure of this growing exit trend is provided by data on Japanese foreign direct investment. From a level so low it barely registered, Japanese foreign investment grew to around $5 billion a year in the late 1970s and then to a level topping $50 billion in many years in the late 1980s through the 1990s (see figure 4.4). Although the initial surge in the late 1980s was in part a product of the bubble economy, with much of it concentrated in the financial services sector, the durability of the trend is revealed by the way foreign investment continued to flow out of Japan through the depths of the Japanese recession in the 1990s. In fact, levels of manufacturing FDI grew in the late 1990s to heights that exceeded those of the bubble years—despite the fact that firms were having to make investment choices in a lower profit environment (see figure 4.5). Outward flows were particularly large

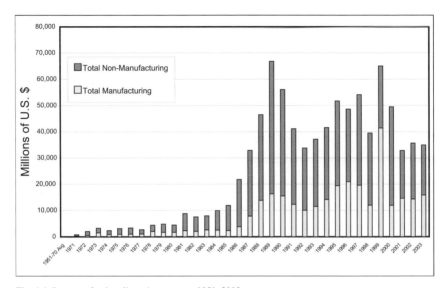

Fig. 4.4. Japanese foreign direct investment, 1951–2003
Source: Based on data from Ministry of Finance, *Zaisei kinyū tōkei geppō*, various issues; data for 1993 forward converted from yen to dollars at the average exchange rate for the year.

in transport and electronics, the sectors that were home to internationally competitive firms such as Toyota, Sony, and Canon.

The surge in Japanese outward investment was so rapid that it transformed Japan from a nation populated mostly by firms producing in Japan for domestic consumption and export to one that was home to many of the leading transnational corporations in the world. In the early 1980s, Japanese firms were major exporters and had high foreign sales, but they remained minor league players in foreign production. Dunning and Pearce report that in 1982 foreign sales accounted for 28.6 percent of the sales of Japan's leading industrial companies. That same year, overseas production accounted for just 5.6 percent of these firms' total sales.[35]

This same pattern can be seen in the share of foreign-affiliate value added in the foreign sales of Japanese manufacturing firms in 1977 and 1980 (first two columns of table 4.2). In those years, foreign affiliates added just 15 and 13 percent, respectively, to the total foreign sales of Japanese firms. Although foreign affiliates in a few sectors such as foods, wood and wood products, and textiles included manufacturing operations and produced higher value added, foreign affiliates in most sectors merely provided distribution and marketing—which in 1977 added 20 percent in electrical machinery, 16 percent in chemicals and metals, and just 4 percent in transport equipment. The final column of the same table shows the impact of Japan's surge in outward foreign investment. By 1995, foreign affiliates of Japanese manufacturing firms were providing 40 percent of the value added to the foreign

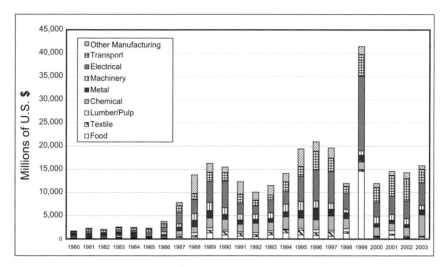

Fig. 4.5. Japanese manufacturing foreign direct investment, 1980–2003
Source: Based on data from Ministry of Finance, *Zaisei kinyū tōkei geppō,* various issues; data for 1993 forward converted from yen to dollars at the average exchange rate for the year.

TABLE 4.2.
Share of Japanese affiliates in total foreign sales by Japanese manufacturing firms

Sector	Year					
	1977	1980	1986	1988	1989	1995
Food	44	28	59	73	74	83
Chemicals	16	16	37	52	51	51
Metals	16	14	29	39	38	46
Nonelectrical machinery	5	5	12	11	15	15
Electrical machinery	20	19	28	38	37	42
Transport equipment	4	5	16	25	29	45
Textile and apparel	36	29	35	46	43	45
Wood, paper, and pulp	46	42	46	58	50	58
Total	15	13	23	31	33	40

Source: Adapted from Magnus Blomström, Denise Konan, and Robert E. Lipsey, "FDI in the Restructuring of the Japanese Economy," in *Japan's New Economy: Continuity and Change in the Twenty-First Century,* ed. Magnus Blomström, Byron Gangnes, and Sumner LaCroix (Oxford: Oxford University Press, 2001), 25. By permission of Oxford University Press.
Note: Share of foreign affiliates is calculated by taking the foreign affiliate value added (sales by foreign affiliates of Japanese manufacturing firms minus affiliate imports from Japan and affiliate exports to Japan) as a proportion of total foreign sales by Japanese firms and their foreign affiliates (Japanese manufactured exports plus sales of foreign affiliates minus foreign affiliate exports to Japan).

sales of Japanese firms, and the foreign affiliate share had risen to 42 to 51 percent in the electrical, transport, chemicals, and metals sectors.

While Japanese transnational firms were especially quick to expand the foreign affiliate share of their foreign sales, the strategy inevitably spilled over to give overseas production a larger and larger share of these firms' worldwide sales, including their sales back in Japan. In 1985, the share of foreign manufacturing value added to total manufacturing value added for all Japanese firms was just 3 percent. By 1995 this figure had grown to 9 percent, and by 2003 it had reached 18 percent. Growth in the foreign manufacturing share was especially rapid for Japan's two most successful and internationalized industries, electrical machinery and transport equipment. From 1993 to 2002 the foreign production share for electrical machinery grew from 12.6 percent to 26.5 percent and that for transport equipment grew from 17.3 percent to 47.6 percent. Almost half of all Japanese transport equipment was now being produced overseas.[36]

This transformation at the macro and sectoral levels showed up as well at the level of the individual firm. In 1980, Toyota was still producing most of its motor vehicles at home. The few produced abroad were assembled in small-scale "screwdriver" operations made necessary by high tariffs or tight quotas that precluded sourcing fully assembled cars from Japan. The other Japanese auto firms were similarly limited to Japan-based production. Honda, the pioneer in overseas production in this industry, had begun producing motorcycles at a plant in the United States in 1979, but it did not begin assembling automobiles there until 1982.

The leading electronics firms were equally slow to move abroad. Sony was a pioneer among all Japanese manufacturing firms in its willingness to experiment with overseas production. As early as 1959, it set up small-scale assembly operations in both Hong Kong and Ireland, but both of these were shut down within a few years after they proved not to be profitable. The company tried again in 1972, when it set up a large production operation in San Diego, motivated primarily by concerns about protectionist sentiment in the United States.[37] Even after this plant and a similar operation in Wales were up and running, however, 80 percent of Sony's production work remained at home. Only after the firm opened nine plants in Asia in the second half of the 1980s did Sony begin to transnationalize its entire production process.[38] Other electronics firms moved overseas at a slower pace. Canon located its first assembly plant overseas, in Taiwan, in the 1970s, but it was not until the 1980s that it began locating several facilities in North America and Europe.[39]

By the late 1990s and early 2000s, this picture had changed completely. Honda now bragged of a "glocalization" (global localization) strategy with 100 factories in thirty-three countries.[40] In 2003 alone, it opened new automobile assembly plants in Taiwan, Malaysia, and Indonesia. While Toyota had been slower to ramp up overseas production, by 2003 it too had emerged as a truly transnational firm, producing 33.4 percent of Toyota vehicles overseas.[41] The Japanese electronics firms were even more transnational. By 2001, Canon was operating a growing number of manufacturing plants in Asia, along with those it opened in the 1980s in Europe and the

United States. Thirty-four percent of its production was being done overseas, and the firm had announced plans to raise this figure to 40 percent.[42] With a large number of Asian, European, and North American plants in operation, Sony also ratcheted up its foreign production, setting a target of 35 percent for the 1990s.[43]

These companies were merely the most prominent among a long list of Japanese firms that shifted production overseas in recent years. By 1999, Japanese firms accounted for eighteen of the world's top one hundred transnational companies, almost as many as the United States (twenty-six) and more than the double the number from the United Kingdom (eight).[44] These firms are listed below (table 4.3). As the table shows, most of these firms were now transnational, not only in terms of sales but also in terms of production and employment. Toyota alone now had over $56 billion in foreign assets and ranked sixth on the list of transnational companies. Other leading Japanese transnational companies had lower total foreign assets but were even more transnational in terms of asset and employment shares. Over 60 percent of Sony's employees were now overseas, as were 53 percent of Canon's and 50 percent of Matsushita Electric's. Of Honda's total assets, 58 percent were located overseas. The proportion was reported to be just as high at Sony,[45] and was almost as high at Canon (48%). These were just the most prominent of Japan's transnational companies. Many more firms, operating on a somewhat smaller scale and frequently producing parts and subassemblies for the leading manufacturers, maintained similar proportions of their assets and workers overseas.

Though Japanese firms have been moving a growing share of their productive operations abroad, we need to be careful not to assume that all of this FDI is a product of the "race for the exits" dynamic that is the focus of this book. Firms locate production overseas for a wide variety of reasons, many of them having very little to do with concerns over production costs at home. Many are interested, for example, in expanding overseas sales by getting closer to their foreign customers. Others aim to protect themselves from currency risks by producing in a number of different locations. Another group is motivated by political concerns, such as the desire to mollify protectionists in their overseas markets by locating production and jobs there. Just as we need to be careful not to assume that all women who do not have children are trying to escape the Japanese family system, we need to be careful not to assume that all firms engaged in FDI are trying to leave behind the costs of the Japanese system of convoy capitalism.

For this very reason, Japanese policymakers have had a great deal of difficulty agreeing on whether the investment trends summarized above add up to a hollowing-out phenomenon. If FDI is driven primarily by business reasons such as those enumerated in the previous paragraph, it clearly is inappropriate to characterize the pattern that way. On the other hand, if many firms are reducing investment at home while increasing investment in low-cost overseas locations in an effort to get around the high costs of labor, energy, and social insurance contributions, that suggests that something more like a "race for the exits" is going on. In the next chapter, I will return to the debate over how to interpret the evi-

TABLE 4.3.
Leading Japanese transnational corporations in 1999

Rank*	Firm	Assets** Foreign	Assets** Total	Assets** Share	Sales** Foreign	Sales** Total	Sales** Share	Employment Foreign	Employment Total	Employment Share
6	Toyota Motors	56.3	154.9	36%	60.0	119.7	50%	13,500	214,631	6%
13	Nippon Mitsubishi Oil	31.5	35.5	89%	28.4	33.9	84%	11,900	15,964	75%
22	Sony Corp.	N/A	64.2	N/A	43.1	63.1	68%	115,717	189,700	61%
26	Mitsubishi Corp.	24.6	78.6	31%	15.8	127.3	12%	3,437	7,556	45%
29	Honda Motors	24.4	41.8	58%	38.7	51.7	75%	N/A	112,200	N/A
34	Nissan Motors	N/A	59.7	N/A	N/A	58.1	N/A	N/A	136,397	N/A
45	Mitsui & Co. Ltd.	17.3	56.5	31%	57.8	118.5	49%	N/A	31,250	N/A
50	Fujitsu Ltd.	15.3	42.3	36%	17.5	43.3	40%	72,851	188,573	39%
53	Sumitomo Corp.	15.0	47.6	32%	12.6	103.5	12%	N/A	33,057	N/A
55	Hitachi Ltd.	14.6	91.5	16%	15.4	77.7	20%	N/A	323,827	N/A
56	Matsushita Electric	13.9	72.5	19%	34.0	68.9	49%	143,773	290,448	50%
60	Itochu	12.4	55.9	22%	18.4	115.3	16%	N/A	40,683	N/A
61	Canon	12.3	25.4	48%	18.0	25.7	70%	42,787	81,009	53%
67	Marubeni Corp.	10.8	54.2	20%	31.9	99.3	32%	N/A	8,618	N/A
81	Nissho Iwai	9.1	38.5	24%	12.9	68.7	19%	N/A	18,446	N/A
97	Toshiba	7.1	53.8	13%	17.5	54.2	32%	46,500	190,870	24%
98	Mitsubishi Motors	7.0	25.4	28%	16.8	29.1	58%	N/A	26,749	N/A
99	Bridgestone	7.0	15.7	45%	11.6	18.3	63%	70,000	101,489	69%

Source: Data from UNCTAD, World Investment Report, 2001.
* Rank in terms of total foreign assets among all TNCs in the world.
** In billions of U.S. dollars.

dence and the way it has played into the policy process, but in order to get a better sense of how business has responded to high costs, we cannot avoid wading into this evidence in a preliminary way here.

The evidence is indeed mixed and muddy. At the same time Japanese firms were doubling manufacturing investment overseas in the late 1980s, they were also doubling manufacturing investment at home, a pattern that hardly conforms to the idea that Japanese firms were trying to escape high costs in Japan.[46] Only after domestic investment declined during the long recession of the 1990s did overseas manufacturing investment rise as a share of total Japanese investment. The share of overseas investment rose to a plateau of about 18 percent in the late 1990s after many years in which it had held steady at around 10 percent (see figure 4.6). The Asian financial crisis slowed the upward trend in this ratio, but it spiked again in 2002 to a level of almost 27 percent. It is only in the last several years, with overseas investment shares at sharply higher levels, that one can begin to make out a pattern in which FDI might be locating production overseas at the expense of investment in domestic operations.

Aggregate data of this kind can only hint, however, at what might be motivating FDI decisions. Fortunately for our purposes, the Ministry of Economy, Trade, and Industry (METI) annually surveys the overseas affiliates of Japanese firms to get a sense of what is shaping their investment decisions, and their replies shed further light on the mix of motives behind these decisions. The 2003 survey showed that "maintaining and expanding sales in the overseas market" was the number-one motive cited by overseas affiliates as a whole and in almost every business sector. Given a choice of reasons and asked to pick one, 30 percent cited this motive, which has no direct connection to efforts to escape the high costs of doing business back in Japan. Nevertheless, substantial proportions of the respondents cited "cost advantages" (12%) or "plans to expand reverse imports into the Japanese market" (5%) as the primary motivations behind investment decisions, answers that suggest that the attraction of lower costs in the overseas location was the primary factor driving at least some Japanese FDI. The proportions choosing this reason were particularly high in the textile, electronics, and farm products sectors.[47]

With at least some Japanese firms using FDI as a means to get around high costs back in Japan, the expansion of these firms' overseas manufacturing capacity eventually began to eat into Japan's domestic production levels. The domestic Japanese automobile industry at the end of the 1990s was producing 25 percent fewer automobiles than it was at the start of that decade, and electronics production in Japan fell to half the level of its mid-1980s peak.[48] METI statistics showed, moreover, that the share of "reverse imports"—Japanese firms' imports of manufactured goods that had formerly been made in Japan from their overseas factories—grew from just 4.2 percent of imports in 1990 to 14.8 percent in 1999.[49]

Meanwhile, FDI was not the only route by which Japanese firms found their way around high domestic production costs. While FDI offered Japanese firms the most complete exit option, allowing them to escape a broad range of costs associ-

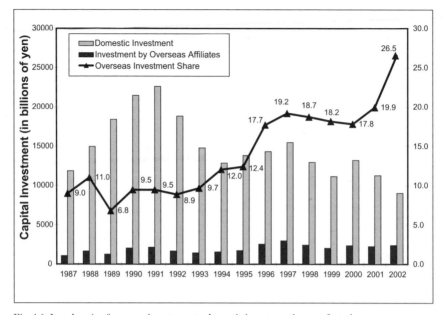

Fig. 4.6. Japan's ratio of overseas investment to domestic investment in manufacturing
Source: Adapted from Ministry of Economy, Trade and Industry, *Summary of the 33rd Survey of Overseas Business Activities,* March 31, 2004, 15; data prior to 1993 from earlier volumes of this series.

ated with convoy capitalism, they also took advantage of a variety of intermediate exit options that did not require them to relocate production overseas. First, they shifted procurement of goods and service inputs to take advantage of substitutes available in the domestic market that are less encumbered by the costs of the system of social protection. For example, when steel users found Japanese integrated steel mills were charging prices much higher than those available overseas, some began shifting procurement to domestic minimills, which were able to charge lower prices in part because, as smaller and newer firms with fewer relational obligations, they were less burdened by "convoy" commitments. Large-scale users of electricity, faced with high prices charged by Japanese electric utilities that are heavily burdened by convoy commitments, were able to produce electricity for their own use at a much lower cost. Finally, firms burdened by the high prices charged by NTT for telecommunication services were able to find newcomers (some of them foreign firms) who were able to connect large-scale users to alternative networks and provide service at much lower costs.

Second, firms could exit by turning to imports from foreign firms as an alternative to domestic sourcing. Discount retail firms frustrated at the high cost of domestic goods, for example, dramatically increased direct importing of items such as clothing, towels, and food products. The firm Fast Retailing, known for its Uniqlo stores, was among those that pursued this strategy, using it to expand rapidly from a chain with just a few stores in western Japan at the start of the 1990s to one with five hundred stores nationwide and sales of $2.1 billion in 2000. It was able to grow this rapidly in large part because its direct importing strategy cut through two levels of inefficiency in the Japanese economy. The Chinese factories it bought from could produce clothing much more cheaply than Japanese ones, *and* its direct importing operation cut out several layers of inefficient Japanese wholesalers.[50] Other retailers used the same strategy to get around high production and distribution costs in the food industry, bringing to market imported products such as mushrooms, leeks, and even beer at a fraction of the price charged by domestic producers.

Finally, firms were in some cases able to slash the cost of services that were expensive to procure domestically because of convoy-related regulations simply by conducting the transaction overseas. This pattern was most prominent in the financial services area where the cost of relocating transactions was particularly low. Japanese firms seeking lower-priced bond issuance, for example, were able to get around regulations that fixed domestic conditions and prices at a high level simply by making the same deal (often with the same Japanese securities firm) in London. This became so easy to do after revisions to the Foreign Exchange and Control Law in 1980 that Euro market bond-issuance soared. Whereas bond-issuance in Euro markets accounted for just 1.7 percent of Japanese corporate financing in the early 1970s, by 1985 they accounted for fully one-third of all Japanese corporate finance. By this time, domestic bond-issuance had slowed to a trickle, with such issues accounting for just 4 percent of corporate funds.[51]

While liberalization measures adopted in the mid-1980s and the frenzy of the bubble brought a great deal of financial market activity back to Tokyo—by the end of that decade share-trading volume matched levels in New York and was higher than in London—the 1990s saw another exodus. By 1997, trading volumes in Tokyo were down to one-fifth New York levels, and Tokyo was even being eclipsed in some market segments by other exchanges in Asia—especially Singapore.[52] Concerned that Japan had fallen behind all of these markets in terms of innovation, infrastructure, costs, and transparency, authorities began using the term "hollowing out" to refer to Japanese financial markets, and not just to manufacturing.[53]

At one level, the exit phenomena described here were a measure of the liberalization that has been implemented in Japan. Some of these forms of exit were simply unavailable prior to 1980 because international transactions were so rigidly regulated. These same liberalization measures, however, also created ways for firms to escape, individually and without coordination, the sheltered sectors that remained unreformed. As we will see when we look more closely at how hollowing out played into the political process in chapters 5 and 6, whether exit accelerated reform via regulatory arbitrage or slowed it down by deflating political pressure for change depended on how costly the specific exit strategy was to carry out.

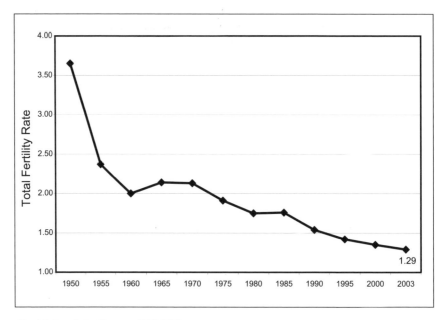

Fig. 4.7. Japan's fertility rate, 1950–2003
Source: Based on data from the National Institute of Population and Social Security Research, *Population Statistics of Japan* (Tokyo, 2003), 24–25, updated with the total fertility rate reported by NIPSSR for 2003.

Women Turn to Exit

One by one, women too have opted for exit strategies. The most basic marker of this trend is the falling fertility rate (see figure 4.7). Up through the late 1970s, Japan's total fertility rate was above or near the population replacement rate of 2.08.[54] Since 1980, however, the rate has been falling steadily, reaching a low of 1.29 in 2003, far below the rate in the United States and on a par with the most demographically challenged nations of Europe (see table 4.4). Already the number of live births recorded in Japan has fallen from a peak of 2 million a year in the early 1970s to 1.2 million in the late 1990s. If the current fertility rate is sustained, just 865,000 children will be born in 2025 and just 667,000 in 2050.

That fertility rates have fallen sharply, of course, does not necessarily mean Japanese women are "exiting." Indeed, some women who are not having children are certainly making this choice because they prefer to be childless. A significant portion of the decline, however, cannot be attributed to a shift in Japanese women's preferences toward not having children. The survey of unmarried women cited above (figure 4.1), for example, showed that there has been only a slight increase in the proportion of unmarried women for whom not having children is their "ideal life course." Between 1987 and 2002, the proportion of young women saying they hoped to remain unmarried without children or married without children grew

TABLE 4.4.
Japan's fertility rate in comparative context

Country	Total Fertility Rate	Year
United States	2.13	2000
France	1.79	1999
Britain	1.65	2000
Sweden	1.57	2001
Germany	1.38	2000
Japan	1.29	2003
Italy	1.24	2000

Source: Data on Japan from Ministry of Health, Labor and Welfare Statistics Bureau; data on other nations from the United Nations, Population Division, *World Fertility Report*, 2003.

only slightly from 6.2 percent to 9 percent. If 30 percent of these women end up childless, as the government now projects, that result would suggest over 20 percent ended up this way because they could not live out their ideal life course.

Indeed, the poll asking unmarried women aged twenty-five to thirty-four to describe their ideal life course suggests that many women have already given up on achieving their goals. After asking them to describe their ideal, the poll went on to ask what life course they actually expected to live. Many reported they expected to live out life courses quite different from their ideal. Of those hoping to work continuously after having children, just 27 percent said they expected to be able to live out this preferred life course. The proportion expecting to be able to live out the life course where they leave work for a period after having children but return when the children are older was higher at 46 percent, but even here over half expected to settle for another path. Fully 16 percent of the women polled who *hoped* to have children *expected* to end up childless.[55]

Although it is therefore quite clear that the trend toward declining fertility is not just a reflection of a growing preference for childlessness on the part of women, we still cannot be certain this trend grows out of women's frustration with the marriage and family norms embedded in its system of social protection. To get a better sense of why women are having fewer children, we need to turn to the voluminous data on the reasons for declining fertility, much of it gathered by Japanese bureaucrats anxious about this trend.

First, there is a consensus that the proximate cause for declining fertility in Japan lies in women's decisions to postpone or opt out of marriage.[56] Japanese women who marry continue to aim for and have a stable number of children. Most hope for and have exactly two.[57] Japanese fertility levels are falling because a growing number of women are remaining unmarried into their thirties, which for almost all of these unmarried women—in a society with an extremely low number of babies born to single women—means they are also remaining childless well into their period of fertility.

These trends show up clearly in figures 4.8 and 4.9. The first figure shows the

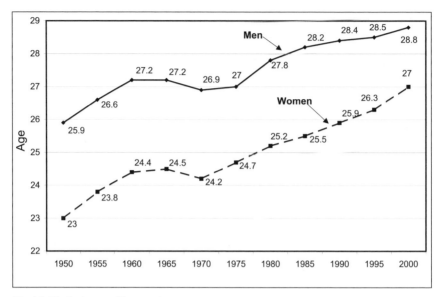

Fig. 4.8. Rise in the age of first marriage
Source: Based on data from the NIPSSR, *Population Statistics of Japan* (Tokyo, 2003), 71.

rise in the age of marriage for women and men. In the case of women, it has risen from 24.2 in 1970 in a straight line up to 27.0 in 2000. The second shows the rise in the proportion of women who remain single well into their child-bearing years. Whereas the majority of women born in the late 1950s were married before they were twenty-five (just 30.6 percent remained single), recent cohorts of women have remained unmarried into their late twenties in increasing numbers, now up to 54 percent. The higher the proportion single at this age, the higher the share of these women who remain single into their late thirties. Almost 14 percent of the cohort who reach this age most recently remained single. The record of younger cohorts up to this point suggests that they are likely to remain single to the end of their child-bearing years at rates of 20 to 30 percent.

This delay in marriage matters because late marriages inevitably produce fewer children. Japanese data show that women married when they were twenty-nine to thirty had 1.78 children, whereas those married at twenty-one to twenty-two had 2.34.[58] The number of children born to women who marry later or not at all is much smaller. This is particularly true in Japan because of its extremely low level of co-habitation and out-of-wedlock births. In the mid-1990s, just 1 percent of Japanese women aged twenty-five to twenty-nine were cohabiting (outside marriage) with a partner, compared to 31 percent in Sweden, 24 percent in France, and 17 percent in Canada.[59] Partners that do not live together are very unlikely to have children.[60] In Japanese society, where marriage and children are so closely linked, the decline of marriage has directly contributed to the fall in Japanese fertility rates.

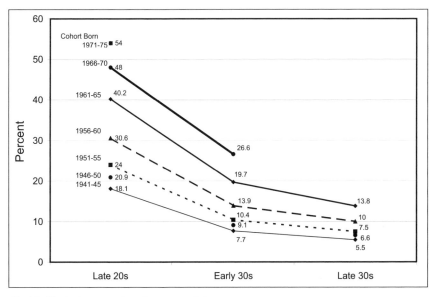

Fig. 4.9. Rise in the proportion of never-married women
Source: Based on data from the NIPSSR, *Population Statistics of Japan* (Tokyo, 2003), 77.

Why are young women putting off or opting out of marriage? Government de-mographers have made great efforts to learn the answer, and much of what they have found implicates young women's frustrations with the "opportunity costs" of marriage, the costs they expect to pay in terms of lost freedom and lost income or quality of life once they tie the knot. When unmarried women aged twenty-five to thirty-four are asked why they have not married, the largest proportion reply be-cause they "haven't met the right partner yet" (52.3 percent), but almost as many answer that they have not married because they "don't want to lose the freedom and comforts of their single lives" (38.2 percent). A similarly large number explain their delay by saying they "don't yet feel any urgency" (34.7 percent), while an-other 19.6 say they haven't married because they are "concentrating on their work or studies." The latter three replies all suggest these women are holding off on marriage because they see few benefits and high costs in terms of lost income and freedom. Moreover, it is quite likely that many of the women who "have not met the right partner yet" are also frustrated by the family and work systems that put most of the burdens of family care on women's shoulders. For many of these women, not finding the right partner means not finding one who is willing to help them hold onto their freedoms and careers after marriage.[61]

While the poll cited above did not ask women whether the availability of child-care and other costs associated with children was a factor in their decisions not to get married, no doubt this is on the minds of women making choices about marriage—especially because of the continuing strong social pressures on married couples to have children. Social pressures on young people to marry have recently declined, but it is still widely expected that couples that do marry will have children.[62] Though we do not have direct evidence of what single women think about the costs of raising children, the replies married women give to surveys on this topic are suggestive. A growing number of married women who are asked why they have not had their "ideal" number of children stress the burdens associated with child rearing. In a 1997 poll, women cited the overall costs of raising children (36%, up from 24% in 1982); the educational costs of raising children (33%, up from 22%); conflicts with their employment obligations (13%, up from 11%); and the physical and psychological strains of child rearing (20%, up from 17%). Interestingly, the only one of the eleven possible replies showing a decline over time was the answer: "because I cannot have children" (14%, down from 18%).[63] Among married women—and probably even more so among unmarried women who are putting off marriage—there is a growing sense that having children is financially, emotionally, and psychologically costly given the lack of support from husbands and society.

The causes of Japan's declining fertility are complex. Indeed, as I describe in greater detail in chapter 7, the debate over the cause has delayed a bold policy response from the government. Nevertheless, it is telling that after many years of studying the problem the Ministry of Health and Welfare finally concluded in 1997 that the falling fertility rate has been caused by individual responses to social and economic changes that have raised the costs of marriage and children, especially for women who want to work. The official interpretation is summarized by Bandō Mariko, the director general of the Gender Equality Bureau of the Cabinet Office:

> We understand why Japanese women don't want to have children. Once they're married, they have to do all the housework. Japanese husbands may help some, but they won't share the burden. Also, if women work as hard as men they can be promoted—not always, but it's possible—but if they have children and stop working, it's virtually impossible to re-enter the workforce. Many well-educated women quit and become housewives whether they want to or not. So instead, women are postponing marriage and/or childbirth.[64]

In this analysis, the declining fertility rate is clearly linked to exit by women who would prefer, if they could, to have both a family and a work life outside the home, but do not do so because of the difficulties of combining family and career.

While the focus so far has been on this type of exit by one group of women, another group has settled for the opposite trade-off, choosing to exit from their careers in order to have a family, giving up on their dream to have both. The clearest measure of this pattern is the famous "M-curve" defining female workforce participation rates as they age: Japanese women work in high numbers in their twenties

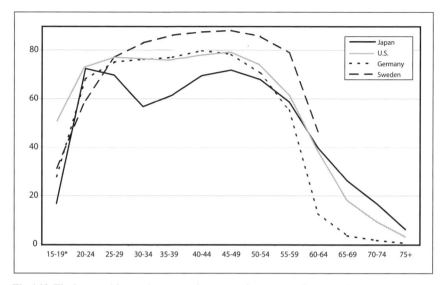

Fig. 4.10. The Japanese M-curve in comparative perspective: percent of women who were economically active, by age group, in 1999
Source: Modeled on Prime Minister's Office, *Danjo kyōdō sankaku hakusho—Heisei 12-nen-han,* 2000, 38, with updated data from the International Labour Organization, *ILO Yearbook of Labour Statistics* 2000.
*Data for the United States and Sweden covers ages 16–19 rather than 15–19.

before they marry and have children, work at much lower rates in their thirties as their family responsibilities grow, and then return to higher rates in their forties and fifties when their children are older. Japanese M-curve patterns stands in stark contrast to workforce participation patterns in other advanced industrialized nations (figure 4.10).

The M-curve, however, actually understates the degree to which women exit the workforce when they marry and have children, because of the way it aggregates women who take these steps at different ages. Between 1997 and 2001, one million women quit their jobs because of marriage and another 1.2 million quit to care for their children.[65] The work rate for women goes from 92 percent for unmarried women twenty-five to twenty-nine down to 22 percent for women with children younger than three, with just 12.3 percent working thirty-five or more hours a week. Even this last figure overstates the number of women who avoid "exiting" the career track after they have children, since some of those working over thirty-five hours are in temporary jobs.[66]

As in the case of exit from family, of course, we should not make the mistake of categorizing all departures from the workforce by new mothers as "exit" from a preferred work-plus-family lifestyle in response to frustrations with the difficulties

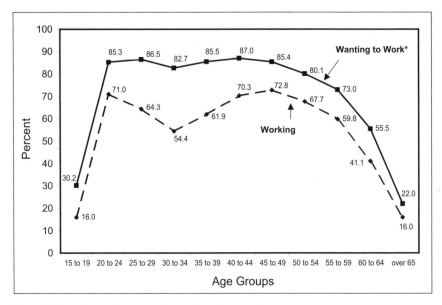

Fig. 4.11. Proportions of women working and wanting to work
Source: Based on data from Ministry of Internal Affairs and Communication, Statistics Bureau, *Shūgyō kōzō kihon chōsa*, 1997.
* The proportion wanting to work is calculated by adding those working to those reporting they would like to be working.

of balancing these two roles. Many Japanese women *prefer* to be full-time housewives. Though this proportion is falling (see figure 4.1), the proportion of young unmarried women who aspire to this life course remains near 20 percent. Nevertheless, data on women's work preferences suggest that much of the dip in the M-curve is a product of frustrations on the part of women who would ideally like to be working. Graphing the M-curve onto the graph representing the share of women who would like to be working if they could (figure 4.11) shows that this gap is almost as many as 30 percentage points for women in their early thirties, a huge potential labor force that Japan will need to tap if it wishes to ease its demographic transition to an "aged society." But rather than struggling to work in an environment where working mothers get little support from husbands and society, a very large number of women have simply given up on careers.

These two types of exit (opting out of marriage/children and opting out of work) are the main focus of my analysis, but there is another form of exit that deserves at least brief mention. Though I described the growing prevalence of Japanese women studying, traveling, and working abroad as part of the cultural process that is changing women's aspirations, it is also possible to view these trends as a *product* of their frustrations. In fact, using language similar to the "exit" terminology employed in this book, Karen Kelsky describes these behaviors as examples of "defection" from Japan by cosmopolitan young Japanese women. Just as Japanese firms are increasingly deserting the domestic economy in favor of foreign production and sales, a growing number of Japanese women are defecting from Japan by studying and working abroad, by working for foreign firms in Japan, and by dating or marrying foreign men.[67]

At present, however, most of those defecting in these ways appear to be doing so only temporarily. Though statistics do show a sharp spike in departures from Japan by young women aged eighteen to twenty-six, they show net inflows for all ages after twenty-seven, suggesting that those who leave to study and work as young women are returning around the time they reach marrying age.[68] International marriage rates for Japanese women are rising, but they are rising more slowly than for Japanese men, who tend to marry women from other Asian nations.[69] Finally, even the foreign dating patterns discussed by Kelsky are mostly temporary "flirting with the foreign" by Japanese women who, in the stories told by her informants, frequently plan on eventually marrying Japanese men.[70] These behaviors remain significant for how they shape Japanese women's attitudes toward their society, and are clearly symptomatic of their frustrations, but their small scale and temporary nature (for most women) has limited their impact on Japanese society relative to the broader exit behaviors that are the focus of this chapter.

Nevertheless, it is possible that the latest generation of young women, or future ones, will respond to continuing frustrations with their limited options in Japan by engaging in these types of exit on a broader scale and by making their defections more permanent. In fact, one research institute in Japan specializing in projecting future trends has imagined a worst-case future for Japan, *The Long Hollowing*, in which talented young Japanese women leave the country in large numbers.[71] If this were to happen, one of the most important effects of the trend would be to exacerbate both of the problems caused by the forms of exit I highlight in this chapter: an increase in the number of women emigrating from Japan would cause the labor force to shrink further while at the same time causing a further decline in the birthrate.

Although this last form of exit remains only a future possibility, the misfit between the convoy capitalist system of social protection and Japan's changing socioeconomic environment had by the 1990s produced three very real exit trends. The first, known in Japan, as in the United States, by the term "hollowing out" (*kūdōka*), hung like a dark cloud over the stagnant Japanese economy. Even as the government struggled to repair the damage caused by the implosion of the speculative bubble economy, Japanese firms were busily relocating a growing proportion of their productive operations overseas, making the job of engineering a recovery more difficult. When the costs of securing key inputs domestically were too high, firms simply conducted their transactions overseas where costs were lower. Most disturbingly, the firms migrating abroad included the leading firms in some of Japan's most important sectors: Sony, Canon, Honda, and Toyota.

The second exit trend is known in Japan as *shōshika,* literally "the shrinking number of children," but often translated as declining fertility. Unlike hollowing out, which threatens jobs now, this trend promises to have its biggest effects several decades in the future. In terms of economic costs and benefits, fewer children today is a plus because a decline in the number of boys and girls in the unproductive ages means working adults have fewer mouths to feed and care for. The trend is foreboding, however, because it means that in two or three decades, just when the full cohort of the nation's baby boomers has retired and created a bulge of thirty-five million elderly citizens in need of care and income transfers, there will be a shrinking number of working-age citizens to provide that support. This forecast has stumped government officials charged with figuring out how to sustain health and pension benefits. Not just officials but individuals looking ahead to retirement are expressing growing worries about what this demographic tidal wave will mean for them.

The third and final exit trend, the exodus from careers by women, has faded into the background during the long recession but remains a latent challenge. As suggested by the graph mapping the M-curve against the curve showing how many women want to work (figure 4.11), the number of women involuntarily taking themselves out of the workforce numbers in the millions, as many as 5.5 million according to one simulation.[72] Although the current economic slump and the associated rise in the unemployment rate have temporarily quelled worries about the looming labor shortage, the shortage has not gone away. In part due to the falling fertility trend, Japan is slated to lose twelve million working-age adults by 2020 (a contraction of almost 15%), meaning the nation will soon be in desperate need of its underemployed women.

Taken together, these three exit trends suggest the contours of a solution. Japan needs to retool its economy to focus on high-value-added, high-productivity manufacturing and services, making optimum use of its shrinking labor supply and abundant capital by focusing on the most capital-intensive, skills-intensive sectors and relentlessly improving efficiencies and profits. This step would minimize the nation's exposure to its shrinking labor supply while supplying the returns to capital that will allow it to finance the retirement of the baby boomers. At the same time, the nation needs to create an environment that encourages women to work *and* start a family, to plug the labor supply gap in the short term with underemployed women, while also assuring that the labor supply of the future does not shrink too rapidly.

Some of the best and brightest Japanese who are thinking about the economic challenges facing the nation have arrived at a vision pretty close to the one just summarized. Even the male-dominated METI signaled its appreciation of the critical role that will be played by women in determining whether Japan can work around the coming challenges by appointing Ōsawa Mari, a leading feminist labor economist, to the panel that produced its most recent *Vision on Industrial Policy for the Twenty-first Century.* Among its recommendations: improved systems of leave for childcare, work-sharing, flex-time, and other reforms designed to keep women with children in the labor force.[73] Will the exit trends drive Japan toward a solution of this kind, or will they sap the reform movement of support as suggested by Hirschman's thesis? In the next three chapters we examine the nation's response to industrial hollowing out (chapters 5 and 6) and to the two exit trends involving women (Chapter 7).

Chapter 5

The Policy Impact of Hollowing Out

The conventional wisdom ascribes powerful influence to those who have the ability to move capital freely across borders. As Henry Laurence writes:

> There are three pathways to regulatory reform where direct influence is used. First, mobile-asset actors can explicitly threaten to leave the country as a bargaining chip when negotiating with policymakers. In this way, the threat of exit simply gives mobile-asset actors a louder voice in the political market-place and translates into more-favorable lobbying outcomes for these actors. But they do not even have to make threats. The mere fact that they are able to leave will be well known to policymakers, who may make preemptive regulatory concessions in order to prevent an ultimately unwinnable political battle. Finally policymakers may be forced to make reactive regulatory reforms in order to entice back mobile-asset actors who have already exercised their exit option and left the country.[1]

To hear Laurence tell it, the ability to exit, threaten to exit, and offer to return gives holders of mobile assets quite a trump card. Investors looking for opportunities to invest in equity markets and firms with the resources to locate production in many different countries around the world merely need to dangle their capital in front of policymakers and they will jump: "They do not even have to make threats." The mere possibility that they may pull out will lead governments to revise regulations to suit the interests of these capitalists or to throw special favors their way—anything to keep the owners of footloose capital happy.

Laurence makes these claims in a book about financial reforms in Japan and Britain, but his view of how capital mobility gives owners of financial assets the power to force through fundamental changes in everything from regulations to social welfare programs is echoed in much of the literature on globalization.[2] Does exit really work so magically that owners of mobile assets merely need to point to their ability to leave to get their way? Laurence and this broader literature clearly imply that at a minimum exit works in tandem with voice to empower capitalists. They may not get their way initially, but once they start shifting assets overseas and threaten to continue doing so, this should amplify their voice in the political arena and help them obtain desired policy changes.

In this chapter, I subject this oft-repeated claim about how exit and voice work in tandem to accelerate economic liberalization to scrutiny by examining how the Japanese government has responded to the hollowing-out trend detailed in the last chapter. Exit via FDI, I argue, has *not* accelerated reform. On the contrary, it has provided internationally exposed firms with an opportunity to escape (or at least cut their exposure to) Japan's high-cost structure in ways that have reduced their incentives to seek policy change in Japan. Rather than leading the charge in favor of liberalization, the firms that have the most to gain from liberalization have allowed Japanese politics to be dominated more than ever by interests with a stake in preserving convoy capitalism. The power of these "vested interests" in the political arena certainly is part of the explanation for Japan's slow pace of reform, but an equally important part of the explanation lies in internationally competitive firms' ability to escape high costs in Japan through FDI. If they had "no way out," like the steel firms in the late 1960s and early 1970s discussed in chapter 3, these firms would have been forced to confront the LDP and use their economic and political clout to pressure the party to implement cost-cutting regulatory reforms and broader changes in Japan's outmoded system of social protection. This "regime shift" hasn't happened, I argue, because limited exit opportunities available to firms have reduced their motivation to battle the LDP in the political arena.

In this chapter I focus on the overall pattern of economic reform since Japanese firms began accelerating their rate of foreign investment in the mid-1980s. Rather than ringing alarm bells and prompting liberalizing reforms, this initial surge in investment was applauded and encouraged by Japanese policymakers. It was not until the mid-1990s that "hollowing out" began to be defined as a "problem." Delay in diagnosing the problem was compounded by uncertainty about how best to stem the outflow of productive capacity. Which regulatory reforms would cut costs the most? Did Japan need to abandon its convoy system of supporting banks? Did it need to give up on the long-treasured lifetime employment system? With leading manufacturing firms preoccupied by efforts to survive by moving production rapidly overseas, the task of diagnosing the problem, answering these questions, and pushing market-oriented reforms through the political arena was left, ironically, to Japanese bureaucrats. Not surprisingly, the result has been uneven and uncoordinated reforms that have failed to chart a path out of Japan's period of stagnation.

Early Signs of Trouble

The first strains in the system of convoy capitalism began to appear in the 1980s under the combined impact of rising energy prices (after the two oil shocks of the 1970s) and the boost in relative prices of labor and virtually all other domestic inputs due to the abrupt strengthening of the yen after the 1985 Plaza Accords.[3] Industries that used a great deal of energy in their production process and those with large labor costs faced the challenge of trying to maintain their competitiveness in an environment where convoy capitalism constrained their restructuring options. They could not lay off members of their core workforce or modify the seniority wage system without the cooperation of their unions, and they could not switch to imported basic materials, parts, or services because of their relational contracts with long-term domestic business partners.

At this early stage, virtually no firms considered abandoning the Japanese model of coordinated capitalism or campaigning for reforms in its basic structures. In 1993, the electronics firm Pioneer attempted to pressure thirty-five middle managers into "voluntary" early retirement without consulting their union, but after being ostracized by the media, criticized by its peers, and shunned by new recruits, it backed down and offered to postpone the retirement deadline while it worked to find them alternative employment. To atone for their offense, Pioneer's top managers accepted salary cuts of 5–20 percent and agreed to consult the union before implementing any such employment plan in the future.[4] After seeing the way Pioneer was treated, few other firms stepped forward to challenge basic features of the system.

Instead, the predominant pattern across a wide range of industries involved a fervent embrace of convoy capitalism. Struggling manufacturing firms turned to their keiretsu partners and their banks for support, as seen in the case of Tōyō Kōgyō discussed in chapter 3. The steel industry relied on its cartel to coordinate gradual cuts in production that would allow its members to survive without having to violate their commitments to their workers. The cement industry relied on its cartel too, forcing the construction industry to abide by an interindustry refusal-to-deal agreement that assured construction firms would not import cheaper Korean cement.[5] Most of these industries also drew heavily on support from the government, which put in place regulatory barriers to imports, administered cartels under the Structurally Depressed Industries Law, and extended credit and tax breaks to struggling industries.

But not all industries could pull this off. Already in the early 1980s, there were several Japanese industries, including aluminum and apparel, that could not remain competitive as Japan-based producers—even with the help of keiretsu partners, banks, and the government. Rather than seeking changes in Japanese structures and policies that made it difficult for them to restructure locally to reestablish their viability as domestic producers, however, these firms became the first to begin moving a large share of their production overseas.

The shift overseas was particularly rapid in the case of the aluminum industry. Up until the 1970s, this industry had been aggressively expanding its refining capacity in Japan. Once the oil price hikes of that decade pushed the price of Japanese electricity way up relative to the price of this critical production cost in other nations, however, the local aluminum industry was in trouble.[6] By 1980, production costs in Japan were 25–50 percent higher than the production costs of aluminum ingot imported from the United States.[7] Rather than campaigning for price reductions in the heavily regulated energy sector in Japan or other changes in the business environment that might have cut its costs, this industry decided to shut down its Japanese production capacity and move overseas as quickly as possible. Japanese producers invested aggressively in overseas production facilities—in Canada, the United States, and Brazil, among other places—and Japan saw imports of aluminum rise as a share of the total market from 40 percent in 1980 to almost 100 percent in 1987.[8] Japan's aluminum firms survived, but they emerged from the 1980s as multinational companies producing almost all of their aluminum overseas.

The textile industry also took a large hit when the oil shocks pushed up the price of petrochemicals that serve as the basis for manufacturing synthetic fibers and as the appreciation of the yen pushed up Japanese wages relative to those of other textile-manufacturing nations. Although the industry was able to adapt in a surprisingly flexible way to the first of these shocks in the 1970s, by the next decade many firms were finding it difficult to hold on to their export markets with Japan-based production and were beginning to face import competition at home. Particularly hard hit was the apparel sector, where wages make up a large share of production costs.[9]

When pressed to the wall, this industry too turned to the exit option rather than working to achieve greater wage flexibility, loosen immigration laws, or otherwise alter the constraints of convoy capitalism at home so that it could survive as a domestic industry. Between 1988 and 1992, the textile industry made 233 investments overseas, with 78 percent of these concentrated in the hardest hit apparel sector.[10] Firms invested $5.2 billion in overseas textile production in the ten years after the Plaza Accords, with the bulk of this going into apparel-manufacturing capacity in China.[11] As Richard Katz has pointed out, this FDI surge led to a remarkably rapid restructuring of the Japanese textile industry in the 1990s, with the industry eliminating 30 percent of its domestic production capacity.[12] By the end of the decade, the workforce in the textile industry was only half what it had been at its peak.[13]

FDI clearly played an important role in accelerating structural adjustment in these two sectors. In both areas, Japan was able to reduce the share of its capital and labor invested in uncompetitive sectors, freeing it up for use in expanding production in more competitive, growing sectors. Indeed, many analysts see the two cases as ones where Japanese firms were able to adjust remarkably rapidly—at least as fast, if not faster, than similar industries in other nations.[14] It is tempting, therefore, to conclude that "exit" in these cases truly did work in tandem with voice to challenge systems of social protection in the way the globalization literature assumes.

What such an analysis overlooks is that all of the adjustment described above was achieved *without challenging* Japan's system of convoy capitalism. Neither the aluminum industry nor the textile industry sought to revise labor laws or get out of their commitments to their core male labor force under the Japanese employment system. They didn't attempt to get out of their relational contracts with domestic suppliers. And they did not attempt to fight for deregulation or competition policy enforcement aimed at lowering electricity or petrochemical prices.

On the contrary, both industries relied on key features of the established system of social protection to help them escape the high costs of producing in Japan. We can see this pattern, first, in the case of the aluminum firms, which used this system to survive and relocate in a way firms from other nations would never have been able to duplicate. These firms had expanded inside Japan by amassing ¥1 trillion ($4.5 billion in 1981 dollars) in bank debt, which they had no hope of repaying given their sudden loss of competitiveness.[15] They had to compete with foreign firms that could produce aluminum ingot for 25–50 percent less and faced a tariff of just 9 percent. Firms caught in this position in most other nations would have faced bankruptcy and dissolution, with their workers left out on the street.

Japan's aluminum producers were able to pull off their Houdini act only because they had help from virtually all of the key players in their convoy network. The banks kept open their credit lines and did not raise interest rates despite the risk of default. Their keiretsu partners agreed to take on most of the firms' Japanese employees so that the aluminum firms could scale back production rapidly without violating their promise to look after their workers. In addition, the government stepped in with a "tariff rebate" (refunding the tariff charged on imports of aluminum coming from the overseas plants of Japanese aluminum firms). This program gave the Japanese firms a subsidy that offset some of their losses on domestic production while also encouraging their investments overseas. Finally, the government supported the firms' relocation abroad with large loans from the state-run Export-Import Bank and even bigger loans through the government's foreign aid program to finance infrastructure connected to overseas projects in places like Brazil and Indonesia.[16]

The Japanese textile industry's consolidation at home and shift abroad was aided in different ways by its own position in the convoy system. Some segments of the industry, especially the synthetic spinning and weaving sectors (which tend to be made up of larger firms), received support from banks, keiretsu partners, and government credit programs that helped them consolidate at home and expand overseas production starting in the 1970s.[17] At the same time, government-supported cartel arrangements helped this segment of the industry slow down its domestic consolidation to a speed it could accommodate without violating its commitments to its core workforce.[18]

The apparel sector, made up of numerous small firms, had difficulty replicating the strategies adopted by the larger upstream firms, but they found alternative ways to take advantage of the convoy system. As Mireya Solis reports, these firms received an extraordinary degree of support from Japan's trading companies (*sōgō shōsha*), which helped coordinate their movement overseas—especially to China—by providing information and capital. They were assisted too by government loans, especially from the Japan Finance Corporation for Small Business, along with loans from the Japan Export-Import Bank.[19] Unable to coordinate domestic consolidation to the degree the large firms were, the apparel makers relied much more on the flexibility afforded by their reliance on a large proportion of part-time, temporary, and female workers. Workers in these categories could be dismissed quite easily without running afoul of the rules and norms of the lifetime employment system. The firms were generally able to work with unions affiliated with the Japanese Federation of Textile Industry Workers' Unions (Zensen), because this union represented only the core (disproportionately male) work force.[20]

That both the textile and aluminum industries were able to work *with* the system of convoy capitalism to reduce production at home and expand overseas meant that they had little motivation to challenge the public policies and economic structures that composed this system as they began moving overseas. We cannot observe exit and voice working in tandem in these cases because there simply *was* no voice in favor of reform coming from these sectors.

Neither did exit work on its own to propel reforms in labor law or deregulation aimed at lowering petrochemical and electricity prices, because the surge in FDI in these sectors was not seen by anyone as a "problem" that required solutions of these kinds. As noted above, labor unions worked with the struggling firms to help them survive through FDI. Bureaucrats in charge of these sectors similarly *promoted* FDI, rather than treating it as a hollowing-out problem that needed to be addressed. Government financial institutions ranging from the Japan Export-Import Bank to the Overseas Economic Cooperation Fund to the Japan Finance Corporation for Small Business provided capital to aid aluminum and textile firms in their efforts to relocate production abroad. The first two industries to face competitiveness problems because of high costs in Japan therefore exited, stage left, without generating any drama in the form of efforts to address the high cost structure that continued to plague the industries that remained behind.

Core Industries Begin Moving Offshore

The surge in foreign investment in the period after the Plaza Accords was not generated entirely, however, by desperate industries seeking to relocate production abroad in order to stay in business. Two very large and quite successful Japanese industries, automobiles and electronics, were responsible for the largest shares of FDI. These two sectors alone invested over $100 billion overseas, accounting for

43.3 percent of Japan's total manufacturing FDI between 1986 and 2000.[21] Most of this investment, by firms such as Sony and Nissan, was designed to expand the firms' total production—not to replace Japanese productive capacity—by locating factories in the firms' major export markets. Nissan and the other leading Japanese automakers opened large new plants in the United States and Europe.[22] Sony and the leading electronics firms similarly opened numerous plants in these places, along with many more in Southeast Asia and later China.

The circumstances surrounding many of these investments show that much of the initial surge was driven by concerns about rising protectionist sentiment in the United States and Europe. In the early 1980s, the Japanese automakers were bound by voluntary export restraints that limited the total number of automobiles they could export from Japan to their leading overseas markets. Locating factories in these markets was a way to expand their sales beyond these voluntary limits while mollifying protectionist sentiment by creating American and European jobs. Once these investments were made, the automakers learned to appreciate how they helped them hedge against the risk of currency movements. If the yen surged, overseas plants in the dollar and euro zones would help the firms avoid having to raise their prices. But economic considerations of these types arose after the initial surge in investment.

Japanese electronics firms faced voluntary export restraints too, on products such as television sets, which motivated them to locate production of those items outside Japan. Even for those products not covered by voluntary restraints (cameras, copiers, VCRs, fax machines), concerns about protectionism were an important motivation behind the firms' decisions to open American and European plants. They realized that locating production in these major markets, and creating jobs there, would buy them some insurance against the risk of protectionist trade restrictions in the future. One executive involved in strategic planning for a leading electronics producer told me that his firms' investments in American factories made little sense in economic terms. Production costs in the United States were *higher* at that time than in Japan and remain higher today. His firm decided to locate factories in the United States anyway because that was the price they had to pay to ensure the United States would not close off its lucrative market.[23]

Given this context, the initial surge of auto and electronics investment was not associated with either voice- or exit-driven demands for reforms in the system of convoy capitalism, much less pressure from the two forces operating in tandem. If anything, this FDI was seen as necessitated by the extraordinary *success* of the Japanese model of capitalism. It was so successful that it had sparked a protectionist backlash overseas; this FDI was the price Japan had to pay to avoid economic sanctions. Neither the automobile firms nor the electronics firms advocated policy changes designed to lower costs in Japan. Restrictions on labor mobility were not an issue, since these firms, at least until the mid-1990s, had no intention of *substituting* foreign production for domestic production. Leading electronics firms like Fujitsu and Toshiba, for example, continued to expand production at factories in Japan as late as 1994, even as they invested heavily overseas.[24] The firms were locating the next generation of factories abroad, but they had every intention of modernizing and making full use of their domestic factories and employees as well. Neither were the high costs of Japanese electricity, steel, or other inputs a motivation behind these firms' FDI strategies, so the leaders of Toyota and Sony made no statements calling for economic reforms in these areas either.

There were some statements in the late 1980s from Keidanren, the big-business federation, about the need to lower trade barriers in such areas as agriculture to appease the Americans, but these statements did not arise because of the firms' concerns about high costs in Japan. They arose because Japan's large exporters hoped that opening domestic farm markets would alleviate protectionist pressure in the United States that might lead to sanctions on their goods.[25] Some leading automobile and electronics firms did adopt "import doubling plans" during this period, but these plans too had less to do with concerns about high costs and trade barriers in Japan than they did with concerns about *U.S.* trade policy.[26] The Japanese firms decided to establish affirmative action programs for imports, purchasing parts that they described as inferior from foreign producers, in order to demonstrate that the Japanese market was "open" to imports.

If this significant component of Japan's FDI surge in the auto and electronics sectors did not correspond with political mobilization in favor of economic reform, neither did it prompt an exit-driven policy response. Once again, no one inside Japan—not the unions, the media, or bureaucrats—saw automobile and electronics FDI as a "problem" when this trend first became apparent in the late 1980s and early 1990s. Rather, most saw it as part of the solution that would help Japan sustain its system of convoy capitalism by ameliorating protectionist pressure overseas. Japanese firms would continue to produce the newest, most profitable product lines at home and transfer overseas, to Europe, North America, and the rest of Asia the older, more standardized product lines.

Ozawa Terutomo, the leading academic proponent of this view, argued that FDI served as a "house-cleaning-and-renovating vehicle for Japan," helping it move industrial activities that could no longer be performed competitively at home to offshore locations, even as it pushed firms to upgrade to higher-value-added operations producing higher profits and paying higher wages.[27] Rather than constituting a problem for Japan, Ozawa argued, "there has been a strong measure of harmony between the private and national interests in Japan's FDI."[28] It supported a system in which Japan was the lead goose in an Asiawide "flying geese formation"—a formulation that was great for Japanese business while also offering benefits to Japan's trading partners.[29] Given the dominance of this frame in discussion of Japanese FDI, few bureaucrats or other observers even used the phrase "industrial hollowing out" in connection with the surge in outward investment up through the middle of the 1990s.

A Turning Point?

Even after the implosion of the bubble economy slowed growth to a crawl, manufacturing output began to shrink, and the unemployment rate began to rise, few Japanese economists or officials pointed to hollowing out as the culprit. The cause of the economic slowdown clearly lay in the macroeconomic tightening needed to cool down the bubble economy. Foreign direct investment was actually down significantly from the bubble years (see figures 4.4 and 4.5 in the previous chapter), so it was hard to blame capital outflows for the difficulties manufacturers were starting to face.

The relaxed attitude of Japanese officials toward hollowing out can be seen in the language used by the Ministry of International Trade and Industry's Industrial Policy Bureau in a report on the subject in 1994:

> As the comparative advantage of various industries changes dynamically in response to changes in both the internal and external economic environment, a certain degree of overseas transfer of manufacturing activities and substitution of domestic production by imports is unavoidable, because such developments are part of the process of structural adjustments inherent in economic development. That process should not be regarded as constituting the hollowing out problem.[30]

Hollowing out was only a problem, the report argued, when "excessive appreciation of the yen or wide price differentials between Japan and other countries" led industries in which Japan "should normally enjoy a comparative advantage" to move overseas. The report did not see the foreign direct investment that had taken place as an unwarranted transfer of manufacturing, but it did warn that industries needed to remain vigilant and engage in self-help efforts to avoid hollowing out in the future.[31]

This relaxed attitude began to change only in 1995, a full decade after Japanese FDI began to flow out of the country in significant sums. The specific trigger that led some government officials and economists to begin to call hollowing out a problem was the extreme strengthening of the yen that brought the exchange rate to the ¥80–90 range and kept it there from April to August of that year. This spike in the exchange rate, which sharply increased the price of manufacturing in Japan while making the acquisition of foreign production capacity cheaper, caused a new surge in outward direct investment, this time concentrated in manufacturing (see figures 4.4 and 4.5). Large sums of investment flowed into Southeast Asia and China starting in the mid-1990s, along with continued investments in North America and Europe. Between 1995 and 1997, Japanese firms notified the government of plans to invest $153 billion in overseas operations.

In subsequent years, the term "hollowing out" began appearing in government reports, media reports, and book titles with increasing frequency. The MITI Industrial Policy Bureau, for example, wrote in 1998 that "there is concern about 'the hollowing of industry' where domestic employment and production will decline as Japanese companies transfer their production bases to other low-cost countries."[32] Books written by journalists and scholars for the public were even more willing to call the FDI trend a problem. There were over a dozen books issued between 1995 and 1997 with "industrial hollowing out" in the title, including *How Shall We Respond to Industrial Hollowing Out?* and *Thinking about the Industrial Hollowing-Out Problem.*[33]

Continuing Uncertainty and Ambivalence about the Hollowing-Out "Problem"

Nevertheless, the question of whether Japan had reached the point where FDI now constituted a "hollowing-out problem" remained the subject of vigorous debate. Some government reports worried that the latest surge in manufacturing investment would substitute for Japanese exports and displace domestic production as products began flowing back into the country in the form of "reverse imports," but others echoed Ozawa's view that FDI remained a "house-cleaning-and-renovating vehicle" for Japan. As late as 2002, Ministry of Economy, Trade and Industry official Nakamura Yoshiaki surveyed the most recent FDI patterns, which show that firms were moving high-value-added operations overseas and beginning to locate R & D there as well, and concluded nevertheless that "the issue of divergence of individual corporate benefit and social benefit is not such a significant issue."[34]

This continuing uncertainty and ambivalence about whether hollowing out was a "problem" was critical because the exit of capital via FDI would only produce a vigorous policy response when there was agreement on this point. Contrary to the assumptions behind Henry Laurence's assertions quoted at the start of this chapter, it was not at all self-evident that firms' decisions to move capital overseas were a "problem"—even after FDI surged into Southeast Asia and China beginning in the mid-1990s. Before there would be agreement on this point, the firms themselves, their workers, or state officials would have to actively make the case for why FDI was now a problem when it had been greeted initially as evidence of the strength of Japanese-style capitalism. For various reasons, none of these key participants in the elite debate about economic policy was eager to take the lead in making this case.

This hesitation was apparent, first, in the way firms locating operations overseas explained their decisions. Firms were indeed struggling to deal with high production costs in the late 1990s and were increasingly choosing to locate production overseas in order to lower their costs, but that does not mean they were eager to draw attention to these decisions or call them a "problem." On the contrary, corporate executives announcing major investments overseas took pains to reassure their domestic workers and the media that they were not doing so at the expense of production in Japan. The jobs of the core domestic workforce would be protected. Valuable technology would not be made available to overseas partners.

Almost every press release announcing new overseas investment by a Japanese firm played up the benefits of the project for the corporation and the host country—and said absolutely nothing about potential costs at home. For example, when NEC announced plans to build a factory in the Philippines producing hard drives (its first factory of this type outside of Japan), it emphasized how it was creating two thousand jobs in that country. Philippine engineers would be trained in the latest production methods. The press release did not say anything about how the overseas production would affect factories at home, but it implied that there would be little effect by pointing out that the new factory was designed to meet growing worldwide demand for this NEC product.[35] Similarly, when Mitsui Chemical announced in 2000 its plans to expand production of PET bottle resins at its plant in Indonesia to 75,000 tons a year, it emphasized how the increased production would supplement and not replace production at its two Japanese plants, which would continue to produce 159,000 tons of this product.[36]

This tendency to emphasize the positive in press releases is certainly a constant for corporations around the world, but for most Japanese firms this commitment to maintain domestic production (at least in factories employing their own core workers) was more than rhetorical. As Mireya Solis argues in her detailed study of Japanese FDI patterns, much of Japanese foreign investment has involved "expansion of overseas manufacture of the more standardized products" concurrently with "attempts to move into higher-value-added segments in domestic production."[37] She found this pattern to be common especially in the electronics industry, but it has also been common in automobiles, petrochemicals, steel, and many other industries that are dominated by large firms with lifetime employment systems.

Canon's approach to FDI, explained by the head of the company's corporate planning unit in a 2002 interview, nicely illustrates this pattern.[38] When Canon first began moving production to Southeast Asia and China in the early 1990s and faced the question of what to do with domestic factories, it decided not to close these plants but to convert them to the manufacture of higher-value-added products. More recently, it has converted factories into facilities that work closely with engineers to work the bugs out of the production process for the firm's newest product lines. Once the process is standardized, production is immediately transferred to China. A growing proportion of the firm's production is being done in China, but because Canon always has new products coming on line, it has a constant stream of products that need the attention of domestic engineers and experienced factory workers.

Canon's efforts to avoid laying off workers as it expands production overseas obviously makes it difficult for it to present its actions as part of the problem of hollowing out—even if it wanted to. The manager I interviewed did not use the term and showed no interest in characterizing his firm's decisions as part of a problem. He did admit, however, that his firm's actions have contributed to the decline of manufacturing employment in Japan as the firm has brought in-house some of the work that it used to subcontract to smaller factories located near its major production facilities. These moves, and similar ones by other firms opening factories overseas, eventually led to a sharp contraction in the number of manufacturing workers in Japan—down from 15.19 million in 1990 to 13.21 million in 2000.[39] They have also led to a sharp contraction of manufacturing activity on the part of small subcontractors in districts like Tokyo's Ōta Ward (the location of Canon's headquarters), and similar neighborhoods in the Kansai region. The number of small firms operating in Ōta Ward fell by 25 percent between 1983 and 1995, and employment fell by over a third.[40]

These effects of Japanese firms' decisions to locate production work overseas, however, have all been indirect—negatively affecting small firms that are sometimes several subcontracting steps removed from the major firm moving overseas, with effects that show up months or years after the foreign venture begins production. Canon and other Japanese firms leading the expansion of overseas operations have shown no interest in claiming credit for these negative effects of their business decisions or in using them to extract concessions from policymakers in Tokyo. Unlike U.S. firms, which have been known to announce the closing of domestic plants on the same day they announce a plant opening in Mexico and have sometimes threatened to move factories across borders in order to extract concessions from their workers, Japanese firms have hesitated to call attention to their role in shrinking the domestic manufacturing sector. They have been even less inclined to aggressively use a threat to close plants and lay off workers in order to extract policy concessions.

Largely because union workers have been able to work with large firms to protect their jobs from the effects of overseas expansion, organized labor has also failed to take a lead in calling attention to the hollowing-out problem in Japan. In the United States, those who did the most to publicize the problem of hollowing out were individuals with close ties to the labor union movement. Both filmmaker Michael Moore, writer, director, and producer of the movie *Roger & Me,* which focused on the effects of General Motors's plant closings in Michigan, and economist Barry Bluestone, the author of the best-selling book on hollowing out, have been close to the union movement in the United States.[41] In their unsuccessful campaign to defeat the North American Free Trade Agreement (NAFTA), these champions of the American auto worker as well as official union leadership put foremost emphasis on their concern that NAFTA would accelerate the movement of factories and jobs across the Mexican border.

In contrast, Japanese labor unions have yet to take a lead in accusing firms of exporting jobs through overseas investment. The relatively low level of emphasis on hollowing out can be seen, for example, in the annual policy statement issued by Japan's largest union federation, Rengō, in 2003. In a two-hundred-page document covering the gamut of issues of interest to Japanese labor unions, the topic of hollowing out gets only brief mention in two subsections. Listing it fifth in a discussion of eight causes of deflation, the union calls for stabilizing exchange rates at an "appropriate level" in order to stem this trend.[42] Hollowing out is not mentioned again until it is given as one reason the government needs to invest more heavily in research and development.[43] The statement makes no attempt to rally popular opinion against globalization, and does not even take issue with government policies that promote foreign investment, such as those providing financing for firms that set up factories overseas.

With neither firms nor labor unions interested in ringing alarms to call attention to the hollowing-out trend, the task of defining the problem has been left to government officials—many of whom have been just as ambivalent about publicizing and exploiting this issue. METI and other agencies have occasionally called attention to statistics that show a contraction in manufacturing employment, a rise in small business bankruptcies, and other evidence of deindustrialization. In a 1998 report, for example, METI mentioned the hollowing-out trend as a concern motivating its call for the government to use deregulation and other economic reforms to lower the costs of doing business inside Japan.[44] Yet the discussion of the problem in the report is very brief, with most of the ministry's analysis devoted to the question of how to revitalize the economy.

METI official Nakamura Yoshiaki offers a clear explanation for METI's reticence in a 2002 essay. The government needs to be careful about how it defines the hollowing-out problem, he explains, because in the past worries about structural adjustment led regulators to get in the way of market forces. "On this occasion," he writes, "the government should, above all, strictly eschew a response that would obstruct corporate activities and the progress of globalization."[45] One can only surmise that his conclusion in this essay—that FDI remains consistent with the national interest and that there is no real hollowing-out problem—is motivated at least in part by his worry that a contrary finding might be used to justify increased state interference in the market.

Debate over How to Solve the Hollowing-Out Problem

As Nakamura's comment makes clear, government officials' ambivalence about whether to define hollowing out as a problem—if and when it is acknowledged to exist—has been inextricably intertwined with their views on the policies that might be used to address that problem. Should the problem of hollowing out be addressed by further reducing government involvement in the economy, by privatizing public corporations and reducing government regulations in order to lower the costs of doing business in Japan? Or should it be addressed by *increasing* government involvement, in pushing down the value of the yen or placing new regulatory hurdles in the way of firms that might want to move overseas? Which costs of business have been the most critical in motivating firms to relocate production abroad? And which of these costs can and should be lowered through government policy?

These are all critical questions that must be answered before public policy can target the causes of hollowing out, but once again exit via FDI has not spoken for itself in identifying causes and solutions. On the contrary, firms' ability to escape many of the high costs of doing business in Japan by moving production overseas has reduced their incentive to get actively involved in the process of campaigning for economic reform, so once again the task of answering these questions and trying to figure out how to make Japan more business-friendly has been left to government officials.

The pathologies inherent in a program of "bureaucracy-led deregulation" were on vivid display every time the government attempted to take the lead in regulatory reform and other economic reforms during the 1990s. When the government formed a high-profile deregulation subcommittee of the Administrative Reform Committee in 1995, it was unable to find a single representative of the traditional manufacturing sector to serve on the subcommittee. The subcommittee was headed by a retired bureaucrat and included a number of economists from academia. The only business representatives were "the head of a supermarket chain, a research consultancy, the Japanese chairman of an American firm called Polyfibron Technologies Inc., and the French chairman of the Tokyo subsidiary of Louis Vuitton Moet Hennessy."[46] If manufacturers were seriously concerned about high costs and the need for deregulation, they should have insisted on being on this subcommittee, but they did not. The result was a report that was long on philosophy (some passages could have been written by Milton Friedman) but short on big concrete reforms.

The next chapter, which examines case studies in economic reform, offers more detailed analysis of firms' failure to press for reforms to restrain and bring down their costs of production. The three cases examined—labor market reform, electricity reform, and public sector reform—all illustrate the pathologies summarized in this chapter.

Chapter 6

Case Studies in Economic Reform

The overall pattern of Japan's response to hollowing out has been one of limited exit leading to less exercise of voice and little reform. When we look more closely at the policy response to specific areas of high costs, we see that the dynamics of the reform debate followed this pattern closely in several critical areas: labor market reform, electricity market reform, and public sector reform. The high costs borne by firms in each of these areas were all ones that firms were able to escape, but not easily, through the time-consuming process of moving manufacturing facilities overseas. Consequently, there has been little concerted pressure on the state to implement reforms in these areas and very little change.

Labor Market Reform

Labor costs are the single largest component of the costs of production for almost all firms in Japan, as in every other country. While Japanese manufacturers for many years had the advantage of lower labor costs than most other industrialized nations, after many years of steady raises (magnified by the effects of an appreciating value of the yen) Japanese wages grew to be among the highest in the world by the middle of the 1990s. Japanese hourly compensation costs in the manufacturing sector were above those in almost every other industrialized nation in 1995 and 2000 (table 6.1).[1] They were above those in the United States, France, and Britain, and were almost triple the labor costs in Korea and Singapore. The table does not show the even lower manufacturing labor costs in China, where wages paid to workers at facilities in export-oriented zones were estimated to be just 5 percent of those of their counterparts in Japan.[2]

Hourly compensation costs, however, were just the beginning of the labor cost disadvantage facing Japanese manufacturing firms, for employers saw costs not

TABLE 6.1.
Hourly compensation costs for production workers, with Japanese costs indexed at 100

Country	Year					
	1975	1980	1985	1990	1995	2000
Germany, former West	211	221	149	170	136	106
Japan	100	100	100	100	100	100
United States	213	179	204	116	74	88
United Kingdom	113	137	98	99	60	76
France	151	162	118	121	84	70
Korea	11	18	18	29	31	36
Singapore	28	27	39	29	31	34

Source: Based on data in U.S. Department of Labor, Bureau of Labor Statistics, *International Comparison of Hourly Compensation Costs for Production Workers in Manufacturing*, http://www.bls.gov/fls/hcompreport.htm (accessed June 14, 2004).

merely in terms of how much workers cost per hour but also in terms of how flexibly workers could be deployed. Most Japanese firms employed a large proportion of their workers as "permanent" employees, with regulations, agreements with unions, and social norms all making it very difficult to lay off these workers for any reason short of bankruptcy. These rules also committed firms to a seniority wage system that constrained firms' restructuring options.[3] In other advanced industrialized countries, in contrast, firms had more flexible wage structures and could lay off workers with only short notice (a common condition in the United States), secure the assistance of the state in retraining workers for new jobs (Sweden), or offload expensive older employees onto unemployment, disability, and pension programs when they became redundant (Germany and France). Conditions governing hiring and firing were even more lax in developing countries such as China, where most manufacturing workers were hired on short-term contracts and could be dismissed with very short notice.

During the period of rapid economic and demographic expansion, as discussed in chapter 3, Japanese employers found their employment system to be quite efficient. Once Japan began to experience stagnant growth and a shrinking population of new young workers, however, rigidities inherent in the system began to constrain the ability of firms to retain their competitiveness. During the 1990s, labor began to command a larger share of national income, growing from 67.2 percent in 1990 to 74.6 percent in 2001.[4] Japanese firms that had been rated among the most competitive in their industries, such as Toshiba and Hitachi, began to bleed red ink, in large part because they could not get their labor costs under control as their sales stagnated.

The situation forced Japanese firms to take action, but the predominant response was *not* to use voice through the political process to seek labor market reforms that would transform the Japanese employment system into a much more flexible one. Instead, manufacturing firms sought to cut their exposure to the Japanese employment system by locating a growing proportion of their production work overseas. Significantly, when they went overseas, they did not duplicate the employment system they had at home. In the United States, they chose to locate primarily in right-to-work states such as Tennessee and Kentucky and fought hard to prevent the unionization of their workforce so that they would be able to take full advantage of the ease of dismissal afforded by U.S. labor law. In their plants in Southeast Asia and China, they offered only short-term contracts (and very few benefits) to their production workers.

The choices Japanese firms have made when given the leeway to choose how to manage their human resources overseas suggests that most firms would, if given the chance, modify the labor market constraints they face at home. The chief of corporate planning for Canon admitted as much when asked why his firm had not attempted to shrink its domestic work force as it expanded overseas production.[5] It made little economic sense, he admitted, for his firm to retain the twenty thousand domestic production workers it employed (in a workforce of forty thousand Japan-based employees). Their wages were twenty times those paid to Chinese workers, but the Chinese employees working in Canon plants were "just as productive, are grateful to have a job, and work hard." In addition, Canon had to pay the social insurance costs of its Japanese workers but had no such obligation for its contract workers in China. The only reason the firm has not laid off production workers in Japan (none of whom are quitting), the manager explained, "is because Japan has a lifetime employment system."

Why not seek to change that system, then? After all, Canon's president, Mitarai Fujio, has been actively involved in Keidanren affairs for some years and is a well-respected figure in business circles. Since 2002, he has served as one of Keidanren's vice-chairs, and he has also headed several of the group's committees. Rather than use his position to fight for a more fluid labor market, however, Mitarai has spoken up in defense of the lifetime employment system. While Mitarai worked for many years in Canon's U.S. subsidiary (where he became familiar with U.S. human resource practices) and has shown he is willing to close unproductive units of his firm in order to increase profits, he stubbornly defends the Japanese employment system as one which helps foster loyalty to the company.[6] Barring the sudden emergence of a fluid labor market in Japan, the Canon executive I interviewed predicted, the firm would keep its current cohort of full-time production workers on the payroll until they retired. The average age of this group is currently forty-two, and since the firm is not hiring any new production workers, this cohort is aging by about one year every year. Canon has decided that it is easier to carry these workers on its books for twenty more years—subsidized by the extra profits it can make by concentrating its production work in low-cost China—than to use its political clout to change the system.

Indeed, few Japanese business leaders or groups have stepped forward to lead the campaign for far-reaching labor market reforms. After reading a comprehensive collection of business group and firm proposals for labor market reform during the 1990s, Miura Mari found that *none* proposed changes that would make it easier for firms to fire or lay off their workers.[7] Many reports published by the Japan Federation of Employers' Associations (Nikkeiren) in the late 1990s extolled the tradition of emphasizing employment security in Japanese human resource practices.

In 1999, Okuda Hiroshi, the chair of Toyota Motors and the incoming head of Nikkeiren, explicitly supported maintaining the lifetime employment system in the face of pressures to move away from it. He recalled that his own firm's bond rating had been downgraded by Moody's investor service the year before specifically because Toyota refused to move away from the lifetime employment system. Toyota refused, he said, because the system "provided for the stability of labor-industrial relations, which was conducive to teamwork in the workplace."[8] In another speech, he urged Japanese firms not to succumb to pressures to lay off workers to increase their profits: "Cutting jobs is the last thing management should do. If you do so only to raise profitability or the value of shares, that's wrong in light of Japan's style of management."[9]

That no business leaders called for an abandonment of lifetime employment does not mean the business sector made no demands for labor market reform. Such reforms were on the policy agenda for much of the 1990s, with business groups pushing for some more specific changes. Among the reforms they sought were the following: (1) flexibility for firms in retirement law to allow them to work out their own arrangements with unions rather than obliging them to extend employment privileges to age sixty-five; (2) reforms of the pension system to minimize the increase in social insurance premiums paid by workers and employers as Japan dealt with growth in its elderly population; (3) reforms in labor standards to allow employers to assign managers to "discretionary work hours" that obviate the need to pay them for overtime work; and (4) a set of reforms designed to shrink the proportion of workers covered by the lifetime employment system while increasing the proportion employed under much more flexible (and cheaper) arrangements.

Although the full agenda, if realized, had the potential to reduce employers' overall wage bill, the business community was unable to prevail in many of these areas. Far from being the aggressor, leveraging its ability to move jobs overseas to force labor and the government to agree to its demands, firms were often on the defensive, seeking to avoid policy changes that would *add* to their labor costs. This was especially true in retirement law and pension reform. In other areas, employers either came up empty handed or settled for modest regulatory reform that did not fundamentally increase fluidity in the employment system.

Retirement Age Policy

Firms were on the defensive from the start in the first area of labor law to receive attention in the 1990s, the government's plan to extend the retirement age in order to minimize the state's burden of paying for pensions and health care for the burgeoning population of elderly.[10] Pension reforms in the 1980s had encouraged employers to extend corporate retirement ages, typically set at fifty-five, closer to sixty. In 1994, over the objections of some employers, the government made it illegal to set the retirement age below sixty. This extension of the retirement age, in a system where many full-time production workers were covered by lifetime employment and seniority wage rules, sharply increased costs for employers, which now had to retain their most costly employees for an extra five years just as the recession was making many of these workers redundant.

Their experience with this earlier round of pension reform made firms even more eager to avoid another extension in the mandatory retirement age to accompany the government's extension of the age of entitlement under the Employee Pension System from sixty to sixty-five, which began with a one-year extension in eligibility for the basic portion of the pension for male employees in 2001 and will conclude when eligibility for both the basic and income-related portions of the pension will be set at sixty-five for women and men in 2030.[11] So far, they have avoided an extension of the state-mandated floor on retirement ages. However, as firms have confronted labor unions over the issue of how workers are expected to bridge the years between retirement at sixty and pensions at sixty-five, they have been forced to come to accommodations that have extended the de facto obligations of most large firms. At many firms, workers over sixty are asked to accept lower pay as contract workers or to accept out-placement at lower wages, but they are typically guaranteed some income beyond sixty until they reach the pensionable age.[12]

Pension Reform

Employers have been similarly on the defensive in the most recent high-profile battle over pension reform. Faced with demographic projections showing that Japanese are both living longer and having fewer children than projected in the past, the Ministry of Health, Labor and Welfare faced a 2004 deadline for revising its pension policies to make sure projected income matched projected payouts. Employers had much at stake in this debate in that employee pensions already added 13.6 percent to the wage costs of full-time employees. Absent any reductions in promised benefits, the MHLW projected, firms could expect pension premiums to rise to 23.1 percent in 2025 due to demographic trends, even if the state increased the proportion of basic pension expenses covered by general tax revenue from one-third to one half.[13] After 2025, premiums were expected to rise even higher. With the social insurance burden of health care expected to rise as well, the questions of whether to cut pension benefits and the way they were financed became critical issues for employers concerned about the costs of domestic labor.

The employers' favored approach, championed by Okuda (by this time the head of Nippon Keidanren, the united big-business federation[14]), was to begin cutting benefits immediately, cap the premium level at 18 percent rather than letting it grow to 23 percent or higher, and radically revise the way the entire pension scheme was financed so that most of the revenue came from an increased consumption tax.[15] Each of these three steps was designed to minimize the financial burden on employers, and so was of critical importance to the business community, but Okuda was only able to win modest steps in his favored direction in each area.

He got the least in the area of benefit reductions. The MHLW favored a formula that promised modest reductions in future benefits through a "macro slide" that indexed benefits to *total* wages (which will go down as the number of workers declines) rather than *average* wages (which may go up). Keidanren objected to relying entirely on this formula to deliver benefit reductions because this approach had the effect of delaying reductions in benefits until the baby boomers have retired in large numbers (the 2020s). By continuing generous payouts in the meantime, the approach fails to build up reserves that Keidanren argued are needed to minimize the financing burden on workers in the future. Nevertheless, the MHLW and LDP refused to budge from this feature of the reform, and it passed as proposed in the final legislation adopted in June 2004.

Okuda was similarly stiffed in his attempt to cap future premiums at a low level, ideally below 18 percent. The MHLW initially proposed raising premiums annually at the pace required to maintain promised benefits until the premiums reach a cap of 20 percent. At that point, predicted to occur in the 2020s, benefits would be cut to match available revenues. Under strong pressure from the business community, the LDP lowered the cap to 18.3 percent, but it undercut the effect of this policy by insisting on a companion provision in the final legislation that promised retirees their benefits would never fall below 50 percent of their preretirement wages. Although 50 percent is lower than the current benefit level of 59 percent, it left unanswered the question of what would happen if the two promises came into conflict because of a further deterioration in demographic or economic trends. The business community is quite sure, based on prior experience, that politicians will end up honoring the pledge to retirees and raising premiums above 18.3 percent when that time comes.

The final tack pursued by the business community was its attempt to convince the government to shift much of the burden of financing social insurance costs (including pensions) away from payroll taxes and onto a broader-based source of revenue. In December 2002, Okuda outlined what he called his "Okuda vision," calling for future social welfare costs to be financed through steady annual increases in the consumption tax from 5 to 16 percent.[16] The aim was to shift some of the burden of financing pensions for the baby boomers from a shrinking base of salaried workers to the entire population of consumers, including the elderly themselves. If this could be arranged, the payroll tax for pension purposes could be cut sharply from current and projected levels, lowering labor costs relative to what they would be without this reform. Prime Minister Koizumi Jun'ichirō was completely cold to this proposal, refusing even to discuss raising the consumption tax while he was in office.[17] The final pension law that passed in 2004 fudges the issue of financing by calling for an increase in general revenue support for the basic pension program without specifying where this revenue will come from.

Discretionary Work Hours

In this third area of labor market reform, employers sought modifications in labor standards that would allow them to switch managers paid on an hourly basis (entitled to overtime pay) to "discretionary work hours" that would allow them to pay these white-collar workers a set salary for a given number of hours (typically forty) without any obligation to pay them for any extra hours they might work. Under labor standards in place before these reforms were proposed, some specific professionals, such as engineers working in research and development and information technicians, could be paid through discretionary work hours, but white-collar managers working in the core divisions of companies could not. Employers pushed hard for this reform and succeeded in getting legislation similar to their proposal to the Diet floor. Faced with firm opposition from labor unions and support for the union position from virtually all of the parties in the Diet other than the LDP, however, they were forced to accept modifications that gutted the intent of the reform. Under the terms of the legislation, the Ministry of Labor (now part of the MHLW) was obliged to consult with an advisory council with statutory representation for labor unions before preparing implementing ordinances. In addition, employers were required to win workers' consent before they could be switched from hourly status to discretionary work hours, a requirement very few employers have been able to meet. Firms had once again failed in their bid to lower labor costs through this tactic.[18]

Expanding the Flexible Segment of the Labor Market

This final area of reform was the one where advocates of labor market reform had the highest hopes of success. The goal was to avoid challenging the lifetime employment system head-on but instead to expand the range of jobs that employers could fill with workers hired under much more flexible arrangements. The employers' federation, Nikkeiren, and the big-business group, Keidanren, both endorsed this strategy in key policy documents in the late 1990s. It was also endorsed by a variety of government agencies and advisory councils as a key strategy for stemming the hollowing-out trend in manufacturing and restoring the vitality of the Japanese economy. The Ministry of International Trade and Industry, for example, touted the potential for fee-charging employment placement businesses to cover an expanded range of professions, thus ensuring "smooth job mobility" and enhancing the competitiveness of Japanese firms.[19] Similarly, the Economic Strategy Council convened by Prime Minister Obuchi Keizō in 1999 stressed the role worker dispatch services could play in facilitating "flexible labor movement." The goal, it said, was "to get rid of the traditional employment policy that stimulated labor-hoarding in individual companies."[20]

As employers and the government began pushing for specific elements of this plan, however, they were faced with strong union objections to most of the specific proposals. The first initiative came in term contracts, which had previously been restricted to one-year with no renewal. This provision limited the range of positions employers could fill under these relatively flexible arrangements because many did not want to have to hire new employees every year. Employers would have liked to be able to hire workers with open-ended term contracts for clerical and skill-specific positions, with contracts that could be renewed as long as firms needed the employee but could be terminated much more easily than in the case of permanent employees.[21] While employers hoped at a minimum to be able to lengthen term contracts to three years without restrictions, they ended up getting even less than that after facing strong objections from unions. Term contracts up to three years are now allowed, but employers can only offer such contracts to "new employees" hired for "new projects," with no possibility for converting regular employees to term contracts unless the employees are over sixty years old. After three years, contract employees are eligible for a single one-year contract after which further renewals imply a permanent contract.[22]

The second initiative, also pursued by employers in the late 1990s, focused on the goal of expanding their ability to contract with temp agencies (*haken gaisha*) to secure the services of temporary workers or, as they are called in Japan, "dispatched workers." If employers could contract for a large number of such workers in a wide variety of positions, they might be able to dramatically shrink the proportion of their work force covered by lifetime employment and seniority wage rules, achieving large savings in their labor costs. Prior to reforms adopted in 1999, however, regulations severely restricted employers' ability to replace expensive permanent employees with dispatched workers. Temps were allowed in only sixteen lines of work (such as translator, broadcast producer, and janitor)—none of them in manufacturing or core white-collar corporate departments. And firms could only fill a position with a temp for nine months to a year (depending on the job category).[23] As a result in 1997 the share of dispatched workers in the employee workforce came to just 0.5 percent.[24]

Employers hoped to greatly expand opportunities to employ dispatched workers by shifting from the "positive list" regulatory system described above, under which firms could only hire temps in a limited number of specified job categories, to a "negative list," under which temps would be barred from just a few specified jobs. They also hoped to make it easier to permanently fill certain jobs with temps, with one temp replacing another when the dispatched worker's term was up, as long as the firm needed someone in the position. The goals of this deregulation drive were endorsed by the leading business associations, the Ministry of Economy, Trade, and Industry, and key government advisory councils, all of which described it as critical to Japan's efforts to make its labor market more fluid.

Nevertheless, the plan encountered fierce opposition from the trade unions, which worried that employers intended to replace permanent workers with dispatched workers enjoying much lower job protection, benefits, and pay. Unions worked to limit the extent of change at every stage of the policy process, and were able to prevent employers from achieving many of their goals.[25] Although the Dispatched Workers' Law was amended in 1999 to convert it from a positive to a negative list regulatory system, manufacturing work was placed on the proscribed list, greatly limiting the potential of the reform to lower labor costs in the sector most affected by hollowing out. Furthermore, the unions succeeded in securing a limit of one-year in the dispatch period (firms could fill a given job with a temp for no more than one year), making it difficult for employers to permanently fill a set of jobs with cheaper temps.

The overall results of the various efforts by employers to expand the proportion of jobs they can fill with irregular workers not protected by the lifetime employment and seniority wage norms have been limited—in both their legislative impact and their impact on employment patterns. There has been some growth in the share of irregular workers in the employee workforce (figure 6.1), but the increase has been very small, especially in the categories that were of greatest interest to employers because they had the potential to apply to skilled workers: contract and dispatched workers. The proportion of employees who are dispatched workers grew from 0.5 percent before the 1999 reforms to 0.7 percent in 2002. The proportion in term contracts grew by a greater proportion, from 1.8 to 3.6 percent. A look at the gender and age breakdown of these irregular workers shows, however, that the majority of these irregular workers are women and older workers (over sixty). Firms have by and large failed to liberalize labor markets for skilled male workers in their prime earning years, even in the manufacturing sectors most subject to hollowing out.

A variety of analysts have surveyed the degree of change in the Japanese labor market and concurred with my evaluation that change has been limited. Economist Genda Yūji notes that "the average tenure of middle-aged and elderly workers within the same firm is becoming longer" and that the proportion of long-term employees in their fifties is growing and concludes that the lifetime employment system is actually becoming more entrenched.[26] Ronald Dore similarly notes the disconnect between the popular discourse about change in the Japanese employment system in which "restructuring has become a buzzword" and the fact that firms continue to employ an estimated two million so-called redundant workers. "There is a great deal of talk about flexible labor markets and merit pay," he writes, "but the proportion of workers on nonstandard contracts has grown only marginally."[27] Finally, after an exhaustive study of the politics of labor market reform over the past decade in Japan, Miura Mari concludes that "Japan's heavy reliance on the labor market for welfare purposes remained untouched or even fortified in the 1990s."[28]

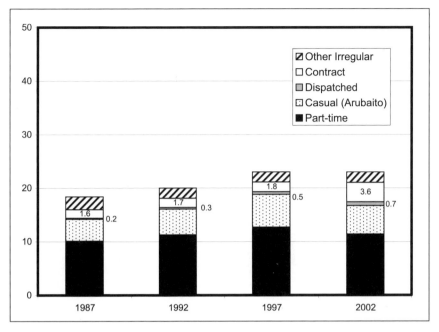

Fig. 6.1. Irregular employment in Japan, 1987–2002
Source: Adapted from Ministry of Labor, *Rōdō hakusho—Heisei 12–nen-han*, 2000, 515, updated with data from the Labor Force Survey, online at http://www.mhlw.go.jp/english/wp/wp-l/29.html (accessed February 25, 2005).

Electricity Reforms

Over the past decade, business groups and government agencies have published countless studies and reports on the "high costs" that are eroding the competitiveness of Japanese producers and driving many of them to relocate operations overseas. Every one of these reports lists Japan's high energy costs, and in particular its expensive electricity, as a major concern for Japanese firms. As we saw, high electricity costs were a major factor impelling Japan's aluminum industry to relocate overseas starting in the early 1980s. Yet despite years of hand-wringing, electricity remains more expensive in Japan than in any other industrialized nation, regardless of how costs are measured or which exchange rate is used.

According to International Energy Agency (IEA) data from the mid-1990s, when policymakers began to focus on electricity prices in earnest, Japan's electricity rates for industry were almost double those paid by firms in most other OECD nations. Japanese households similarly paid 50 to 100 percent more for electricity than households in North America and Europe.[29] Japan's electricity costs are also

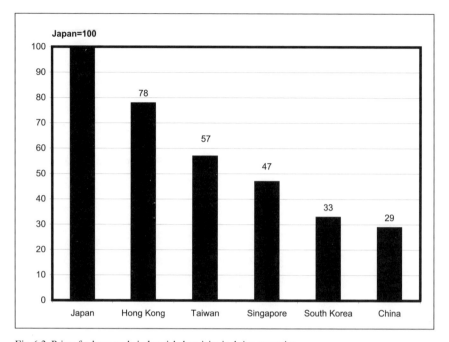

Fig. 6.2. Prices for large-scale industrial electricity in Asian countries
Source: Adapted from Ministry of Economy, Trade and Industry, *Structural Reform Issues and Economic and Industrial Policy,* May 2002, section 5, based on data from the ministry's "Survey on Domestic and Overseas Prices Related to Interim Output," July 2001.

much higher than those in Korea, Taiwan, and China, where many producers of energy-intensive steel, machinery, and petrochemicals have been relocating an increasing proportion of their production work (see figure 6.2). Although Japan has not been the only country to struggle with high electricity costs, some of the other high-electricity-cost countries have succeeded in lowering costs through reforms—while Japan's electricity prices have remained stubbornly high. Britain was able to lower industrial electricity prices by 33 percent in inflation-adjusted terms in the decade after reforms were introduced in the 1980s.[30] Germany, which liberalized its markets all at once in 1998, saw electricity prices fall by 20 percent in just one year.[31]

High electricity prices have been a particular focus of concern in the discussion of hollowing out because they represent a significant share of the input costs facing manufacturers, especially in energy-intensive sectors. They make up 15 percent of the input costs of the iron and steel industry, 8 percent of the costs of ceramics and cement, and 8 percent of costs in the chemical industry.[32] Industry as a whole purchased 254 billion kilowatt hours of electricity from the utilities in 2001, at an approximate cost of ¥4.3 trillion ($36 billion).[33] While all of this would lead one to expect industry to be taking a lead in calling for reforms designed to bring electricity prices down, for reasons that are consistent with the logic of the argument developed here, business has not been pushing very hard for lower electricity prices, and Japan has not adopted far-reaching reforms of the type that would be necessary to bring the nation's electricity prices down to the level of its leading competitors.

Japanese electricity prices have been stubbornly high for a variety of reasons, some more amenable to a policy solution than others. An OECD review of the challenge Japan faces attributes the cost difference at least in part to the geographical and geological environment in which Japanese utilities have to operate: they have to import almost all of their fuel (which means natural gas, for example, has to come into the country in the expensive liquefied form); they have to build plants and transmission lines to expensive specifications designed to make sure the infrastructure can withstand the earthquakes and typhoons that frequently buffet the islands; and they have to pay more for everything from land to site licenses to pollution equipment because they operate in such a densely populated country.[34]

Nevertheless, most analysts stress that Japan's high electricity costs are also a reflection of the permissive regulatory environment in which utilities operate. Japan's ten regional electric utilities are all privately owned, but each has traditionally enjoyed a monopoly on the right to supply businesses and consumers with electricity in its area. The Japanese government has regulated these utility companies, but it has allowed them to set prices on a cost-plus basis, giving them no incentive to restrain (or cut) their costs. As a result, they have been content to retain excess employees, pay some of the highest wages of any industrial sector, pay more for plants and other equipment than utilities in other nations, and ignore opportunities to use their generating capacity more efficiently through load-shifting (from peak to off-peak hours). They have also been willing, at the behest of a Japanese government eager to improve the nation's energy security, to invest heavily in expensive and risky nuclear energy projects.

The OECD, after reviewing the Japanese regulatory system and recent limited moves toward liberalization, argued that lower prices would only be achieved through far-reaching reforms designed to foster genuine competition in electricity markets. Doing so would require not only opening up the transmission grid to independent power producers—something Japan had done in 1995—but also creating a regulatory regime that would prevent the existing firms from using their control of the grid to discriminate against their competitors. For competitive forces to take hold, the ten regional firms would have to be forced to separate their transmission accounts from their power-generation accounts and sell access to the grid at nondiscriminatory rates; anticompetitive practices would be banned and policed; and the regional grids would need to be connected so that utilities operating in one region could be forced to compete with those in other regions. The OECD noted that even these steps might not be enough to jump-start competition in the closed Japanese electricity market. The nation might have to adopt fundamental structural changes of the type other nations have pioneered, including ordering the complete legal separation of the utilities' transmission and power-generation operations.

Reforms along these lines have indeed been on the policy agenda in Japan since the mid-1990s, with the government revisiting electricity policy three times over the past decade, in 1995, 2000, and 2003. The frequency of policy initiatives should not be seen, however, as evidence that large industrial users, frustrated by high prices, have driven the reform process. On the contrary, although Keidanren has issued advice each time the issue has been on the government's agenda, and although large industrial users have been given representation on government advisory councils, industry's advocacy of electricity market reform has been modest at best. Neither Keidanren nor large users have called for the most controversial, but potentially most effective, reform: legal separation of the incumbents' transmission and power-generation operations. In a 1998 report covering the topic of high electricity prices, Keidanren did not even call for accounting separation, better connections between the regional transmission grids, or tougher policing of anticompetitive practices—three reforms that are a prerequisite to fostering competition in the industry. Instead, the report called only vaguely for the introduction of competition in retail electricity markets, for more pricing options (e.g., off-peak pricing) designed to use existing generating capacity more efficiently, and a cut in corporate taxes paid by the utilities.[35]

One of Keidanren's senior staff, Kinbara Kazuyuki, admits that his group has not taken a lead in this issue area and that Keidanren criticism of high electricity prices has been "watered down." One reason, he explained, is that the electric utilities are "important members" of the organization and participate on committees dealing with their sector. These committees operate "on consensus," so when the industry objects, strong and specific language has to be deleted.[36] Indeed, the utilities are giant industrial firms whose size relative to Japanese industry as a whole guarantees them significant stature in an organization like Keidanren. The Federation of Electric Power Companies has its offices in the same central Tokyo building that houses Keidanren's offices. The electric utilities routinely lend staff to Keidanren, and the president of Tokyo Electric Power Company (TEPCO)—Katsumata Tsunehisa—was one of Keidanren's vice-chairs in 2004.

These structural constraints on Keidanren's advocacy of reform, however, cannot explain why user firms and industry associations that are not limited by the need to win the utilities' support for their position papers have not been significantly more vocal in their calls for reform. User firms have regularly been invited to serve on government advisory councils considering electricity market reform proposals, but a variety of observers report that these members have not been vocal proponents of far-reaching reforms in council meetings. According to the METI official who worked most closely with the Electricity Industry Committee between 2001 and 2003, the president of Nippon Steel (a huge user of electricity) was not a vocal champion of reform.[37] Another close observer, a financial analyst covering the electric utility sector for Dresdner Kleinwort Wasserstein (DKW), classified the Nippon Steel executive as "anti-deregulation; largely advocates the status quo."[38] The same analyst rated several other user firm representatives on the panel, including the president of Toyota, Chō Fujio, as "pro-deregulation," but the METI official who staffed the committee characterized Chō as a "very shy" member of the committee who did not criticize the utilities in public. Asked specifically whether industrial users attempted to use their relocation of operations overseas as leverage to push for far-reaching reforms in the electricity market, the METI official was quite clear that they did not: "No one was threatening. Few were even willing to openly support METI's position in favor of reforms."

Why were industrial users so hesitant to complain that they were forced to pay the world's highest electricity prices? Why didn't they campaign more openly and vigorously for electricity market reforms? According to a variety of observers, part of the explanation lay in the political and market power of the utilities. The utilities are extremely influential, not just within Keidanren, but within the Liberal Democratic Party. As private corporations, they have long been free to contribute to political parties and candidates (although legal opportunities to contribute to candidates have been more tightly regulated since 1994), and they have used this opening to establish themselves as one of the leading sources of campaign financing. The utilities have also developed alliances with other influential industries, such as construction and steel, whose goods and services they procure in large volumes when they build power plants and transmission lines. By making it clear to these industries that the high prices they get for construction services and steel are contingent on the protection utilities enjoy from competition, the utilities have secured their support for the status quo in the political and policy arenas. The METI official cited above attributes Nippon Steel's lack of support for reform to the firm's prioritization of sales to the utilities over the price it has to pay for electricity.[39]

The market power enjoyed by the utilities extends beyond its procurement budget for construction and steel. Until partial reforms that went into effect in 2000, the utilities had a monopoly on supplying retail sales of electricity over transmission wires in their regions. In the period since then, as debate over more substantial reforms has continued, alternative sources of supply have emerged, but only very slowly. Most large industrial users of electricity are still very dependent on the utilities for the bulk of the electricity they need. Although the utilities have a legal obligation to supply consumers and firms with electricity, they are free to offer lower prices to large users (or to *withdraw* those offers). Industrial users talking to METI about electricity policy have therefore had to do so while looking over their shoulder at utilities that had the potential to reward or punish them by changing the price it charged them for this critical resource. Toyota, in particular, seems to have been asking its utility, Chūbu, to offer it lower prices, even as it participated in Electric Industry Committee meetings.[40]

Although these structural sources of the electric industry's political and market power should not be discounted, user industries also enjoy significant power in politics and markets. Nippon Steel and Toyota are giant and rich companies that could have challenged the entire monopolistic structure that allowed the utilities to block access to cheaper power if they believed it was crucial to the survival of their firms.

Back in the early 1970s, Nippon Steel prevailed on policymakers to stop forcing it to pay inflated prices for domestic coal and begin using state subsidies to shrink the industry, even though the coal industry was very powerful. An important motivator for Nippon Steel at the time was that the firm was limited to producing in Japan. It was a large exporter competing for customers around the world with a production base that was limited to Japan, and it could not afford to lose sales in order to keep the uncompetitive domestic coal industry afloat.

Today Nippon Steel has operations that span the globe. It has an 18.5 percent stake in the Brazilian steel firm Usiminas, a similar stake in Siam United Steel of Thailand, and it recently swapped shares with its long-time Korean rival Pohang Iron and Steel Works in a move that may foreshadow more cooperation with that firm. In all of these places, Nippon Steel has access to electricity at a fraction of the rate it has to pay for retail purchases from the utilities in Japan. The Japanese iron and steel industry produced 19.4 percent of its output overseas in 2001, making it the third most globally diversified Japanese industry after electronics and trans-portation equipment.[41]

Other Japanese industrial firms in energy-intensive sectors have similarly been slowly moving a growing proportion of their production work overseas. Japan was abandoned as a production base by the aluminum industry. By 2001, the Japanese chemical industry, another energy-intensive sector, was producing 14.5 percent of its output abroad.[42] Even *inside* Japan, the heaviest industrial users of electricity have been able to escape having to pay the utilities' posted price for electricity. The largest users have been free to negotiate their own deals with the utilities, which sometimes give them access to power at prices cheaper than the official industrial rate.[43] In the most energy-intensive sectors, firms increasingly rely on self-generation, producing the electric power they need for their industrial processes on-site. The proportion of power these sectors draw from self-generation has been growing steadily over the past fifteen years, reaching 48 percent in 2001.[44] Nippon Steel is one of the leading self-generators in Japan.

Although the firms most vulnerable to high electricity prices have several exit options, these options have been costly and have taken time to implement. It takes many years and great expense to relocate capital-intensive production operations overseas in lower-cost countries. Even domestic self-generation takes time and space and is not a viable option for many moderately energy-intensive manufacturers. This movement has thus been insufficient to push down electricity prices through market forces. But the limited exit options *have* been sufficient to dampen the motivation to campaign for reform by those heaviest users who otherwise would be clamoring for lower electricity prices. Some firms (and residential customers) have been stuck paying high prices for electricity, but these have been ones for whom electricity makes up a smaller portion of input costs—for example, 4 percent for the auto industry.[45] Most of these firms have decided that it is safer to suffer quietly than to lead the push for radical reform of the electric utility industry.

As a result, the leading "voice" pushing for electricity market reform has come from the ministry that regulates and promotes the sector, METI. Kawamoto Akira, the official who shepherded the 2003 reforms through the policy process, complained that his ministry was often alone in challenging the utilities. "METI is the only one out there publicly criticizing the utilities and pushing for lower prices in the national interest," he said.[46] The agency has frequently published reports that list high electricity prices as a problem for industry and associate them with industrial hollowing out. But Kawamoto noted that the ministry has had a difficult time *proving* that high electricity prices were the cause of hollowing out or in guaranteeing that the trend would turn around if prices were brought down. Surveys of firms moving operations overseas show that "high production costs" are a factor behind their decisions, and electricity prices are lower in places such as China, "but none of this is proof that electricity prices are the critical factor that is causing a specific firm to locate production in China," he said.[47]

Yet the Japanese state, and METI itself, is not of one mind about what kind of electricity policy is in Japan's "national interest." All nations have a mix of interests at stake in energy policy: they value not only low-priced energy but also have concerns about the security of supply and the impact of energy use on the environment. METI has a long history of prioritizing energy security above prices, especially in the years after the energy crises of the 1970s, and the ministry has recently begun putting more stress on environmental sustainability. Both considerations have pushed it to promote nuclear energy, which has the greatest short-term potential to reduce Japan's reliance on imported (and globe-warming) fossil fuels. In the mid-1990s, faced with forecasts of rising electricity demand and convinced that nuclear power was the cleanest and most secure source of power, METI pushed the electric utilities to build sixteen to twenty new nuclear power plants before 2010 and to increase the proportion of electricity generated by nuclear plants from 32 percent to 42 percent.[48] It also continued supporting the development of expensive new specialized plants and facilities that would give the nation the ability to operate an entire nuclear fuel cycle: a new uranium-fuel-fabrication plant, a new and larger reprocessing plant, plants designed to burn reprocessed plutonium in the form of MOX (mixed oxide) fuel; a fast breeder reactor; and a high-level nuclear waste disposal site.

METI was therefore conflicted when it realized, as it began to promote electricity market liberalization, that the utilities might demand in exchange a renegotiation of the arrangement under which they had complied with METI's efforts to promote nuclear power. The utilities became even more eager to use market liberalization as an excuse to reduce their exposure to the rising costs and risks of nuclear power after the nation's nuclear plants had a raft of accidents, scandals, and cost overruns in the late 1990s and early 2000s. The most notorious incident was the 1999 accident at the Tokaimura reprocessing facility one hundred miles northwest of Tokyo, which killed two workers and released radiation into the atmosphere.

Other incidents included the revelation that TEPCO had falsified test reports at a number of its nuclear facilities. An investigation of TEPCO's plants revealed additional lapses and previously unpublicized accidents, raising concern to such a level that the utility was forced to shut down all seventeen of its reactors for testing in the summer of 2003.[49]

Amid these revelations, localities have become increasingly reluctant to approve the siting of nuclear facilities in their areas—especially sites that involve storing nuclear waste, reprocessing plutonium, and experimenting with newer types of nuclear fuel like MOX. Projects in all of these areas have been plagued by mishaps, delays, and huge cost overruns. Because the commercial viability of conventional nuclear power plants owned by the utilities depends on finding a reasonably priced solution to the closely related challenges of reprocessing, burning, and storing nuclear waste, the uncertainties plaguing these projects has raised questions about how to allocate the unpredictable and potentially very large costs between the utilities and the state.[50] If METI wanted the utilities to bear some of these costs, it would have to compromise on plans to force the utilities to accept market competition.

Despite the advocacy of far-reaching reform by some within METI, therefore, the nation has made very little progress toward lower electricity prices even after three rounds of liberalization. The first round in 1995 did little more than set the stage for the more important steps that were still being considered. Independent power producers, including self-generating industrial users like Nippon Steel, were for the first time authorized to sell their surplus power to the regional utilities. The utilities still enjoyed a monopoly in their regions on retailing power, and consequently had no competitive pressure to lower prices, but this step opened up the possibility that independent power producers might someday compete with the power-generation operations of the utilities and bring prices down.

This first round left open the question of how such retail-level competition might be introduced. As suggested above, the government could have ordered the legal separation of the utilities' power-generation and transmission operations in order to prevent them from using their control of transmission to stifle competition. METI ruled that the utilities were private companies and could not be ordered to split themselves in this way. The United States had split the private telephone monopoly AT&T in the 1980s, but this step had required many years of legal wrangling. Since few electric power users were campaigning for the Japanese government to undertake such an effort, and since METI hoped to avoid such a fight, the legal separation option was quickly abandoned.

Another option, pursued by some OECD countries and U.S. states, is to order utilities to carry out mandatory "account unbundling." The aim is to force each utility to separate its transmission accounts from its power-generation accounts, cutting off opportunities for utilities to maintain an advantage over new entrants in the power generation business by using the profits on their monopoly transmission operation to subsidize their own power-generation operations. *If* the accounting separation is done fairly, and *if* the wheeling fees (covering the cost of transmission) charged to power generators are set at an appropriate level, it is theoretically possible to foster market competition in the power generation business without legally splitting the utilities into two parts.

Two other reforms were also critical. First the utilities, which were previously exempt from the Anti-Monopoly Law because they operated a regulated monopoly, needed to be brought under the law and subject to strict guidelines preventing them from using their market power to block the emergence of new competitors. Second, since the supply of power from self-generators was limited and because it took time to build new power plants, it was critical that the reforms facilitate competition *between* the regional utilities if a deep market was to be fostered in the short term. That would only happen if the utilities were forced to invest in enhanced connections between their regional transmission grids and if a utility selling power in another utility's region was exempted from having to pay additional transmission charges to all of the utilities between its own power plant and its customer in another region—a practice known as "pancaking."

Because these steps had the potential to force incumbent utilities to face strong competition from new entrants, the giant utility companies did everything they could to make sure the fine print of METI's reforms did not include these features. There was a fair amount of pressure—from METI, Keidanren, and some large firms—for the introduction of retail competition, at least for the largest users, so the utilities ultimately agreed to accept the first step in this direction in the second round of reform. The 2000 amendments to the Electric Utilities Industry Law allowed large customers (those who receive their electricity in its high-voltage form or have a connected load of at least two megawatts) to choose their own power supplier. On almost every one of the above points, however, the utilities held out for fine print that would prevent the emergence of significant competition. Rather than ordering account unbundling, METI settled for the requirement that the utilities voluntarily disclose their account balances and the basis for their transmission charges—leaving ample room for utilities to set their wheeling rates at a level that would penalize new entrants. The utilities were subject to the Anti-Monopoly Law, but they faced few extra constraints on their business practices despite the fact that they remained infinitely larger than any of their rivals by virtue of their previous monopoly status. The utilities had no obligation to expand connections between their transmission grids, and they were allowed to impose pancaking charges on intraregional sales.

Not surprisingly, given these features of the new regulatory regime, Japan saw very little market competition after the introduction of the 2000 reforms. Although the reforms nominally "opened" the retail electricity market for the nine thousand largest customers that made up 30 percent of the total electricity market, very few have been able to gain access to cheaper power. One customer that was able to do so was METI itself, which put its own electricity contract out to bid and succeeded in convincing a new entrant, Diamond Power, to supply it with power at below the TEPCO price.[51] But most of those who have sought to buy power from new entrants have found that only the local regional utility was interested in bidding.[52] Ten new entrants had emerged as of July 2002, but their combined sales totaled just 140 gigawatt hours, or 0.71 percent of the market. In five of the ten regional markets in Japan, *no* new entrants were operating.[53] The large electricity companies have announced two rounds of price reductions since the reforms went into effect (TEPCO cut its prices by 5.3% in 2000 and another 7% in 2002), but analysts do not regard these as evidence that the regulatory reforms are working. The International Energy Agency calculates that most of the reductions were made possible by the fall in the utilities' interest payments now that Japanese interest rates are near zero. The fact that the reduction was offered to all of the utilities' customers, and not just to those in the "competitive" segment of the market, is also evidence that the reductions were not a product of new efficiencies that were forced on the utility by the need to compete for customers.[54]

When METI officials investigated why new entrants were not emerging more rapidly, they found that much of the fault lay in the structure of the regulatory regime they had settled for in 2000. The regional utilities were not selling in each others' territories, in part because pancaking charges made it impossible for utilities from outside the area to undercut the local incumbent's price. And new entrants were finding it difficult to compete because the voluntary accounting practices prescribed under the regulatory regime allowed the utilities to charge new suppliers a 33 percent "back-up" charge on top of the regular transmission fee. The utilities claimed this charge was justified because they needed to maintain spare generating capacity of their own in case the new entrant's power source went down. Even though METI had evidence the utilities did not need to construct extra capacity for this purpose, the ministry could not force the utilities to eliminate this charge because it had no legal basis to do so.[55]

An additional problem was that the utilities were using their market power to slow down the emergence of competitive rivals. TEPCO and the other incumbents were especially worried when Enron, the U.S. energy-trading firm, began to show strong interest in the Japanese market in the years before it went bankrupt. To keep Enron from gaining a foothold, they reportedly used threats and inducements to dissuade Japanese self-generators from selling power to the company. Similar tactics were used to discourage industrial firms that were capable of developing or expanding self-generated power from becoming new entrants into the power supply business.[56]

METI was thus forced to revisit the issue of electricity market reform almost as soon as the 2000 reforms had gone into effect, to try to expand the segment of the market open to competition and to eliminate some of the barriers to competition. The outcome was another amendment to the Electric Utilities Industry Law passed by the Diet in May 2003.[57] The share of the market open to competition was expanded to 40 percent in 2004 and 63 percent in 2005. In 2007, the government is scheduled to consider opening the entire market, including the residential segment that currently remains subject to price controls. Pancaking charges have been banned. In 2005, METI issued new rules governing account unbundling aimed at making it more difficult for incumbents to discourage new competition from power generators by leveraging their monopoly control of the transmission system.

As of October 2005, it remains too early to evaluate the most recent reforms, but there are reasons to be pessimistic. First, although pancaking charges no longer apply, intraregional competition continues to be limited by the thin connections between the regional transmission grids. The latest investment plans announced by the utilities show that they have no plans to expand those connections in the years covered by the plans (up to 2011).[58] Second, it is unclear whether METI has written the accounting rules strictly enough to prevent the utilities from keeping out significant new competition. Legal separation may be the only real solution, and the ministry does not have the power, and may not have the will, to go that far. Finally, little has been done to scrutinize utilities' anticompetitive practices. Until the Japan Fair Trade Commission investigates the sector and writes tough, detailed guidelines placing limits on the utilities' business practices that are stricter than those imposed on weaker competitors, it is likely the incumbents will be able to scare off significant competition.

Public Sector Reform

In other advanced industrialized and developing nations that have struggled to achieve economic reform, trimming the size of the public sector through privatization and making the remaining public sector more efficient by bringing market forces to bear on public services have been at the top of the agenda, domestically and through the IMF. This area of economic policy is the central focus of the debate over the future of the welfare state in Europe where, some argue, exit and threats of exit by capital are driving governments to trim the size of the public sector and shrink social welfare programs and public services.

Because the Japanese state has historically been much smaller as a segment of its economy than most European states, the debate over public sector reform there has taken a different form. Unlike Europe, where many nations started the 1980s with state ownership of steel, coal, oil, gas, electricity, the automobile industry, railways, airlines, and telecommunications, Japan began with nationalized industries in just the last three of these sectors. The government privatized Japan National Railways in the mid-1980s and committed to privatizing telecommunications and airlines soon after. Despite this record of success in keeping much of the economy in private hands, however, Japan has struggled to rein in a public sector that has ballooned in other ways, notably through a massive public works budget, a state-owned postal savings system, and a tradition of bailing out failing banks. Together these features of Japan's public sector combined to increase government expenditures to a level approaching that of Europe at the end of the 1990s (see figure 6.3). While Britain, Germany, and the United States were all shrinking their public sec-

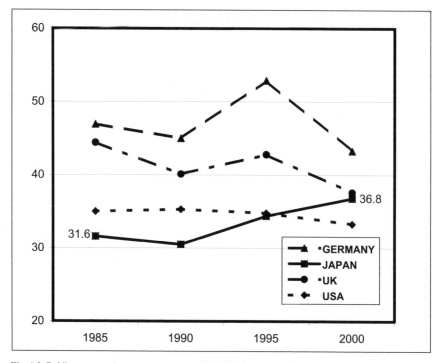

Fig. 6.3. Public sector outlays as a percentage of GDP in four countries
Source: Based on data from data on total government outlays (excluding consumption of fixed capital) and GDP from SourceOECD National Accounts Statistics, *Historical Statistics—Structure or Composition of Certain Economic Aggregates,* vol. 2002, release 01.

tors during this decade, Japan let its state expenditures grow from 30 percent of the economy to 37 percent. Neither exit nor the threat of exit by Japanese firms seemed to have any impact on this trend.

The size of the public sector is a critical issue for private firms in all advanced industrialized nations because firms, in one way or another, bear much of the cost. They have to pay higher corporate taxes and see their wage bills inflated by higher social insurance premiums. Even income taxes and taxes on consumption increase the cost of doing business by eroding the purchasing power of wages.

In Japan, rising public expenditures are a concern for business even though taxes have not kept pace with the rate of government spending. In 2000, tax revenues were 27 percent of GDP, far below the 36.8 percent of GDP the government spent.[59] Japanese firms know that this situation is temporary, however, for after years of spending much more than it collects in taxes, the government's finances are in precarious shape. In 2003, the nation's gross public debt was equal to 166 percent of its GDP.[60] Long-term interest rates that have hovered between 1 and 2 percent for several years have allowed the government to finance this massive debt while devoting just 1.7 percent of GDP to debt service, but this number is likely to rise quickly in coming years as the government exhausts its ability to cut interest payments by replacing high-interest debt from ten years ago with new lower-interest bonds. When that happens and interest rates rise, the state will have no choice but to cut spending, raise taxes, or inflate away its debt.

During the first three decades after the war, the Japanese business community fought hard to slow the expansion of the state. It blocked state efforts to nationalize key industries and opposed the creation of generous social welfare programs. While these efforts suffered a setback in the mid-1970s, when Prime Minister Tanaka Kakuei went to work "remodeling the Japanese archipelago" with expansive public works projects while also increasing state spending on health and pension programs, the business community pushed right back in the early 1980s by supporting the Rinchō (Administrative Reform) campaign of prime minister Nakasone Yasuhiro. Led by the hard-charging Dokō Toshio, the former president of Tōshiba and Keidanren leader, Rinchō pressed for the privatization of the national railways and reductions in state spending on welfare and public works.[61] In large part due to the business community's strong support for this effort, the government cut spending on public sector fixed capital investment from 9.5 percent of GDP in 1981 to 7.7 percent in 1985–90.[62] The business community did not secure any large tax reductions (since fiscal deficits made these difficult to defend), but Dokō's committee minimized the burden borne by the business community by insisting that a tax increase should be a last resort, after budget cuts. The tax that was eventually adopted in 1989 to close the budget gap took the form most favored by the big-business community. The new 3-percent consumption tax promised to reduce the state's dependence on corporate taxes and taxes on salaried workers by establishing a source of revenue that would fall broadly on the entire population of consumers.

Given this record of successful advocacy for public sector restraint and reform, the business community's failure to advocate more vigorously for this cause in the 1990s is puzzling. Business leaders have been represented on a series of high-profile economic reform councils, some of them modeled explicitly on Dokō's Rinchō, and several have taken a personal interest in specific budget-busting policy areas, but no individual has been able to marshal firms' political energies behind the kind of effort seen a decade earlier, and the few personal efforts have come up largely empty-handed. The leading spokesman for fiscal rectitude and public sector reform in the current period has been a young academic, Takenaka Heizō, rather than a senior business leader, and he has not surprisingly lacked the heft necessary to head off the looming fiscal train wreck.

Any evaluation of the business community's involvement in the cause of public sector reform in the 1990s must be sensitive, however, to the way in which the economics and politics of this issue area were complicated during that decade by the advent of Japan's huge bad-loan crisis, deflation, and recurrent recession. In the immediate aftermath of the stock and land market crashes early in the decade, when the economy slowed sharply and banks were saddled with large sums of bad loans, few economists in Japan or elsewhere called for fiscal restraint. Fiscal stimulus, along with lower interest rates, was seen as the appropriate remedy that would help Japan through the post-bubble downturn. Even later in the decade, after the banking crisis reached a crescendo and ushered in an era of deflation, many economists continued to call for fiscal stimulus aimed at placing a floor beneath the fragile economy.[63] If deflation continued and more banks became insolvent, Japan faced the prospect of being caught in a liquidity trap (deflation makes it difficult to lower real interest rates to stimulate the economy since nominal rates cannot be lowered below zero). If Japan could not engineer an end to deflation, it faced the prospect of a deep economic depression with high unemployment rates and widespread bankruptcy.

These considerations meant that simple fiscal restraint—lower state spending and immediate moves to balance the budget—was never the rational policy for the Japanese business community to push. If firms wanted to avoid being saddled with much higher taxes down the road, however, they had an incentive to make sure the recession-fighting fiscal stimulus and bad- loan cleanup were structured so they would put the economy on a sustainable recovery path as soon as possible. Specifically, they had incentives to make sure that (1) fiscal stimulus was not composed mostly of useless public works projects; (2) the postal savings system and associated public corporations were reformed so that they did not produce additional public debt in the future; and (3) public money put into struggling banks actually cleaned up the bad-loan mess rather than prolonging the process. A review of the record of business activism and reform in each of these three areas shows that there has been little of either.

Fiscal Stimulus and Public Works

Even after the Rinchō campaign had succeeded in lowering public works spending relative to rates that prevailed in the early 1980s, Japan still devoted a much higher level of public expenditure to construction projects—dams, bridges, and roads—than any other OECD nation (see figure 6.4).[64] In the high growth era, when Japan was struggling to build the public infrastructure that would support its rapid advance to the front ranks of the industrialized nations, it made sense for Japan to devote unusually large sums to public works. By the 1990s, however, Japan's growth had slowed and the projects that promised the highest social benefits (the bullet train and expressways along the heavily-traveled Tōkaidō route, dams for hydro-electricity, and Narita International Airport) had been built. And yet the state continued to spend large sums of money on projects with diminishing, and even negative, returns. It built not one but three bridges between the main island of Honshū and Shikoku. It extended the expressway network and the bullet train to the most remote reaches of the archipelago. It finished covering most of the banks of Japan's rivers and a large portion of its coastline with concrete (for erosion and flood control), so it began spending money to remove concrete in areas where it was causing

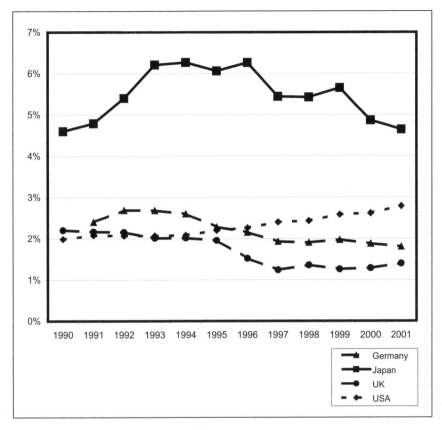

Fig. 6.4. Public works spending in four countries
Source: Based on data for government gross fixed capital formation and GDP from SourceOECD National Accounts Statistics, *National Accounts of OECD Countries: Volume IV—Summary of General Government Aggregates and Balances,* vol. 2003, release 01.

environmental damage. Public works were so central to what the Japanese state did that it was known as the "public works state" (*doken kokka*).[65]

Given the centrality of public works in the Japanese system of social protection and consequently in the political system, it was not surprising that politicians would favor emphasizing this mode of spending when economic conditions in the early 1990s called for fiscal stimulus. Yet infrastructure spending was not the most efficient way to give the economy a boost. Most economists recommend tax cuts over public works spending because tax reductions tend to have a larger multiplier effect, cause less market distortion, and restrain the growth of the public sector.[66] These arguments should have had particular resonance with the business community in Japan, especially with leading manufacturing firms like Toyota and Sony. These firms, like the nation as a whole, had an interest in bringing about an eco-

nomic recovery as soon as possible with the minimum possible growth in the size of
the public debt. They also stood to gain more from an income tax cut, which would
put money in the pockets of a broad range of Japanese consumers (who might buy
automobiles and electronics), than they would from public works spending, which
would mostly go to the construction, steel, and concrete industries.

Nevertheless, leaders of these firms and business organizations, including Keidanren, raised virtually no objections when, in 1992, the government began announcing a string of supplemental budgets that relied on public works spending for
virtually all of their stimulus effects. Adam Posen, who extensively analyzed the
supplemental budgets adopted in these years, calculated that these fiscal stimulus
programs pumped an extra ¥23 trillion ($200 billion) into the economy, almost en-
tirely in the form of public works spending.[67] These budgets reversed the decline in
public works spending and made Japan even more unusual in its propensity to
spend heavily on concrete (figure 6.4). The only major tax reduction adopted during these years, an income tax that went into effect in 1995, was offset entirely by an
increase in the consumption tax that went into effect in April 1996.

After the government faced another, deeper downturn in the economy in 1997–
98, business leaders once again failed to raise objections when Prime Minister
Obuchi issued a plan that relied almost entirely on public works spending to boost
the economy. Obuchi took over as prime minister after his predecessor Hashimoto
Ryūtarō resigned after the LDP's defeat in the 1998 upper house election. This was
the low point in the Japanese economy's disastrous decade. The economy was
shrinking, deflation had set in, several financial institutions had already gone bankrupt and another large one (the Long-term Credit Bank) was on the verge of collapse. Fiscal stimulus and a plan to clean up the banking mess were urgently
needed, so the prime minister called together a group of economic advisors under
the leadership of the honorary chairman of Asahi Breweries, Higuchi Hirotarō.
Also on the committee were Okuda Hiroshi of Toyota and three other business
leaders.

Consistent with the pattern observed in 1992–95, however, the businessmen on
the Economic Strategy Council said little to challenge the public works emphasis of
the prime minister. The supplemental budget adopted in December 1998 and the
budget for fiscal year 1999 both included substantial increases in public works
spending, with an extra ¥3.5 trillion ($30 billion) in the supplemental budget
alone.[68] In its final report published in February 1999, Obuchi's advisory council
raised concerns about how to "restore fiscal sustainability" after this surge in debt-
financed spending, but it failed to target the largest category of wasteful spending,
public works, for future cuts. Instead, it proposed reducing the number of public
employees, revising the public accounting system, and selling state property.[69]

The selection of Koizumi Jun'ichirō to replace the inept Mori Yoshirō in April
2001 shifted the contours of the debate over public works dramatically—although
not because the business community had backed Koizumi in hopes that he would
bring the LDP's "public works state" under control. Koizumi came to office be-

cause the public saw him as a leader who might be able to "change the LDP in order to change Japan." Campaigning under this slogan in the 2001 upper house elections and calling for cuts in spending on highways and an end to wasteful public works projects, Koizumi won by a large margin. He presented himself as the antithesis of the old Hashimoto wing of the LDP, with its deep ties to the construction lobby. Koizumi put a lid on government spending on public works, retaining this stance even when the economy relapsed into recession in 2001–02. Nevertheless, the most recent figures for public works spending show that Japan continues to devote far more resources to this category of expenditure than other OECD states. As Koizumi has attempted to cut deeper, he has run head-on into the structures that are at the root of Japan's continued public works profligacy: the system of special public corporations financed by postal savings, postal life insurance, and public pension reserves.

Postal Savings and FILP Reform

Japan's network of 24,778 post offices, located in every small village and neighborhood in the nation, do much more than sell stamps, collect mail, and deliver packages. They also serve as financial institutions offering savings accounts with the best interest rates and the most rock-solid guarantee in the nation; they have Japan's largest network of automatic teller machines; they sell life insurance; and they provide bill-paying services. Their ability to offer one-stop financial services in such convenient locations has made the Japanese postal service the largest financial institution in the world, with ¥250 trillion ($2 trillion) in deposits at the end of fiscal year 2000. In that year, postal deposits accounted for 35 percent of all household deposits in Japan.[70]

What makes the Japanese post office distinct from private commercial banks is that it turns over most of its money to the Japanese state for investing in projects that reflect a political, rather than market, logic.[71] Until reforms implemented in 2001, the post office turned over most of the savings and life insurance premiums it collected to the Trust Fund Bureau (TFB) of the Ministry of Finance. There this immense sum of money was joined with additional funds from the public pension reserves to supply the TFB with the money it needed to compile the Fiscal Investment and Loan Program (FILP), which totaled ¥418 trillion, or 82 percent of Japan's GDP, in 2000.[72] Much of this program was composed of investments made in earlier years, but even in *flow* terms FILP was massive. In 1998, the new money FILP injected into the Japanese economy was equal to 10.9 percent of GDP.[73]

The postal savings/FILP system played a critical role in perpetuating Japanese politicians' public works profligacy by creating the pretense that the large sums of money being spent on bridges, roads, and dams would not place any burden on taxpayers. The funds FILP turned over to special public corporations such as the Government Housing Loan Corporation and the Japan Highway Public Corporation were designated "investments" that would yield financial returns over the lifespan of the funded projects that would more than repay the sum being spent. The money was only being borrowed from postal savings depositors and pension reserves and would be repaid in whole by the public corporations, so taxpayers would not have to contribute anything.

The problem was that public corporations funded in this way were subject to very little monitoring to assure that their investments were actually yielding adequate returns. Public corporations based their claims of expected future returns from toll road and bridge projects, for example, on wildly inflated estimates of future users. They assumed that almost all small business loans made by the Japan Finance Corporation for Small Business would be repaid in full, even though significant numbers of borrowers were defaulting. These claims were not subject to the usual disciplines of bond markets, which rate bonds devoted to specific investment projects and charge higher interest rates when claims of solvency are discovered to be dubious. Neither were they subject to the discipline of the electoral process, since the politicians of the ruling LDP preferred to know as little as possible so that they could go on pretending that FILP funds placed no burden on taxpayers.

By the end of the 1990s, however, it was clear to most elites and to many members of the public that the FILP system concealed significant bad debt that would eventually have to be made whole through the use of taxpayer money. The public had received a sense of the proportions of the problem when taxpayers had been asked to cover ¥28 trillion in unrecoverable debt left over after Japan National Railways was privatized in the 1980s.[74] Takero Doi and Takeo Hoshi estimate that the unrecoverable debt on the FILP books at the end of fiscal year 2000 came to at least ¥78.3 trillion, or 15 percent of Japan's GDP.[75] Others have estimated the sum may be as high as ¥100 trillion.[76] What was clear was that the FILP system had allowed Japanese politicians to saddle the nations' taxpayers (including the business community) with significant future obligations. If the system was not reformed, the amounts involved could be expected to balloon even higher.

Reform of FILP and the postal saving system have therefore been on the agenda of Japan's economic reform debate for over a decade. As a first step, reformers proposed, the postal saving system should end its practice of delivering most of its funds to the TFB. Instead, public corporations previously funded by FILP should be turned into "independent agencies" that raised funds in bond markets where they would be subject to the disciplines of rating agencies and forced to pay higher interest rates when found to be on the verge of insolvency. While this first reform enjoyed relatively broad support, many economic analysts questioned whether such a reform would be sufficient. As long the postal savings system continued holding ¥250 trillion in deposits, it would have to send the funds somewhere. If significant sums of postal money continued to flow to the "independent agencies," or if markets did not believe the state would allow these supposedly independent agencies to default on their obligations, there would be little market scrutiny of these institutions and no constraint on the ability of politicians to continue channeling postal money into pork barrel projects with dubious financial prospects. What was required, these analysts argued, was the sale to the private sector of the postal finance system (or its dissolution), and the privatization of remaining public corporations.

Japan's private banks have long supported most of this reform agenda, motivated less by their concerns about the impact of the system on taxpayers than by their desire to eliminate what they see as unfair competition from the postal savings system. The business community as a whole, however, has been content to sit on the sidelines of this debate, despite its implications for public finances.[77] When the first stage of the reform described above (the elimination of the TFB and the switch to FILP agencies financed by bonds) was considered as part of broad administrative reforms in 1998, FILP reform ranked low on the list of business priorities. The law mandating the first set of reforms was pushed through in large part due to concerns of MOF officials that the FILP system needed to be brought in line with the "big bang" reforms of private sector financial regulation.[78] Academic economists and officials from MOF and other concerned agencies (Posts and Telecommunications, Health and Welfare) were the guiding forces of the first-stage reforms, although Keidanren supported the steps being planned in position papers issued after the direction of reform was established.[79]

As feared, however, the first-phase reforms did not go far enough to constrain the flow of pork through the FILP system.[80] The Trust Fund Bureau was gone, but most postal savings funds continued to flow to the public corporations through other channels.[81] In the first two years after the TFB was abolished, the postal service continued to use the bulk of its funds to purchase FILP bonds, which gave the FILP plenty of money to continue funding each of the public corporations at close to the levels they had received before the reform. The FILP shrank only slightly, from ¥423 trillion in fiscal year 2000, the last year before the reform, to ¥368 trillion in 2003.[82]

The reform aimed to push the public corporations to rely increasingly on FILP agency bonds, sold directly to financial markets without a government guarantee, and some public corporations issued small volumes of these bonds to make up for the slight reduction in funds coming from FILP, but most of the agencies were charged interest rates only nominally higher than what they paid the TFB under the old system. The small size of the interest rate differential for public corporations that many analysts judged to be insolvent suggested that bond market analysts did not regard the absence of a formal government guarantee as a concern. That there was no system in place to close a poorly performing public corporation no doubt contributed to the market's continuing confidence that taxpayer funds would be used to prevent any of the public corporations from defaulting on their bonds. The rules of the new system also forced the public corporations to provide the markets with more transparent accounting statements, including a summary of the long-term "policy costs" (the subsidy they expected they would need from taxpayer funds), but the policy costs they identified were much smaller than those estimated by independent analysts.[83] As Doi and Hoshi conclude in their analysis, "A comparison of the old and new systems reveals that, the government's claim that the reform is 'fundamental' notwithstanding, the new system may in practice not differ substantially from the old after all."[84]

Because the first stage of FILP reform failed to rein in the public corporations, the second set of reforms—privatization of the postal savings system and the public corporations—rose to the top of Japan's economic reform agenda in the first years of the new century. Koizumi was well known for his stance in favor of privatizing the postal services even before he became prime minister. One of his first acts upon securing the top job in April 2001 was to appoint an advisory council to consider postal privatization. He also announced his intention to slim down some of the largest public corporations, including the Japan Highway Public Corporation and the Government Housing Loan Corporation.

These reforms were never going to be easy. The privatization of the postal finance system threatened to cut off the flow of investment funds to public corporations that built roads, dams, and urban development projects. It threatened to limit the funds available to the Japan Finance Corporation for Small Business, which had become a critical source of funds for struggling small firms that were unable to obtain funds due to the credit crunch. These programs were vital to the economic survival of some of the LDP's most loyal constituencies, and they were at the very heart of the traditional Japanese system of social protection. In addition, the post offices enjoyed support from the LDP for their ability to mobilize voters on the party's behalf through a network of highly organized postmasters, and from the public sector unions for their ability to offer a large number of well-paid, high-benefit, secure jobs. If the postal finance system was separated from the mail delivery network and sold off, some post offices would have to be closed and workers laid off, since delivery operations alone could not sustain the dense post office network.[85]

An additional challenge was the absence of popular support for postal privatization. Many members of the public had postal savings accounts and appreciated the convenience and relatively attractive interest rates offered by the system. They also considered postal savings to be a safe haven at a time when several private banks had gone bankrupt and even the biggest banks were struggling to clean up massive volumes of bad loans. If Koizumi was going to succeed, he would need support from the segment of Japanese society that faced the most concentrated costs (in the form of future tax obligations) from a failure to rein in the public corporations: the big-business community.

Unfortunately, the business community failed to make this second stage of reform a priority. At a speech given on the topic of "structural reform of the economy" just as Koizumi was launching his postal privatization advisory council in May 2001, Keidanren head Imai Takashi devoted just one vague line, buried at the very end of his comments, to the topic. He and Keidanren thought it was important that reforms "allow the private sector expanded opportunities to enter the postal businesses." In other words, he supported the aspect of the proposed reforms that called for the postal service to give up its monopoly on letter delivery. Nowhere in the remarks did Imai touch on the critical issue of whether and how the postal financial operations should be privatized.[86] Koizumi's advisory council on this topic was dominated once again by economists and pundits with interests in economic affairs. It included just two businessmen: Kasai Yoshiyuki of Central Japan Railway Company (a former public corporation) and Morishita Yoichi of Matsushita Electric.

In the end, this council was not able to come together behind a far-reaching plan for reform. Instead, it examined three broad options, only one of which promised to shrink postal savings and life insurance operations.[87] When Koizumi turned to the task of formulating legislation to move the process of postal reform forward in the spring of 2002, he was not able to win support from his party for this option, or for a second option calling for the privatization of all current postal services (including savings and insurance) as a single unit. Instead, he settled for the most modest reform proposal, calling for the postal services to be turned into a "special company" (now known as Japan Post) with all of its stock owned by the government and facing competition for the first time in the mail delivery business. Further compromises agreed to during the legislative process in the summer of 2003 placed such onerous conditions on firms that might want to compete in mail delivery that even this provision—largely unrelated to the goal of curtailing the financial operations of the post office—promised little relief for businesses tired of paying high mailing costs.[88]

In 2005, Koizumi made one more attempt to reform the postal services. Despite the absence of support for this effort from either the public or the business community at the start of the effort, Koizumi was able to maneuver his opponents into a corner and turn the issue into an election winner. Expelling thirty-seven members of his own party after they voted against his postal privatization plan, he called a snap election, which he won decisively. Just one month later, in October, the Diet passed Koizumi's postal legislation. Captivated by the political drama, few noticed that Koizumi, in order to win the support of key LDP opponents earlier in the legislative process, had watered down the plan to such an extent that it was unlikely to make a significant dent in the flow of postal savings into the public corporations. That motivation for reform had virtually dropped out of the political debate.[89] Under the legislation, the government will split Japan Post into four units and sell off its equity stake in these operations gradually over a ten year period. Some post offices may have to close and a few postal workers may lose their jobs, but the reforms contain no provisions that guarantee that the flow of postal savings to the FILP agencies will stop, or even slow. Koizumi had essentially given up on the core issue in postal finance reform in order to devote his energies to winning one last symbolic victory over his LDP rivals.

Having realized how difficult it would be to shut off the flow of postal savings to the public corporations through postal finance reform, the prime minister had from the start of his tenure conducted a simultaneous offensive on another front. By privatizing the public corporations and forcing them to account accurately for their unrecoverable debts, he aimed to force them to stop putting any additional taxpayer money at risk. While he aimed his fire at several public entities, his chief target was the Japan Highway Public Corporation. In his first months in office,

Koizumi pitched the idea of diverting some road tax revenues, long reserved for highway construction and maintenance, to other uses as a means of depriving Japan Highway of subsidies it needed to continue expanding the road network. Almost as soon as he had proposed this idea, however, he dropped it under heavy fire from LDP colleagues who were close to the highway lobby.[90]

Stymied in this effort, the prime minister switched gears in June 2002, deciding to set up a high-profile advisory council that would examine whether and how the Japan Highway Public Corporation and three other road-related public corporations should be privatized. To prevent antireform LDP members from stacking the council with individuals who would sabotage the reform, he insisted on naming the council members himself without seeking Diet approval. Recalling the important role Dokō had played in pushing through the privatization of the national railways, Koizumi looked for a leader from the business community who might play a similar role in helping him push through the privatization of the road corporations. He thought he had found the ideal candidate in Imai Takashi, the chairman of Nippon Steel and the honorary chairman of Keidanren. Not only did Imai agree to serve on the committee, he agreed to chair it, joining another business community heavyweight, Matsuda Masatake of East Japan Railway Company.

The council went to work immediately, settling quickly on a plan to divide the public corporations into two parts. One part would remain public and would retain both the assets and the debts of the highway companies. Debts totaled ¥40 trillion ($333 billion), far more than could be serviced by private companies that had to pay taxes on their landholdings. The operation of the roads and bridges, however, would be taken over by new private road companies. These companies would collect tolls, using these revenues to maintain the roads and pay large rents to the public road holding companies, payments that would be used to pay down the debt.

Just as quickly, however, the council split into two factions over critical details of the plan. One group, which hoped to use the privatization plan to slow road building, called for the following conditions: (1) the road holding company should not be allowed to make decisions on building additional roads; those decisions should be made by the private road operating companies, which should be free to make decisions based on the profitability of specific road projects; (2) the government should immediately assume a large portion of road debt, perhaps as much as ¥8 trillion, using tax revenues to pay this off; (3) rent payments should be set at a level that would allow the remaining road debt to be paid off in ten to fifteen years, at which point the private road companies would take over ownership of the roads; this would force the private companies to use the bulk of their toll revenues to pay rent and leave them unable to build many additional roads; (4) the private companies should not be allowed to use toll revenues from existing high-profit roads to build additional roads; they should have to finance new road construction by issuing bonds on private markets—effectively preventing them from building new roads that could not deliver sufficient cash flow. The other group favored an alternative arrangement that would allow the public road holding companies to influence road building plans, would stretch the repayment period to fifty years in order to create leeway for continued road building, and would let the private firms use revenues from profitable roads to build new roads in low-traffic areas.

Although Matsuda of Eastern Japan Railways emerged as a supporter of the more reformist position, his efforts to convince the panel to give unqualified endorsement to a road-limiting proposal were undercut by the other business leader, Imai. As the committee tried to wind up its deliberations in December 2002, Imai refused to let the committee decide the contents of its report by majority vote, even though Matsuda had lined up five of the seven council members on his side. When Matsuda pressed his point, Imai left the council room in disgust and resigned his chairmanship. Although the council proceeded to publish a report favoring road-limiting reforms, its proposals were heavily modified in succeeding stages of the legislative process. When road-privatizing legislation was finally adopted in June 2004, it included compromises on almost all of the reformist conditions and a commitment by the government to build every one of the 2,352 additional kilometers of expressways that were planned before the reform began. Instead of helping push the reform through, Imai ended up caught between the reformers on the council and the LDP's road caucus. By quitting, he helped sabotage the reform plan by creating the impression of a hopelessly divided council.

Koizumi's inability to get strong business support for his postal savings, FILP, and public corporation reform plans doomed his public sector reform efforts. Why Imai and other business leaders did not go to bat for the prime minister as Dokō had in the early 1980s is hard to say. No doubt they were intimidated by opposition from the prime minister's enemies in the LDP. Many businesses, including Imai's firm, Nippon Steel, also stood to lose from a sudden halt to highway construction. Nevertheless, the business community's failure to fight for reforms in structures that were generating massive public debt and saddling firms with future tax obligations suggests that businesses felt less need to be concerned about the effects of a future debt crisis. Leading Japanese firms had the option of raising funds overseas, so a hike in Japanese interest rates due to competition with a heavily indebted public sector didn't seem a great worry. And most firms' sales were globally diversified, meaning that macroeconomic disruptions caused by future efforts to tax or inflate away Japanese public debt did not threaten their bottom lines the way this prospect worried a more Japan-centric business establishment in Dokō's day. Imai certainly did not explain his actions in this way, but his behavior suggests that he was not seriously concerned about Japan's mounting public debt.

Cleaning Up the Bad-Loan Mess

The mountain of bad loans left behind when Japan's bubble economy imploded at the start of the 1990s was technically a private sector problem. The banks were private, and so were the insolvent borrowers. As other nations faced with similar crises have discovered, however, a banking crisis on this scale inevitably has implications for society as a whole that often means a bailout with public funds is required. Economists broadly concur that the most efficient way to handle such a crisis is for the government to intervene as soon as it becomes apparent that the sum of bad loans is too great for banks to write off using their own capital. Rather than letting troubled banks limp along, carrying bad debts on their books and curtailing loans to new customers, it usually makes sense for the state to intervene by nationalizing banks and cleaning them up itself using public money or by forcing banks to accept new capital from the state in exchange for commitments to use this money to write off bad loans and sell off distressed assets. These steps allow banks to make new loans and get the economy on a growth path again.

Once the property and stock markets collapsed in the early 1990s, leaving behind bad debts estimated at ¥100 trillion, or 20 percent of GDP, there was never any question that public funds would be needed.[91] The question was whether the bailouts would be structured to minimize the burden on taxpayers (by acting quickly and requiring banks to use funds to write off bad loans rapidly) or would instead be structured to drag out the process at great cost to the public treasury. The worst outcome from the point of view of taxpayers would be for the bailouts to be structured so that banks received a continuing series of capital injections, each one used by the banks to buy time to *avoid* writing off bad loans. This would mean that public money would end up being used to keep insolvent borrowers ("zombie companies") alive for a few more years instead of being used to clean up the banks' balance sheets to make room for new loans to companies with growth prospects. It was indeed possible to structure a series of these bailouts in such a way that the state would spend a huge sum of the taxpayers' money without cleaning up the bad-loan mess at all.

The last scenario describes Japan's actual policy in dealing with the bad-loan crisis through most of the decade after the problem emerged. At the start of the process of capital injections in the mid-1990s, the government estimated that 5 percent of bank loans were nonperforming. A half-decade later, after the state had devoted ¥60 trillion ($550 billion) in public funds to reconstructing the banking system,[92] the government estimated that the proportion of bad loans had grown to 10 percent.[93] Richard Katz summarized the situation in 2002 as follows: "Despite a write-off of ¥35 trillion ($284 billion) worth of bad debt over the past decade—7 percent of GDP—the remaining pile of non-performing loans is larger than ever."[94] The costs to society were greater even than the sum of taxpayer funds consumed by the banks without solving the problem. The delay in cleaning up the bad-loan problem had slowed down the economy for an entire decade at significant cost to Japanese national income, and desperate price-cutting by zombie companies kept in business by banks too short of capital to write off their loans helped create an environment in which deflation could take hold.

The Japanese hesitated to act decisively to clean up the banking system, despite these costs to society as a whole, because cleaning up the banking mess threatened to impose concentrated costs on certain segments of the economy. Writing off loans required banks (or the government agency taking over this responsibility) to force firms that were operating in the red to restructure—closing factories, retail stores, hotels, and other operations and laying off workers. When it was clear firms could not survive, cleaning up bad loans required that firms be pushed into bankruptcy so that their assets could be sold. Given the central role banks, firms, and the life-time employment system played in the traditional Japanese system of social protection, calling for an aggressive cleanup of bad loans was tantamount to calling for an abandonment of this entire system.

While the lack of enthusiasm for a more timely resolution of the bad-loan crisis by insolvent firms, their workers, and banks is perfectly understandable, the failure to resolve the crisis imposed costs on other segments of Japanese society, especially profitable, tax-paying businesses. As large taxpayers, these firms had reason to worry that the government was being asked to spend massive sums of public money cleaning up the banks without imposing sufficient conditions to guarantee that the money would solve the problem. The absence of sufficient conditions meant the public was likely to be asked again and again to keep the weak banks and zombie borrowers afloat. A failure to clean up the financial system also promised a delay in the recovery of the Japanese economy, at significant loss of sales.

Despite these incentives to pressure the government to act more decisively, firms like Toyota and Sony and the big-business organization Keidanren did not take a lead in pushing for a rapid cleanup of the banking system at any stage of Japan's decade-long struggle to extricate itself from the bad-loan crisis. This absence of pressure certainly characterized the early years after stock and property markets tumbled in 1990–91. Though few Japanese at this stage were aware of the scale of the bad-loan overhang, leaders in the business community did know that losses were threatening to overwhelm the first group of financial institutions, the home-loan companies (*jūsen*) that had made some of the riskiest loans at the peak of bubble mania. In 1992, leading banks that had financed the *jūsen* told MOF regulators that the institutions were insolvent. They proposed to set up liquidation companies to dispose of the *jūsen* bad loans, covering losses out of their own capital.[95] If the *jūsen* problem had been handled in this way, the same approach had been applied to the banks' own bad loans, and the state had stepped in with an injection of public money into the banks, Japan could have recovered from its post-bubble recession much more quickly. MOF officials, however, refused to accept the plan. Taking an approach they would adopt repeatedly during the next decade, they insisted that banks keep the *jūsen* and their borrowers afloat by cutting the interest rates they charged on their loans to these institutions.[96] The banks made no attempt to appeal this decision.

The next turning point came in 1995 when the failure of stock and property markets to rebound made it clear that the banks had been right about the *jūsen*. The size of *jūsen* losses had ballooned in the intervening years to the point where the banks that had loaned them their initial capital could no longer afford to absorb all of the losses. The problem was that the farmers' cooperatives, which had provided significant funding to the *jūsen* during the peak bubble years, were unwilling to accept a liquidation deal in which they absorbed their own share of the losses. MOF officials, faced with pressure from LDP lawmakers who would not allow the politically powerful farmers' cooperatives to take any losses, were forced to use ¥695 billion ($6.3 billion) in taxpayer funds to cover the farm cooperatives' portion of the losses. The banks, in contrast, were made to absorb more than a pro rata share of the costs of cleaning up the *jūsen* mess, forcing them to eat into their capital.[97] The result of this short-sighted deal was that bank capital was severely depleted even as the public became suspicious of any use of taxpayer money to resolve the banking crisis. Despite these flaws in the *jūsen* deal, the Japanese business community defended it.[98]

The unpopularity of the *jūsen* bailout delayed consideration of a systematic taxpayer-funded cleanup plan for banks for several years despite growing official estimates of bad-loan volumes and analysts' estimates, as early as 1995, that the total of bad loans might range from ¥60 trillion to ¥100 trillion. Instead of proactively nationalizing insolvent banks, creating a public body to acquire and liquidate bad loans, and recapitalizing the surviving banks, the government ended up reacting to events. After the shocking failure of one of Japan's city banks (Hokkaido Takushoku Bank) and one of the big four securities firms (Yamaichi Securities) in November 1997, the government threw together a bank recapitalization plan that asked the nations' largest banks to accept an infusion of ¥13 trillion ($108 billion) in public money. In their eagerness to reassure the public that the large banks were safe, however, the nations' financial authorities handed the funds over indiscriminately. Much of the ¥13 trillion was squandered on two banks that turned out to be beyond hope: Nippon Credit Bank and the Long-term Credit Bank. They failed within the year. The weak conditionality of the capital infusion also meant other banks had no obligation to use the money to rapidly write off their bad loans. They could use it instead to carry weak borrowers if they preferred. This first capital infusion into the largest banks thus did little to help get the banking system back on its feet.

When it became clear in the summer of 1998 that Nippon Credit Bank and Long-term Credit Bank were already back on the brink of failure, it was apparent the government would have to devote a great deal more public money to a more systematic cleanup of the banking system. The markets were charging a large "Japan premium" on financial deals with Japanese banks, telegraphing their worries about the possibility of runs on weak banks. The only question was whether the financing would be provided in a way that forced banks to write off their bad loans rather than letting them use the capital to carry weak borrowers for a few more years before returning for another bailout. Even though Japan's large export-oriented firms, as taxpayers, had a huge stake in how this question was answered, they were not a prominent part of the debate. Nor did Keidanren emerge as an advocate for an efficient cleanup of the banking system. Instead of calling for a strict timetable for the write-off of bad loans, it called on banks to "voluntarily disclose their non-performing loans as soon as possible." Instead of demanding that the regulatory authority responsible for assuring that banks were rigorously evaluating the quality of their loans be made independent of the Ministry of Finance, Keidanren called for MOF to remain in charge.[99]

In the end, the government was able to act in time to avert a crisis, making available sufficient funds to restore confidence in the solvency of the banking system. A total war chest of ¥60 trillion ($500 billion) in public money was made available for deposit insurance, for the cleanup of nationalized lenders, and for the recapitalization of viable banks. The legislation governing bank nationalization included strict conditions that made it impossible for the managers of Long-term Credit Bank and Nippon Credit Bank to buy any more time. Both were nationalized in late 1998, with the value of their outstanding shares reduced to zero and their loans sold off to new institutions.[100] The legislation creating the fund for recapitalizing viable banks, however, did not set strict enough conditions to guarantee that the banks would write off bad loans aggressively. How quickly they would clean up their balance sheets depended on how closely the financial authorities monitored the quality of the banks' loan portfolios and how willing they were to use their regulatory authority to compel write-offs.

In the years after the adoption of this bank rescue package, therefore, the question of whether taxpayer money would be once again squandered or would instead be used to clean up the bad-loan overhang depended on the actions of the Financial Services Agency (FSA).[101] For much of this period the FSA used its authority to pressure lenders to extend more loans to weak companies and to forgive loans to zombie firms, instead of pressuring banks to clean up their balance sheets.[102] Nevertheless, there was very little pressure from firms or Keidanren to protect the taxpayers' investment by assuring that banks rigorously accounted for and wrote off nonperforming loans. When Koizumi asked economist Takenaka Heizō to take over the FSA portfolio in the fall of 2002, apparently endorsing his plan to pressure banks to clean up their bad loans more rapidly, he was not responding to demands from the business community. On the contrary, when asked about the Takenaka appointment at a press conference, Keidanren chairman Okuda made it clear that he would prefer that the government focus on "anti-deflation measures such as tax reform, on the securities transaction tax, land related taxes, corporate tax, rebalancing between gift and inheritance taxes, and other measures that could prop up the stock price" instead of accelerating the bad-loan cleanup.[103]

The absence of support from the business community, combined with strong opposition from inside his own party, led Koizumi to stop short of endorsing Takenaka's boldest bank clean-up plan in the fall of 2002.[104] Instead, Takenaka was forced to use his discretionary powers, including his power to order tough inspections of the banks' loan portfolios, to cajole and pressure banks into writing off loans more rapidly. Assisted by a recovery in stock prices in 2003, which bolstered bank capital, the largest Japanese banks have made some progress in writing off bad loans in the period since Takenaka took over bank regulation. After all of the efforts of the past decade, however, official figures show that ¥35 trillion in bad loans remain on the books of Japan's deposit-taking financial institutions—an estimated 6.3 percent of all loans.[105] Taxpayers may well be asked for bailout money again in the coming years.

The catalog of aborted economic reform efforts in this chapter fleshes out the overall pattern described in chapter 5. Japanese businesses face high and inflexible costs for labor, the highest prices in the world for electricity, and a growing tax burden linked to government policies that subsidize inefficient segments of the economy, but they have done very little to change these policies. A review of Keidanren reports, the statements of company executives, and the role business leaders have played on advisory councils in each of these areas suggests that business leaders have not attempted to use their leverage in the political system to push for reform in these elements of the traditional Japanese system of social protection. Business leaders have defended the lifetime employment system rather than seeking to weaken it. They have used positions on advisory councils to block electricity market liberalization. And they have hesitated to use their influence to push for more aggressive FILP reform, postal privatization, or the efficient use of public funds devoted to cleaning up the banking system.

As we have noted throughout, many Japanese manufacturing firms have been moving operations overseas in order to escape these high costs, but what we have seen in this chapter is what an inconsequential impact this trend has had on the debate over specific economic reforms in Japan. As METI official Kawamoto noted, it has been very difficult to link a given Japanese firm's decisions to relocate overseas to high electricity prices. Policymakers are aware that some FDI is motivated by the desire to gain access to lower cost inputs, but they cannot promise that a marginal reduction in electricity prices will keep any segment of this FDI at home. Similar uncertainties get in the way of efforts to tackle high labor costs. With Chinese wages costing just 5 percent of those in Japan, officials have not been able to demonstrate that more flexibility in the home labor market will keep any of the China-bound investment from leaving. Finally, what we saw in the section on public sector reform is that hollowing-out concerns were virtually a nonissue. At no point in the prolonged debates over FILP reform, or how to privatize Japan Highway Corporation, or how to handle the bad-loan crisis, was firms' exit via FDI given as a reason for pressing ahead with reform.

Another kind of exit, sales of stock by panicked investors, did influence policy in one area: the bad-loan cleanup. At several points during the banking policy saga, especially in the fall of 1998 and just before book closing in September 2002, policymakers were forced to consider the reaction of equity markets when deciding what to do. The markets strengthened the hand of reformist politicians in 1998 when they sought to forestall Prime Minister Obuchi's efforts to use public money to buy more time for the Long-term Credit Bank rather than nationalizing it. And the fact that the markets liked the idea of appointing Takenaka to head the FSA in 2002 probably gave Koizumi the impetus to stick with his choice in the face of opposition from inside his party.

The influence of markets at critical moments like this should not be confused, however, with sustained policy impact. Between these episodes of stock market turmoil when policymakers felt constrained by market reactions, financial authorities made numerous microdecisions affecting bank policy: how to handle the looming bankruptcy of specific borrowers like MyCal, Sogō, and Daiei; how to deal with tax-deferred assets; how strictly to audit a given bank's books. More often than not, at moments like these, Japanese policymakers responded to the vested interests that were making the most noise in the policy process. The absence of sustained countervailing pressure from taxpaying, export-oriented, large Japanese firms like Toyota and Sony facilitated the dominance of this antireform coalition.

Chapter 7

The Policy Impact of Exit
by Women

To hear Shimomura Mitsuko, director of the Gender Equity Center in Fukushima Prefecture, tell it, women's decisions to put off or opt out of having children should be having a profound impact on public policy:

> I think it's a good thing. The parasites have unintentionally created an interesting movement. Politicians now have to beg women to have babies. Unless they create a society where women feel comfortable having children and working, Japan will be destroyed in a matter of 50 or 100 years. And child subsidies aren't going to do it. Only equality is.[1]

Politicians now have to "beg women to have children," and these policymakers have discovered that nothing less than "equality" will do the trick. Meanwhile, some women's decisions to give up careers out of frustration with the difficulties of balancing family and work responsibilities aggravated labor shortages during the bubble economy years and are predicted to create even more serious shortages once the economy recovers from its long period of economic stagnation. In this case too, one might expect an exit-driven response from policymakers and employers as they beg women to continue working.

Does the policy process really work this way? Does it respond so smoothly to exit trends of these kinds that such behavior substitutes for political mobilization by a women's movement? Alternatively, do exit trends of these kinds at least work in tandem with political mobilization to bring about change? In this chapter I examine Japan's policy response to exit by women and find that limited exit of the kind we have seen so far has actually delayed an effective policy response. Women who exited by opting to remain single and childless or by opting to give up careers after having children lost personal incentives they might have had to mobilize in the political arena to make it easier for women to balance work and family roles. As a result, formulating a policy response has been left almost entirely to bureaucrats whose inherent conservatism and caution has slowed them down at every stage of the process: from diagnosing the problem to formulating policy alternatives to mobilizing political support for proposed changes.

In the first section of this chapter I summarize the overall pattern of Japan's response, focusing on how bureaucrats have failed to put in place the far-reaching reforms needed to encourage women (and men) to balance work and family roles, and explaining why women have not taken a larger lead themselves in this reform movement. In the second section, I illustrate this pattern by examining developments over the past decade in the main issue areas involved: leave for child rearing, childcare services, labor standards, child allowances, and tax and benefit rules. Although there have been important changes, they have failed to create an environment that makes combining full-time careers with child rearing an attractive choice for Japanese women.

The Overall Pattern

As was the case with hollowing out by firms, policymakers were very slow to identify the problem later known as "the shrinking number of children". The job of following fertility trends within the Japanese government falls to a research institute affiliated with the Ministry of Health, Labor and Welfare: the National Institute for Population and Social Security Research (NIPSSR). Every five years, this institute examines population trends and issues fifty-year population forecasts that are used by the MHLW officials responsible for maintaining the solvency of government social insurance programs. As we saw in chapter 4, the Japanese fertility rate has been falling almost continuously since 1950 and has been below the population replacement level of 2.08 since 1980. Nevertheless, it was not until the late 1990s that the NIPSSR began to accept the fact that a growing number of Japanese women were opting not to bear any children.

The slow pace with which the NIPSSR came to terms with Japanese women's changed behavior patterns can be seen clearly in figure 7.1, which shows how its population projections sagged over time. Initially, government demographers were confident the decline in fertility rates was a reflection of women reducing the size of their families, with fewer women having three or more children. Such a trend suggested the fall in fertility rates would stop once the rate reached 2.0, and indeed they did level out at that level for about a decade. In the 1980s, when fertility rates began dropping again, demographers posited that they had dipped below replacement level only temporarily: women were merely postponing marriage and childbirth. During a period when women are postponing childbirth, the total fertility rate necessarily dips due to the way in which it is calculated.[2] If the typical woman goes from having two children between twenty-five and thirty to having the same number of children between thirty and thirty-five, the total fertility rate is destined

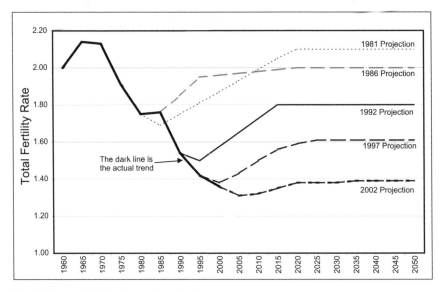

Fig. 7.1. Japanese fertility rates, projected and actual
Source: Adapted from Yashiro Naohiro, *Shōshi kōreika no keizaigaku* (Tokyo: Tōyō Keizai Shimpōsha, 1999), 16, updated with the 2002 NIPSSR population projection.

to dip while women are postponing childbirth but will rise again once these women reach the age when they are ready to start a family. Thus when government demographers first began mulling over the implications of a total fertility rate below the population replacement level, they predicted this trend would soon reverse itself, projecting in 1981 and 1986 that the rate would fall only briefly before rising again to the replacement level over the next two decades.

Over the succeeding years, however, government demographers were forced to come to terms with a fertility rate that kept falling below their worst-case projections. In 1992, they admitted the rate would likely stabilize below the replacement rate at 1.8, and in 1997 they lowered this projection to 1.6. Finally, after the total fertility rate had stood below 1.4 for a few years at the end of the 1990s, government demographers accepted the fact that Japanese women had fundamentally changed their behavior. Whereas only 10 percent of women born in 1950 completed their period of fertility with no children, projections issued in 2002 expect 31.2 percent of women born in 1985 to complete their period of fertility without having a child and predict another 18.5 percent will have just one. The projections based on these assumptions have led the government to expect fertility levels to stabilize at roughly 1.4 over the long term.[3]

This issue of projected fertility rates is significant because falling fertility rates only create economic problems when the rate dips well below replacement level and stays there for a long period of time. A fertility rate that dips to 1.8 for a few years will have almost no effect on long-term population levels, the size of the future labor force, or the sustainability of pay-as-you-go social insurance programs. On the other hand, a fertility rate that falls to 1.4 and stays there for a long period of time promises to cause societies major adjustment problems as the effects of this rate compound over time. When cohorts of women that are already smaller because of a low fertility rate in 1990 have similarly small numbers of children in 2020, the effects will compound. Thus Japan's latest projections of a sustained 1.4 fertility rate promises to reduce by one-third the size of the working age population by 2044 and cut it in half by 2072.[4] Society could expect to accommodate without too much difficulty earlier projections of a temporary dip in fertility rates. It is only the most recent projections of 1997 and 2002 that have presented society with a real long-term policy challenge: the government will find it impossible to pay for the full costs of the health care and pensions of aging baby boomers if its population of working-age and taxpaying adults shrinks this fast.

Beyond these issues of projections and the difficulty of interpreting data on birthrates, Japan's policy response has also been delayed by disagreements over whether a fall in the fertility rate, even if sustained, would actually constitute a "problem." The first cries of alarm began to be heard in 1990 after the government issued its report on fertility rates for 1989. That year the rate fell to 1.57, below the previous record low recorded in 1966, when the birthrate fell abruptly for one calendar year as couples adjusted family planning to avoid giving birth to a daughter during the Chinese zodiac year of the fire-horse (*hinoeuma*). According to superstition, women born in one of these years are likely to gnaw their husbands to death when they grow up, a prospect that makes them unattractive candidates for marriage.[5] That the fertility rate had fallen below the 1966 level even though 1989 was not an unlucky year signaled to many that the falling fertility rate was a real problem. As one government commission noted in 1990, "Just as in the last days of the Roman empire, the decrease in the number of children is a sign of the decline of civilization."[6]

If some saw the increase in the number of women opting not to have children as a civilization-ending problem, however, others applauded the trend. Typical of the reaction of many feminists was that of Ueno Chizuko, a leading academic at the University of Tokyo well known for her feminist criticism of Japanese society. In an article titled "The Declining Birthrate: Whose Problem?" she argued that the increase in the never-married population was only "natural" and to be welcomed for the greater freedom of lifestyle choice it afforded. It was the earlier period when almost all women married, she insisted, that was the aberration. Similarly, she criticized population projections for neglecting the possibility that a decline in births could be offset by rising immigration.[7] Ashino Yuriko, the deputy director of the Family Planning Federation of Japan, was even more direct, arguing, "Population control deserves praise rather than criticism. You won't find today's women having babies for the sake of their country or because someone told them to."[8]

These reactions testify to the historical experiences that have conditioned the way various segments of Japanese society have interpreted declining fertility numbers which, after all, do not speak for themselves. The first to worry about declining fertility were the nationalists and conservatives, who have a history of linking population growth to national strength. Before World War II, the Japanese government was actively involved in encouraging women to "go forth and multiply"—a slogan rendered into Japanese in the memorable words *umeyo, fuyaseyo*. Women were encouraged to give birth in order to provide the nation with a larger industrial labor force as well as military manpower. Abortion was kept illegal with the specific aim of encouraging population growth. Many families, pressed to enlarge their number of offspring beyond their means, went hungry during the war and occupation years because of this pronatalist campaign. Because they realize this history is sensitive, contemporary nationalists and conservatives are generally careful when speaking and writing about population issues. Nevertheless, the habit of linking national strength to population size remains deeply rooted in this segment of society—as suggested by the "decline of civilization" quote above.

This same history, however, has made many others extremely dubious of efforts to characterize Japan's falling fertility rate as a "problem." That the strongest reaction quoted above came from a spokesperson for the Family Planning Federation, a group that supports abortion rights, is not surprising since women involved in this movement have been worried that conservative men will use the decline in fertility as an excuse to tighten up abortion law. Current law allows women to secure abortions not just for medical reasons but also in cases of "economic hardship," a provision that essentially allows abortion on demand. In the 1980s, conservatives attempted but failed to remove this provision, and a few raised this issue again in the early 1990s in connection with the fertility decline. Given this history, it is hardly surprising that women's movement activists have been leery of characterizing the declining birthrate as a "problem."

It is not merely feminists, however, who have been bothered by the memory of *umeyo, fuyaseyo* policies. MHLW officials, when asked whether they considered raising fertility rates a goal, uniformly brought up this historical legacy to explain why the government could not make this an explicit goal.[9] One official who has worked for many years with like-minded officials to advance women's issues within the ministry recalled the "repulsion" (*hanpatsu*) expressed by members of her group when it was proposed that they seek to use the decline in fertility as a reason for advancing policies promoting gender equality. "Many didn't want to say anything that suggested women needed to have more children," she recalled. Over time, they have become more comfortable with using the declining fertility trend as a reason to "create an environment in which women who want to have children can do so," but the goal is always expressed in this way in order to avoid arousing memories of the *umeyo, fuyaseyo* period.[10]

Not surprisingly, the ideological barriers that delayed identifying declining fertility as a "problem" also got in the way of efforts to identify and compare alternative proposals for addressing it. If officials couldn't say the declining fertility rate was a problem, how could they go about evaluating policies to see whether they would reverse this trend? This hesitation merely exacerbated the inherent difficulties involved in doing rational policy analysis in this issue area.

Japanese bureaucrats, like officials in most modern states, prefer to have data and evidence to support their policy proposals before taking them to politicians who might sponsor their legislation. This rationality standard required them to have data that would convince politicians that spending money on certain policies, such as childcare leave or services, would actually cause women to have more children. Proving such a claim was clearly more difficult than the usual burden bureaucrats face when selling policy ideas. One MHLW official pointed out how much easier it was for his ministry to promote long-term care insurance as a solution to the aging-society problem. Everyone knew Japan would soon have a ballooning population of elderly and bedridden citizens who would need care. It was also quite clear what kinds of services this group of citizens would require. The ministry merely had to determine what volume of services would be required and devise a funding formula to pay for them.[11]

In contrast, the declining fertility issue area was fraught with complexities and uncertainties. No one knew for certain whether and for how long the decline in fertility rates would last. Even more dauntingly, no one knew which programs, services, or policy changes—if any—would encourage women to have more children. Over the course of the decade of the 1990s, Ministry of Health and Welfare officials and academics sympathetic to the feminist critique of Japanese society worked hard to argue that a whole package of changes (in childcare leave and services, employment practices, and social norms that viewed child rearing and housework as the wife's responsibility) was needed in order to reverse the decline in fertility. Only when women had the social services and social support from their employers and husbands needed to allow them to keep working or return to work after having children, they argued, would women enjoy the economic security that would encourage them to have more children. This argument took several years to develop, but even when it was expressed elegantly in advisory council reports and white papers issued in 1997 and 1998, it was based more on logic and hope than on social scientific evidence.[12]

Then, just when this argument had been put before the public, it was challenged by a popular alternative theory about the forces driving the fertility decline. According to the "parasite singles" argument, promoted in books, articles, and television appearances by sociologist Yamada Masahiro, young men and women were putting off marriage and parenthood not because they lacked economic security but because they enjoyed too much of it through the generosity of their parents. Living at home rent free, with meals and cleaning provided for them by their mothers, these parasite singles were loathe to give all of this up in order to set up separate households, with all of the associated expenses. Young women in particular hesitated to give up the travel and leisure time activities they could enjoy as singles living at home.[13]

The argument did not completely contradict the one being advanced by the MHW as a basis for promoting a gender-neutral society. After all, single life was attractive to women in part because married life with children, absent support from husbands and the opportunity to go back to work, was so isolating and confining. Nevertheless, the popularity of this argument undercut the rationale for spending large sums of money on childcare services and leave for child rearing by making everyone wonder whether extra money spent on these things would do anything to convince women to give up their carefree single lives. Perhaps the young women putting off marriage were just too selfish to be induced into giving up their freedoms for motherhood.

Yashiro Naohiro, an economist who had been arguing for many years for changes in the Japanese employment system to make it easier for women to stay in the workforce after having children, reports that Yamada's "parasite singles" argument let the air out of the effort to promote this message. The MHW had built up a head of steam with its dire population projections in 1997 and the analysis in its reports and white papers in 1998 and 1999, but after Yamada's argument came out that was all the media and politicians wanted to talk about.[14] His "alternative" explanation for Japan's declining fertility simply fed the uncertainty about whether public policy could make any difference. What if the government spent billions of yen on childcare only to see the fertility rate fall even further? It was easier to scale back funding plans and play it safe.

Many of the problems and uncertainties that delayed the government's response to declining fertility rates also got in the way of its response to the other exit trend: the decisions of many women to give up careers when they marry and have children. If women's fertility decisions were difficult to predict, so were their decisions about work. Showing that a specific policy, such as more generous childcare leave for new mothers, would keep women in their careers was almost as difficult as showing that such a policy would cause them to have more children. It didn't help when the initial (quite meager) childcare leave system introduced in 1992 did almost nothing to increase staying-on rates for new mothers.[15] How generous did the program need to be to induce women to stay in the workforce? Bureaucrats could not give an exact answer based on rational policy analysis.

As in the area of fertility rates, ideological barriers also got in way when policy reform depended on bureaucrats diagnosing this exit trend as a "problem." Japanese feminists have long complained about how the predominantly male bureaucracy has a hard time sympathizing with the difficulties women face trying to balance work and family responsibilities. Indeed, when the labor shortage emerged during the bubble years, most of the Ministry of Labor (MOL) officials assigned to figure out how to convince women to keep working as one part of the effort to deal with this concern were men. Almost all career central government officials are the sole breadwinners for their families, working long hours at the office with the support of a full-time housewife at home. Even the female bureaucrats are usually single or, if they have children, have a mother or mother-in-law at home who takes care of the children. Very few officials of either gender have any experience trying to balance family and career without the support of a full-time caregiver at home.[16] How could they begin to appreciate the degree of change in society that would be required before large numbers of women (without mothers or mothers-in-law at home) could continue careers after having children?

One male MOL official I spoke to provided a glimpse of how the experience gap just described could prevent officials like him from leading a movement to transform society in response to the labor shortage. Asked whether Japan's introduction of childcare leave was a response to International Labour Organization standards, this is how he responded:

> The unions and opposition parties often bring up the ILO, but this organization is really designed by and for the Europeans with their welfare states. It isn't well suited to Japan. Japan has a system where the company takes care of the family. It is characterized by harmony (*wa*). It's designed to help the entire labor force get along. This system is better suited to Japan than a Western one where everyone is paid according to his or her ability.

Just to be sure I had heard him correctly, I asked him more specifically whether he thought it was a problem that part-time workers are paid less than regular employees for the same work. "No," he said, "as long as labor's total share of national income is high enough, it shouldn't really be a problem if part-timers receive less than their share."[17] This official clearly continues to believe that the family wage system—which pays male breadwinners more and part-time women less—is best for Japan. It is little wonder that, despite the government's official commitment to create a "gender equal society" (*danjo kyōdō sankaku shakai*) in response to the labor shortage and declining fertility, officials like him declined to put much energy into the effort.

If women had responded to their frustrations with the established system through political mobilization rather than exit, they would not have needed to rely on bureaucrats to interpret their behavior, figure out what to do, and use rational policy analysis to sell specific proposals to politicians. Through a social movement, they could have gone to politicians themselves and demanded labor market reforms, expanded childcare services, and whatever other policies they needed in order to support their efforts to balance work with family. They could also have demanded more support from employers and worked to convince their husbands to do more housework, shopping, and childcare. Such a movement would not have needed to show that any given policy would increase the birthrate or induce more women to stay in the workforce. It would have spoken for itself in identifying and diagnosing the problem, proposing solutions, and providing the political muscle to push the proposals through the policy process.

The very difficulties presented by the established system, however, led most Japanese women to give up either on motherhood or career, preventing the emergence of a group of women struggling to do both and driven by this struggle to campaign for fundamental changes in the social system. Instead, today there are two distinct women's movements, neither of which is strongly pushing to overturn the male-breadwinner, female-caregiver system with a new one more suited to Japan's present circumstances.[18]

The largest women's organizations today—the Housewives Association (Shufuren); the National League of Regional Women's Organizations (Chifuren); and the Consumer Cooperatives Association (Seikyōren)—are made up mostly of full-time housewives and are committed to causes related to their roles as the cooks and shoppers of their families. These groups campaign for food and product safety, sometimes fight for lower prices, and promote consumer cooperatives.[19] Even the Seikatsu Netto (Daily Life Network), a group that formed and has grown in size relatively recently, has its roots in the Seikatsu Club cooperatives that provide housewives with an alternative means of acquiring food and other products. Though more overtly political than cooperatives that developed earlier, the basic bond between members of the Netto revolves around their roles as cooks and shoppers.[20]

These groups have shown they can mobilize significant support when their consumer interests are at stake, rallying against the consumption tax in the late 1980s, for example, and mobilizing in favor of the Product Liability Law in the 1990s. Neither these groups nor the broader community of housewives committed to these causes, however, is particularly interested in challenging the family system norms or associated policies that place the primary burdens of caregiving and taking care of the home on women. Those who had careers in the past left them long ago. More of them now work part time, but as Ueno Chizuko has argued, women who return to part-time work after their children are in school do not face the kind of fundamental role conflict faced by women who attempt to maintain careers after having children. In most cases their work is motivated primarily by their need to pay for the costs of educating their children, which leads them to see part-time work as an extension of their mother role. Work for the vast majority of these women is a temporary expedient, something they do because they need to help stretch the household budget. Work is not something they value as an expression of their identity as "workers," that leads them to fight for policies that would make it easier for women with children to maintain careers.[21]

Ueno and other feminists are critical of these women for their complacent acceptance of the Japanese family system. They worry that this group, who make up the vast majority of women in Japan, are too comfortable with their housewife lives. As she said in an interview:

> These women make very practical and realistic choices in the context of contemporary Japanese society. . . . They make careful choices between the necessity of household income and their desired leisure time. . . . Lifestyle is a very real concept for these women, but it is a commodity that is purchased

rather than a freedom that is fought for. . . . They are only doing what is reasonable given the limited options available to them. It is the fact that their lifestyle is so comfortable that makes them so unlikely to leave it or do anything that would unsettle it.[22]

Having chosen to concentrate their energies on their roles as mothers and housewives, Ueno explains, these Japanese women have little motivation to go out and fight for the kinds of changes that would be required to make Japan into a "gender equal society." Those concerns are of little relevance to their lives.

Completely separate from this segment of Japanese women are the scattered groups of feminists and unionists that have a deep commitment to issues like abortion rights, equal pay for equal work, and women's representation within the government. These are working women, most of them careerists, and in their commitment to equal pay for equal work they certainly are more interested in making Japan into a "gender equal society" than their housewife sisters. Nevertheless, their interest in achieving strict equal treatment has sometimes worked against the cause of making work easier for women with children.

For example, the prohibitions against discrimination in layoffs and resignation enshrined in the Equal Employment Opportunity Law of 1985 were purchased at the price of giving up Labor Standards Act limits on overtime for female workers and prohibitions against assigning women to night shifts. As many Japanese critics of the EEOL deal have noted, it is unclear whether this "equal treatment" arrangement has actually made it easier for women with children to maintain full-time careers, for the added job protections have come at the expense of forcing women to accept the same constraints on their ability to balance work and family time that working men have had to live with for decades. It is in part due to EEOL changes, therefore, that many women who previously might have worked full time now settle for part-time jobs, where they can more easily juggle childcare and avoid transfers but face even lower pay and protections than in full-time jobs before the EEOL.[23]

That the EEOL deals involved these trade-offs cannot be blamed solely on feminist groups. Indeed, employers were the primary faction demanding a relaxation in overtime and night-shift restrictions, and union women and their lawyers stubbornly resisted giving up special protections for female workers.[24] Nevertheless, the feminists who spoke in favor of reducing protections in the name of "equal treatment" probably did so in part because they were better positioned than most women to deal with the tougher work expectations. Most female academics from the first generation of Japanese women to secure university positions are unmarried and childless. The broader group of careerist women in Japan includes large numbers with children, but many of these (like the bureaucrats mentioned above) rely on their mothers or mothers-in-law to provide childcare.[25] Women who succeed in careers without relying on their mothers remain rare enough in Japan that those who do are hailed as heroes in the media.[26]

As in the case of the full-time housewives discussed by Ueno, the choices these women make are an understandable adaptation to the situation they face. What it means, however, is that this group too has by and large "exited" from the difficulty of trying to maintain careers with children without support from the family system. It is true that careerist women have been much more likely than housewives to campaign for leave for child rearing and childcare services, but without facing the full difficulties of trying to stay on this tightrope without a net, could they appreciate the extent of changes in society that would be required to get the rest of Japan's women to desire careers? To a certain extent, these women too were more complacent than they would have been if they had no exit options.

In reflecting on the effects of exit options on women's propensity to use voice, however, we need to be careful not to limit our analysis to the political movements and groups that exist. We also need to consider those that did not form—the dogs that didn't bark. Japan's leading feminists, most of whom are in their fifties and sixties and have been active for decades, often bemoan the lack of interest in the feminist movement among today's young women. These are women who have been going to college and entering the labor force in rapidly increasing numbers and expressing role aspirations that—as we saw in chapter 4—are much more progressive than their mothers'. Many more young Japanese women today want to have a family and work than was the case in their mothers' generation. They want husbands who will do their share of the housework. They want romantic marriages of equals. These women should be revitalizing the women's movement in Japan, just as an earlier generation of young women who came of age during the late 1960s and early 1970s briefly revitalized the Japanese movement by fighting for "women's lib."[27]

But these younger women are conspicuous for their absence from the contemporary women's movement. Feminists like Ueno routinely note their disappointment with the lack of interest in their cause among young women.[28] Japanese women, especially those in the youngest cohort, remain disconnected from party politics. In 1996, 35 percent of women declined to identify with a party, compared to 28 percent of men, and the share of nonidentifiers was especially high among young women.[29] Political participation rates have been declining steadily for both women and men under forty since the 1980s. As Ito Peng notes, all of these trends are indicative of the tendency of younger women to take the "route of political disengagement"—in sharp contrast to the pattern of engagement she found when she examined the role of older Japanese women in fighting for long-term care insurance during the same period (discussed in chapter 8).[30]

The particular disengagement of younger women, especially in contrast to the behavior of older women faced with the challenge of caring for aging relatives, strongly suggests that this pattern is a product of the different exit options that are available to the younger women faced with choosing how to combine work and family. Those who find the existing system of social protection objectionable because it relies on unpaid female caregiving within the family, who cannot stomach all of the compromises they are expected to make once they marry and have children, can avoid much of this by postponing or opting out of marriage and by deciding not to have children. In part because of the gains made by previous generations of the women's movement, today's young women can enjoy the freedom to study, travel, and pursue their own interests; premarital sexual relations with protection against the risk of unwanted pregnancy; and even rich career opportunities—as long as they opt out of marriage and children. So, rather than protesting against this system, trying to change public policy, society, and Japanese men, they are rebelling by staying out of marriage.

Indeed, many of those who have described Japanese women's recent propensity to put off and opt out of marriage and children as a rebellion have emphasized that it is a rebellion without voice. Mikanagi Yumiko calls it a "silent revolution."[31] The Nakamae Research Institute, in a study that was concerned with the possibility of women turning to new forms of exit such as emigration, called their protest a "quiet rebellion."[32] Ironically, the decision by these women to exit in these ways has kept them silent at the critical moment when the government is considering whether and how to create a "gender equal society" as it attempts to come to terms with the twin exit trends of declining fertility and the looming labor shortage.

As government officials have searched for ways to address these problems, they have sought out women's views. Women have been placed on all relevant advisory councils, female bureaucrats have been assigned to oversee them, and, after drawing up the government's basic plan, the MHW even went so far as to create a People's Committee to Promote a Response to Declining Fertility (Shōshika e no Taiō o Suishin suru Kokumin Kaigi) to mobilize support for reforms from concerned interest groups. These efforts to involve female voices in the policy process, however, have been restricted almost entirely to the usual suspects: lawyers that represent the Women's Bureau of the union federation Rengō; female labor economists; a few moderate academic feminists; and representatives of the housewives organizations. Unlike the groups that sprang up to give voice to women who were suffering under the burden of caring for frail elderly relatives without support, no new groups arose to represent young women struggling to avoid having to choose between work and family.

An MHLW official who headed the ministry's Declining Fertility Response Planning Room argued that his outreach efforts extended beyond contacts with these established groups. Twice a week during his tenure in that position, he explained, he traveled to the suburbs to visit with housewives participating in child-rearing circles (*kosodate saakuru*) and asked them about the challenges of raising children. What would it take to make the environment more attractive? Through these contacts, he learned how isolated they felt trying to raise children without support from their husbands and how this made them unhappy with the experience of motherhood; feedback of this kind led his ministry to increase support for non-profit organizations serving these women as well as for drop-in childcare for full-time housewives.[33] Similar consultations led the Ministry of Labor to embark on a publicity campaign, complete with posters (see figure 7.2), encouraging husbands to take childcare leave to help out with their new babies.

When I asked him whether he ever sought out unmarried women to see what it would take to get them interested in child rearing, however, he admitted he had never done so. These women were not organized. He doubted whether even local governments had means of soliciting feedback from this demographic. The NIPSSR did surveys of unmarried women, he pointed out, and some of these women wrote books and articles. He supposed that their views entered the policy process through these channels.[34] In the end, these women had to rely entirely on bureaucrats, other advisory council members, and the occasional middle-aged politician to interpret why they were holding out on marriage and to prescribe possible solutions. Not surprisingly, the policy solutions they arrived at represented incremental changes, making life a little easier for working women and full-time housewives who already had children. The changes, as we will see in the issue-specific analysis below, fell far short of creating a new system of social protection, one that would make combining marriage and motherhood and full-time work attractive enough to live up to the MHW slogan: "creating a society where child bearing and rearing are something to dream for" (*kodomo o umisodateru koto ni yume o moteru shakai o*).

Specific Policies

The preceding section summarized how young women's tendency to exit in response to their frustrations with the constraints imposed by the Japanese system took them out of the policy process, left decision-making in this area largely to bureaucrats and experts, and thereby slowed down the pace of policy change. We now turn to some of the specific areas in which this overall pattern played out, focusing on each piece of the package of changes reformers have argued will have to be put in place before women, in large numbers, will choose to combine motherhood with full-time work.

Childcare Leave

The first area to receive attention was leave for mothers and fathers to raise newborn children, called in Japan "childcare leave" (*ikuji kyūgyō*). Even before reforms were implemented in 1992, Japanese women enjoyed a period of leave benefits under the Labor Standards Act, which required employers to provide them with eight weeks of paid postpartum maternity leave. Though these benefits were already more generous than those provided by employers in the United States, they were insufficient for most working women, who had difficulty finding childcare services for children that young and often preferred to stay at home with their in-

Fig. 7.2. Ministry of Labor poster encouraging fathers to take childcare leave. The poster declares that men make up only 2.4 percent of those claiming childcare leave. It asks rhetorically, "Which is more important: work or childcare?" Its answer: "Both are important."

fants for a longer period of time. The lack of more generous leave benefits was particularly problematic for new mothers under the Japanese permanent employment system, since this system made it virtually impossible for women to find another career-track job once they left the workforce to care for their children.

The initial impetus for reform in this area did not come from the declining fertility trend or women demanding leave benefits so they could stay in the labor force. Instead, the idea of creating a childcare leave program arrived on the agenda because an earlier policy change, the Equal Employment Opportunity Law of 1986, had called on employers to open up career-track jobs to female applicants and barred them from laying off women because of marriage or childbirth. Ministry of Labor officials realized that these changes meant they needed to do something to make it easier for the new female recruits to keep their jobs after they had children.[35] Policy deliberations on creating a childcare leave program therefore began as a bureaucracy-led process, with MOL officials setting up an advisory council and inviting concerned groups to offer opinions. It was not a process set in motion by demands from female workers, labor unions, or Nikkeiren, the employers' association.

Along the way, however, the twin exit trends discussed in this book did give a boost to the MOL's efforts to create this program. In particular, the labor shortage of the bubble economy years, which was aggravated by the tendency of women to leave the labor force when they had children, reduced opposition to the program from Nikkeiren. When the MOL had first broached the idea of childcare leave in the early 1980s, the employers' association had squelched the plan, but the emergence of real labor shortages in the late 1980s caused employers to become more amenable to the idea. In contrast to the position they had taken earlier, they were now willing to support some kind of leave program, as long as firms did not have to pay women while they were at home with their infants and as long as there was no increase in their benefit costs.[36]

The declining fertility trend, in contrast, played almost no role in shaping the initial childcare leave program. The basic policy direction had already been set by 1990 when the "1.57 shock"—the announcement that the fertility rate had fallen to a record low—raised awareness of *shōshika*. MOL officials explain that this concern therefore played only a minor role in shaping the initial policy, although it has played some role in subsequent policy developments.[37] The Diet passed the Childcare Leave Law in March 1991, and the leave program went into effect on April 1, 1992.

Not surprisingly, given the bureaucracy-led nature of the process and the lukewarm attitude of business, the initial policy was not very generous. Until 1995, firms with fewer than thirty employees were exempted from all requirements. Larger employers were required to offer leave to new parents (fathers or mothers) who requested it, and they were barred from dismissing workers who took leave. Yet there were no penalties for firms that violated these rules, and the workers who took time off were not offered any income support. Even though they were not being paid, workers were required to continue paying into health insurance and pension programs during their time off.[38] Obviously, these provisions guaranteed that few women (and virtually no men) would be attracted to the leave program.

MOL officials were aware when the legislation passed that they needed to make leave more financially attractive, especially since women who *quit* their jobs after having children were able to claim, on average, 100 days of pay at 70 percent of their old salary under the Employment Insurance program.[39] Prior to the passage of the initial leave legislation, these officials made an effort to convince Nikkeiren to support some means of paying workers who were on leave, but they failed.[40] Once the legislation was on the books, they made another effort and were successful this time in convincing Nikkeiren to accept a system under which parents on leave would be paid out of the same Employment Insurance program that was already paying women who quit. The only question was how much.

With decision making at this next phase once again driven by bargaining between the MOL and the employers' group rather than by women's demands for a program that would actually reduce gender segregation in the labor market, the program for paying parents on leave was only marginally more attractive than unpaid leave. The pay level was set at 25 percent of salary for ten months, not because this was judged to be a level that would induce large numbers of mothers (or fathers) to take leave, but because Nikkeiren was convinced by MOL officials' arguments that this formula would minimize the impact on employers' benefit costs. At this rate, women who took leave would receive roughly the same sum of money as those who quit, so the Employment Insurance system would not be stressed. With the Employment Insurance system running a surplus when this decision was made, MOL officials could predict that employers would not have to pay more than they were already to put in place a paid leave program at this level of benefits.[41] With Nikkeiren withdrawing its objections, the Employment Insurance Law was amended in 1994, allowing leave benefits to be paid for the first time on April 1, 1995.[42]

Given the predominant role of bureaucrats and employers in setting leave benefit levels and the uncertainties involved in estimating what level of benefits it would take to influence parents' decisions about taking leave and staying in the workforce, it was probably inevitable that the government would shoot too low. When MOL officials checked labor market statistics several years later to see whether their program had kept more women in the workforce, they found that there had been virtually no change. The proportion of mothers of children from birth to three years in the employee labor force rose only slightly from 20.1 percent in 1990, before any leave benefit was available, to 22 percent in 2000, by which time paid leave benefits had been available for five years. The proportion working full time actually fell from 12.3 percent to 10.3 percent.[43] Surveys of women leaving the labor force showed that childcare responsibilities continued to be the leading reason women in their late twenties and thirties were quitting. In 1997, 236,000 women quit for this reason, down just a few thousand from the 239,000 who quit for this reason in 1994, before paid leave was available.[44] Childcare leave had barely budged the dip in the M-curve.

Labor ministry bureaucrats have continued to tinker with childcare leave policy in hopes of inducing a greater change in mothers' workforce participation. In 2000, they wrote legislation raising the proportion of salary provided to parents on leave to 40 percent as part of a larger package of changes in the Employment Insurance system.[45] Again, however, a technocratic argument related to the structure of the Employment Insurance system limited the extent of the benefit hike. Nikkeiren was amenable to raising leave benefits, but insisted that: (1) benefits for new parents on leave, including the value of health insurance and pension premiums (which they had been excused from paying after 1995), could not be higher than benefits available to the "real unemployed," who were required to pay benefit premiums worth 13 percent of their salary out of the typical 60 percent salary replacement they received while out of work; and (2) the costs of providing increased benefits for new parents had to be offset by reductions in benefits to the "voluntary unemployed," including women who quit to care for their children. The first condition limited the increase in benefits to 40 percent, well below the 60 percent sought by labor union representatives.[46] The second condition meant that economic support for dual-income parents, who were given more generous leave benefits, would be funded by reductions in subsidies to couples who opted to have one parent leave the workforce to stay at home with the newborn.

While the leave allowance has been raised, many women and almost all men continue to decline to take leave benefits to which they are entitled. One reason is the lack of enforcement provisions to back up the law's prohibition of discrimination against employees who take leave. There have been numerous reports of mothers facing discrimination on returning to their jobs, with some subject to "restructurings" that leave them unemployed while others face harassment that has led them to quit.[47] Partly for this reason, just 58 percent of those women who continue working and are eligible for leave take the leave benefits they are guaranteed. The rest go right back to work after eight weeks of maternity leave. The take-up rate for men is much lower, at 0.55 percent, in part because new fathers hesitate to be the first ones at their firms to take time off to be with their children for fear they will be bumped off the fast track.[48]

Throughout the policy-making process up to this point, the main focus was on how to keep new mothers in the workforce—not on how to encourage workers to have more children. A focus on the latter objective would have argued against funding an increase in the leave allowance for dual-earner parents by taking money away from single-earner couples, as was done in 2001. It also would have suggested setting qualification criteria and benefit levels in such a way as to induce *fathers* to take childcare leave, encouraging the greater level of paternal involvement in child rearing that would challenge the mother-must-do-it-all status quo that was turning off so many young Japanese women from the idea of marriage. Rather than attempting to challenge the status quo in this way, Japan's childcare leave rules make the majority of fathers ineligible for any benefits since the program does not require employers to provide leave to workers who have a spouse at home caring for an infant.[49] Even when eligible, fathers are discouraged from taking any leave by a benefit level that provides salary replacement of just 40 percent. For most married couples, with husbands earning much more than wives, a benefit level this low means only the wife can afford to take time off—relying on her better-paid husband to keep the family financially afloat. Though more generous than policies in the United States, Japan's policy remains far less revolutionary than the program in Sweden, which was designed to encourage fathers to take leave by providing a benefit level of 90 percent and requiring fathers to take at least a month of leave if the couple wanted to be eligible for the maximum leave period.

Only in the last few years, after the latest population projections of 2002 made it clear that Japanese women were not just postponing motherhood but opting out of it in large numbers, has the government begun to consider using childcare leave policy to address this more fundamental challenge. Called upon by Prime Minister Koizumi to present a "comprehensive" plan for reversing the fertility decline, the now-merged Ministry of Health, Labor and Welfare began working on a set of proposed childcare leave reforms as part of their "Plus One" package announced in 2003. The title of this latest package of reforms, according to official policy documents, was chosen because this was the latest initiative being constructed on top of two earlier "Angel Plans" (Enzeru Puran) discussed in more detail below. When asked whether the "Plus One" title might also have been chosen to reflect the government's hopes that each Japanese woman would have one more child, however, the MHLW official in charge of the relevant section of the ministry admitted that it was chosen in part because it had this "nuance."[50]

Once again, the modifications to the childcare leave program that were made in the years following this initiative were the product of a top-down process. MHLW officials proposed ways to use the leave program to involve fathers in childcare and thereby lighten the burden on women, and then they bargained with the employers' federation to see how far they could go. The answer: not very far. Legislation passed in 2003 merely obliged employers to fashion "specific plans" for helping their employees balance work and family lives. The ministry encouraged firms to expand leave opportunities for new parents (by giving them a second year off from work, for example, at no pay); it called on them to set up special leave programs for fathers to take brief leaves immediately after their children were born (five days was mentioned as an appropriate duration); and it called on them to set targets for the proportion of new mothers and fathers taking leave (the MHLW announced that it hoped 80 percent of new mothers and 10 percent of new fathers would take leaves). Exactly what was in employers' plans was left almost entirely up to them, however, and employers with fewer than three hundred workers were not even obliged to produce a plan.[51] A survey conducted a year after the legislation passed showed that

97 percent of the firms with a program for encouraging male employees to take childcare leave limited their efforts to "making the system thoroughly known." Just 2.7 percent included a component "encouraging target employees to take such leave," and just 1.4 percent offered financial assistance to fathers who were ineligible for childcare leave because their wives were not working.[52] Even after these latest revisions, the Japanese approach to childcare leave continues to presume that wives will take the bulk of childcare leave, with fathers helping out for just a few days. Eligibility rules and benefit levels, together with the lack of enforcement behind the prohibition of job discrimination, continue to guarantee that few fathers will take any more than the five-day program promoted by the government.

The government is finally trying, in its own timid way, to challenge the gender-role assumptions that are embedded in the Japanese labor market system. This effort to lead change from the top down has been constrained, however, by the absence of a vigorous movement demanding change from below. A look at how childcare leave issues are being handled at the firm level—at Toyota Motor Company—illustrates how policy is being shaped for women by firms that have their own agendas. Since this policy is not being driven by demands from a broad-based women's movement, the changes Toyota is implementing benefit only a handful of elite female workers that Toyota hopes to retain, and do not target fathers at all.

Katō Yoshirō heads a section within Toyota's personnel division that is putting into place what he describes as far-reaching changes in the firm's childcare leave program. The fact that Katō is a man, and the group is called the Josei Kasseika Guruupu (Women Activization Group), already hints at the degree to which this initiative is coming from the firm, and not from female workers there.[53] In fact, Katō admits, the Toyota union did not have a women's division when he and his group approached it to begin a conversation about leave policy. The union, which had not made childcare demands in recent *shuntō* (spring wage offensive) campaigns, had to put together a group that would serve as interlocutors for the team from the management side. "It was a top-down initiative, not something Toyota developed after being approached by female employees," Katō explained. "[Toyota] President Chō had been in charge of operations in Kentucky and was aware of how female workers were treated there, so he took the initiative."

Also absent from the list of motivations for Toyota's policy change was the declining fertility problem. Katō says it played a role, but only a very small one. "Fertility is the government's business, and not really for companies to worry about," he explained.

What motivated Chō and the Women Activization Group was a desire to retain talented female employees that the firm had begun recruiting into career-track jobs a decade earlier. Toyota had long employed a significant number of women in clerical and blue-collar jobs, but it kept its management and engineering tracks completely closed to women until the EEOL was implemented in 1986. Toyota's interest in hiring women was also spurred by the difficulties it began to have in hiring top male college graduates around that time. The top men were going into finance, which allowed them to remain in Tokyo. Toyota found it could recruit some of the top female college graduates who were finding it difficult to get offers from (Japanese) financial firms and who were willing to relocate to Toyota City in Aichi Prefecture. Though the first management-track female employee was not hired until 1992, female recruitment has grown to the point that in 2003 one-third of those hired for white-collar (*jimu*) specialist jobs and 8 percent of those hired for engineering jobs were women. Given the legacy of the earlier period in which women were kept out of these positions, however, Toyota still has just 150 specialist women employees out of fifteen thousand such employees.

Katō admits that Toyota's program is aimed at this elite group of 150 employees, though the benefits are available to all 4,600 female employees who work for the firm, as well as qualified men. That the elite group is the focus is clear from the timing of the initiative. Clerical and blue-collar female employees have been working for Toyota and quitting upon childbirth for years. Until recently, Katō explained, 95 percent of the firm's female employees quit upon marriage or childbirth. This exit did not bother Toyota until it realized that the first specialist female employees were now reaching their child-bearing years. If the firm wanted to retain these valuable employees and recruit more women in the future, it needed to create a childcare leave system that addressed their needs.

What Toyota has introduced is a two-year childcare leave program. Employees can receive the childcare allowance provided through the Employment Insurance system for the first year. The second year of leave is unpaid. After that, employees have the option of going onto a "flex-time with no core" program under which they can put in shorter hours on a schedule that fits their childcare needs. The firm will establish a childcare center on the Toyota City campus for parents who work there. While this package is impressive, it is aimed at a very small group: the elite group of women. Katō expects that many women who are not specialists will continue to quit, since the work is not interesting enough to keep them focused on their careers through their child-rearing years. He noted that, though fathers are eligible, "just two brave guys" out of sixty thousand male employees had taken childcare leave over the past decade. "They just don't ask for it," he reported.

Japanese childcare leave policy has come a long way since 1992 when it was first introduced. Unlike the United States and like some of the more progressive welfare states of Europe, Japan now guarantees paid leave of up to a year for qualified employees. Nevertheless, the program has limitations that have the effect of reinforcing gender and class divisions in the labor force. Very few men take leave, because most are ineligible (because they have a stay-at-home wife), and others face a serious risk of injury to their careers if they step forward to claim this benefit. In many firms, female employees who are not highly skilled risk hurting their careers if they take a full year's leave. The program is aimed primarily at retaining the most valued female workers, the 15 to 20 percent of new mothers who have the skills and the motivation to stay in the workforce through the years when their children are young. Unlike Sweden, and despite growing concern about the declining fertility problem, Japan has made only token attempts to use childcare leave to challenge the mother-must-do-it-all assumption that remains entrenched in Japanese society.

Childcare Services

Whereas Japan's childcare leave program was always more focused on keeping mothers in the workforce than on encouraging women to have children, the rhythm of policymaking for childcare services has echoed much more closely the drumbeat of news about falling fertility rates. The original Angel Plan was adopted in 1994, in large part in reaction to concerns about population projections issued in 1992. Its very name hinted at the government's hope that expanded childcare services would serve as midwife to a new baby boom.[54] The second Angel Plan came in 1999, just two years after another disappointing fertility report. Finally, Koizumi's call for the government to eliminate waiting lists at childcare centers (*hoikuen*) as part of the more comprehensive Plus One initiative came just months after the government issued its most pessimistic fertility projections ever in January 2002. As in the case of childcare leave, however, Japan's policy initiatives in this area have been less substantial than advertised and have had their greatest impact on the 15 to 20 percent of mothers who were already committed to sticking it out in the full-time labor force.

Japan has provided high-quality, publicly subsidized childcare services since 1947. Though the focus at the start was mostly on child welfare, with centers designed to provide care for children who would otherwise be left at home by parents who were struggling to make a living, over time the MHW expanded services to meet the needs of the growing number of mothers who were entering the employee workforce.[55] In the early 1990s, even before the renewed attention to this issue, daycare centers already served 1.6 million children, or about 11 percent of the children under three and 32 percent of those aged three to six.[56] Nevertheless, as discussed in chapter 3, the limited hours of service, waiting lists for those seeking to enroll infants and toddlers, and the lack of services for ill children left many parents underserved. The problem was particularly serious in growing urban areas where working parents often had long commutes and childcare outside the state-supported system was of poor quality and high priced.

Because this program already existed, it quickly became the focus of attention when the government began searching for ways of addressing the declining fertility problem at the start of the 1990s. Parents with children served by *hoikuen* were a natural constituency for expanded hours and services, and providers were eager to secure additional funds to help them expand. The MHW and politicians were also supportive of a program that was popular with these constituencies. Expanded childcare services thus became the core of the first Angel Plan formulated by the MHW, together with the Ministries of Labor, Education, and Construction, in December 1994. In fact, the most specific part of the plan was the Five-year Project on Urgent Daycare Measures, which announced specific targets for increased childcare services of various types: expanding the number of places for children under three from 466,000 in 1995 to 600,000 by 1999; increasing the number of centers offering longer hours from 2,530 to 7,000; expanding the number of centers providing care for children recovering from illnesses from 40 to 500; raising the number of community centers supporting child rearing (*kosodate shien sentaa*) from 354 to 3,000; and expanding the number of after-school programs from 5,220 to 9,000.[57]

The second Angel Plan announced in 1999 continued the government's focus on childcare services, though it slowed down the pace of expansion somewhat. The government's 1999 targets, the level of service actually achieved in 1999, and the new 2004 targets, show that the government failed to create as many spaces for young children by 1999 as it hoped (see table 7.1). It also slowed down the pace of expansion from an average of thirty thousand more spaces a year during the first Angel Plan to just twenty thousand more spaces a year during the second five-year plan. Nevertheless, it redoubled efforts to achieve original targets for community child-rearing centers and drop-in childcare centers, pushed for even higher numbers of centers with extended hours, and added a new goal of building centers with weekend and holiday hours.

According to MHW officials, the ministry's emphasis on childcare services in its response to declining fertility reflected what it was hearing from parents and providers.[58] Officials visited childcare centers regularly to speak with parents, and they made monthly visits to chat with members of "mothers' clubs" to see what kind of support these stay-at-home mothers needed. From the former they heard about waiting lists and the need for expanded hours, which the Angel Plans duly attempted to address. From the latter, they heard about the isolation and difficulties of caring for children all alone in Japan's urban areas, without much support from their husbands or extended families. The second Angel Plan thus redoubled efforts to set up more community centers supporting child rearing as well as childcare centers providing drop-in care, which were designed to serve stay-at-home mothers who needed advice, places to go with their children where they could interact with other mothers, and someplace to leave their children when they needed to go on errands. This was one area, among those involving mothers, work, and children, where officials heard women's voices demanding enhanced services, and they responded as best they could.

Because the voices bureaucrats and politicians were hearing (and not hearing) reflected choices women had already made, however, the government's efforts in this area too inevitably fell short. As we will see in chapter 8, when pressed on the issue of eldercare, the government created a brand-new social insurance program guaranteeing care services to those in need—in part because the group likely to be affected by the lack of care services constituted a very large proportion of society. In contrast, the shortage of conventional childcare was a problem that affected only those women who opted to have children and chose to stick it out in their careers. It was not an issue that concerned very many men, women who were past their child-rearing years, women who had opted to stay at home to raise their children, or

TABLE 7.1.
Angel Plan targets, 1999–2004

Category	1999 Target under Angel Plan	FY 1999 actual	2004 Target under Angel Plan
Spaces for children under three	600,000	580,000	680,000
Centers with extended hours	7,000	7,000	10,000
Community centers to support childrearing	3,000	1,500	3,000
Drop-in childcare	3,000	1,500	3,000
Centers for children recovering from illness	500	450	500
After school programs	9,000	9,000	None
Weekend/holiday childcare centers	none	100	300
Junior and senior high combined schools	none	4	500

Source: MHW, *Shōshika taisaku suishin kihon hōshin to shin enzeru puran*, 1999, 21.

women who had opted not to have children. Though the women most directly affected spoke out in support of longer hours and more spaces, they were not powerful enough to secure a guarantee of care or budgets anywhere near the sum devoted to eldercare.[59]

Consequently, despite the Angel Plans the increase in the proportion of children attending childcare centers was only marginal, and working mothers still faced shortages of subsidized childcare in many urban areas.[60] By the time the government was in the sixth year of the Angel Plans,[61] the proportion of infants under age one attending childcare declined slightly, reflecting the availability of childcare leave, which allowed more mothers to stay at home for their child's first year (figure 7.3). The main focus of the government's efforts was on increasing the availability of care for one- and two-year-olds so that mothers could move seamlessly from childcare leave back into work. The proportion of children of these ages in childcare did rise, but only from 13.2 to 17.5 percent, and waiting lists in urban areas continued to make it difficult for these parents to count on the availability of care. The length of waiting lists actually grew, from 28,400 in 1995 when the Angel Plan was launched to 40,000 in 1997 and 1998 before stabilizing at roughly 32,000 at the end of the decade.[62] Since Koizumi launched another assault on the problem with his 2001 pledge to eliminate waiting lists, they have come down to 25,000 (as of April 1, 2002),[63] but thousands of working mothers continue to be forced into difficult choices by the unavailability of care: quitting work, imposing on relatives, settling for substandard "baby hotels," or spending large sums of money on babysitting services.[64]

Meanwhile, the MHW's attempts to create new kinds of childcare services to meet the needs of stay-at-home mothers, though responding to a real expressed de-

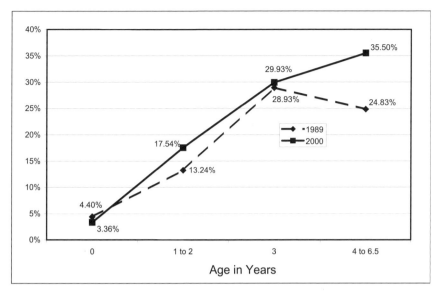

Fig. 7.3. Change in proportion of age groups in childcare centers, 1989–2000
Source: Based on data in Zenkoku Hoiku Dantai Rerakukai, *Hoiku hakusho* (Tokyo: Sōdo Bunka, 1990), 252, and 2002 edition, 274.

mand of women in these roles, props up a social structure in which mothers are still expected to do it all, and husbands and firms do not contribute very much. It may address the needs of stay-at-home mothers, but it does little to make the idea of marriage and motherhood more attractive to the portion of young women who are putting off marriage because they do not find the idea of sacrificing so much of their autonomy appealing. As noted above, when I asked MHW officials whether they talked to such young women to see what they wanted, they answered that they had no way of soliciting their opinions since they were neither *hoikuen* parents nor members of mothers' clubs. To their credit, however, MHW officials gradually came to the realization that their efforts to address childcare service needs, by themselves, were not going to address the deeper causes of the declining fertility problem. Through discussions of the Population Problems Advisory Council (Jinkō Mondai Shingikai), culminating in the publication of its analysis of the causes of declining fertility in 1997, policymakers came to realize that the roots of the problem lay in the structure of Japan's employment system.[65] Even with childcare leave and childcare services, mothers of young children were finding it difficult to meet the expectations of their employers. The system provided little room for such mothers to slow down or take a break while their children were young. If they quit or went part-time, they were likely to find it difficult to move back onto the career track. Neither did the system give these women's husbands much opportunity to help out at home. It was this basic incompatibility between the employment system and child rearing that was causing couples to have fewer children and turning off young women to the idea of marriage.

Mukuno Michiko, the MHW official who oversaw the work of the Population Problems Advisory Council, admits that government officials failed to grasp the extent of social change that would be needed to tackle the declining fertility problem when they began addressing the issue with the first Angel Plan.[66] Only after the publication of this commission's report, and the adoption of a more comprehensive approach to the declining fertility problem with the second Angel Plan, did the government begin attacking the heart of the problem.

Labor Standards and Employment Practices

What Japanese parents and would-be parents needed were changes in labor regulations to make it easier for mothers and fathers to insist that their employers allow them reduced and flexible hours to spend more time with their families while protecting them against recrimination in promotions and layoffs should they choose to do so. Reflecting the lessons Mukuno and others had drawn from their analysis of the declining fertility problem, government policy began to focus more on this area after 1997. Points two and three of the second Angel Plan of 1999, right after point one on childcare services, called for creating an "employment environment making work compatible with child rearing" and a workplace free of gender segregation.[67] The government passed the Basic Law for a Gender Equal Society in 1999. And the most recent Plus One Plan exhorts fathers, with the support of employers, to devote more time to child rearing. What has become clear as the government has tried to address this problem, however, is that there are limits to what it can accomplish by exhorting fathers and employers to change their ways. Even more than in the areas of childcare leave and services, the absence of a strong social movement to back up the government's campaign has limited its impact.

As in many countries, Japanese society has been torn about how to balance the goal of providing equal employment opportunities for women with the need to protect them from employment demands that are seen, by some, as incompatible with women's physical capabilities and family responsibilities. In the 1986 Equal Employment Opportunity Law, Japan struck an awkward balance. On the one hand, the law prohibited employers from discriminating against women in training, benefits, and dismissals—and matched these prohibitions with reduced job protections for women in managerial professions. The message seemed to be that these women should be able to do everything men do and should be treated as equals. On the other hand, the same law opened a gaping hole for employers to continue gender discrimination by stating that firms merely "have a duty to endeavor" to avoid discriminating in hiring, promotions, and assignments—and by giving them a reason to do so by continuing job protections for women in blue-collar and clerical jobs.

These women could not be assigned to night shifts and holiday shifts, and employers could assign them to only a limited number of overtime hours. Firms responded by tracking men and a small number of women into career jobs with long hours, challenging projects, and higher pay, while tracking most women into dead-end jobs, often part-time or under a term-limited contract, with lower pay and benefits. Even women who were initially able to get onto the career track often found that they were pushed out or onto the "mommy track" once they had children, with no opportunity to move back up onto the career track later in their working lives.

The challenge for reformers seeking to make this system more equal and more compatible with child rearing was to beef up the antidiscrimination provisions in the EEOL and reduce the gender-based protections that were giving employers license to discriminate while at the same time giving parents (fathers and mothers) the ability to devote time to their families without suffering permanent damage to their careers. Ministry of Labor officials took the lead on both fronts in the late 1990s, responding to criticism of the 1986 EEOL and to the Population Problems Advisory Council's call for labor reforms that would address the declining fertility problem.[68] Referring the issue to the Advisory Council on Issues of Women and Young Workers, the MOL solicited input from representatives of Nikkeiren and the unions and came out with a set of proposals that were put into law in EEOL revisions and in the Childcare and Family Care Leave Law, both passed in June 1997 and implemented in April 1999.

As in the case of childcare leave policies, policymaking was led by bureaucrats and constrained by the need to come up with a deal that would be acceptable to the two organized interest groups at the table: employers and unions. Consequently, change was incremental on both fronts. Neither unions nor employers pushed for changes in the basic structure of the employment system of a kind that might have addressed the root of the problem, and employers insisted on sharp reductions in protections of women and only limited new protections of parents as the price for their acquiescence to moderately improved antidiscrimination provisions in the EEOL.

The package of policies coming out of the reforms included the following elements: The EEOL was revised to prohibit, for the first time, discrimination in hiring, assignment, and promotion. At the same time, special protections for women were removed, aside from those involving pregnancy. Employers were no longer prevented from assigning women to night shifts, holiday shifts, or long hours of overtime, just because of their gender. Instead, parents of children under six were given an opportunity, under the Childcare and Family Care Leave Law, to petition their employers to exempt them from night shift assignments (between 10 p.m. and 5 a.m.), while parents of children under one who opt out of childcare leave were given the opportunity to request shorter working hours. Finally, in a section instructing employers on measures they should "endeavor" to take, the law asked them to take "necessary measures" on behalf of workers with children under elementary school age and to rehire workers who quit due to pregnancy or child-rearing demands.[69]

While the package of changes moved in the necessary direction, critics have argued that it did not add up to a good deal for women.[70] Women without children or other family responsibilities might come out ahead, but those that did have such responsibilities now faced the challenge of having to face employer demands that they work on holidays and late into the night (as late as 10 p.m. for women with young children, later than that for those with elementary-school-aged children). Because childcare services in most centers are provided only from 7 a.m. to 6 p.m., these work-hour expectations are a challenge to many mothers. While this condition was not affected by the reforms discussed above, an additional challenge for women on the career track was their obligation to move anywhere in the country at their employer's command. These obligations meant many mothers found it difficult to stay in career jobs, even under benevolent employers.

More disturbingly, bosses eager to push mothers out of their jobs had plenty of ways to do so within the letter of the law: they could demand that a young mother work until 10 p.m.; demand that she work every weekend; or demand that she transfer to a new location distant from her current place of employment. Magazines catering to working women were full of tales of exactly these types of abuses. Employers could even violate the specific prohibitions in the EEOL against dismissal and promotions without too much worry. Though sanctions were added to the law for the first time, these merely provided for the government to publish a list of employers that had violated the law.

A final problem with the labor law changes was their failure to make work and child rearing easier for women by protecting fathers from employer demands that forced many of them to get home past 8 p.m. night after night. Men still faced the obligation, under the Labor Standards Law, to work up to 350 hours of overtime a year, and employers faced few penalties for forcing workers to work additional hours of "voluntary overtime" above this limit.[71] Moreover, the lifetime employment system puts workers under tremendous pressure to comply with these demands, since the absence of lateral job mobility means they have few fallback options if they offend their current employer. These circumstances guaranteed that the husbands of working wives, though eligible for childcare leave and limits on overtime for fathers of small children, were unlikely to take the risk of asking for these benefits. Those whose wives were taking care of children full time were not even eligible for these benefits, since flextime, like childcare leave, is offered only to the parent "who is responsible for childcare" and does not have a spouse who is able to take on these responsibilities.

The round of reforms adopted in the late 1990s, however, was not the end of reform efforts in this area. The release of even more dire population projections in January 2001 caused the government to consider whether it had done enough to make working harmonious with family life in the initial round of reform. In May of that year, Prime Minister Koizumi instructed the MHLW to recommend more "declining fertility countermeasures," starting with a "re-examination of working styles, including those of male workers." Specifically, he instructed the ministry to "reduce overtime for those fathers whose children still need care; to encourage all fathers to take at least five days off when their child is born; and to encourage firms to establish systems whereby regular employees can work shorter hours."[72] This initiative resulted in the approval by the Diet in November 2001 of another package of labor law changes: employers are barred from "unfair treatment" of workers who take childcare leave, such as a transfer of an employee to a remote location; employees responsible for the care of children younger than school age can insist that their overtime be limited to 150 hours a year; employers are required to provide the option of shorter work hours for parents of children younger than three, rather than just infants under one in the previous legislation; and they are asked to endeavor to provide leave benefits to employees who need to take time off work to care for sick children.[73]

The latest round of reform reflected a degree of party-political involvement not seen in the earlier periods when policymaking was driven primarily by the bureaucracy. Not only did Koizumi take a particular interest in this issue area, in hopes it would burnish his credentials as a "reformer" and distinguish him from the LDP old guard he was challenging, but the Democratic Party of Japan (DPJ) also campaigned vigorously for labor law revisions to make work more family-friendly. In their party platform released in April 2001, family-friendly policies dominate the top of the list of "21 Key Policies" it supported: (1) helping balance work and family; (2) increasing choice in preschool childcare; (3) providing more after-school care; (4) increasing child allowances; and (5) creating a single system for childcare centers. Under the first point, the party elaborated that "the DPJ will work to change company-centered social arrangements and the idea that men and women should do different work."[74]

Although the competition between Koizumi and the DPJ to take a lead in this issue area, and rapid legislative action in 2001, reflects their political calculations that there is latent enthusiasm in at least a segment of the electorate for family-friendly policies, it is not at all clear that the latest reforms will be effective in changing the actual working environment facing the majority of Japanese. Labor law has been changed to create new programs like flextime for parents of small children, but actual labor practice depends on the balance of power at the shop floor or office level. Given that legislative action in this area has developed top down out of a concern about declining fertility, rather than as a result of a groundswell of activism on the part of working mothers or fathers, there is little organized support for the individual parents (or would-be parents) who are facing decisions about whether to avail themselves of these opportunities. Employers still face little more than a slap on the wrist for discriminating against employees who take leave and flextime, while workers face the very real possibility of losing their jobs and being thrown into a weak labor market where lateral movement remains almost impossible in most fields.

As a result, neither mothers nor fathers are finding it easy to take advantage of the new family-friendly programs. Most of those going on flextime and seeking sick leave, of course, are women. Those that have done so continue to report horror stories of employer discrimination. In a 2003 issue of the weekly women's magazine *Shūkan josei*, a long list of women reported being fired after becoming pregnant, taking childcare leave, or taking off a few days to care for a sick child.[75] Such experiences, combined with the broader pressures coming from husbands, employers, and society have led the vast majority of women working full time before childbirth to leave the workforce after having a child. Today, after all of the reforms discussed in this chapter, the percentage of women in full-time, regular jobs staying in those jobs through marriage and child rearing is actually *lower* than it was in 1992! The proportion working full time is up slightly for those most recently married, but it is down significantly for those married five to fourteen years (table 7.2). Many women with older children return to the workforce, but the vast majority of these hold part-time jobs.

Although fathers of young children (whose wives work) are also eligible for these programs, the take-up ratios have been extremely small. When I asked one MHLW official responsible for this policy initiative whether any father in his office had gone on flextime, he said that none had done so. Neither had any mother. He himself was the father of a young child, but he had not reduced his long hours since the child was born.[76] Despite the most recent changes, fathers are still barred from taking advantage of flextime if their young children have a mother who is primarily responsible for their care. All of these facts on the ground contribute to a working environment where men in their thirties—the prime fatherhood years—are still working more hours than any other group of Japanese: 20 percent work more than sixty hours each week.[77]

Short of a groundswell of parent activism, is there anything the government could do to change this situation? One reform that would make a difference, but has not even been considered in the policy debate, is an end to Japan's system of permanent employment. If the labor market created opportunities for lateral movement into interesting and rewarding jobs, mothers and fathers would have a much greater opportunity to slow down during the period they are raising their children—by shifting into jobs more compatible with child rearing when their children were young, and then shifting again into more demanding and better-paying jobs when they were ready to devote more time to their careers. At the same time, ending this system would encourage workers to take greater advantage of opportunities such as leave and flextime within their current jobs by reducing the penalties employers can impose. Currently, despite the name "permanent employment," employers have the ability to force workers out by demanding unreasonable hours, transferring employees to distant locations, and assigning them to meaningless tasks. Once out, workers have few opportunities to move into rewarding jobs. In contrast, under a labor market with greater lateral mobility, the worst that could

TABLE 7.2.
Proportion of all married women with children who are working

Marriage duration	Survey year	Women with children working (part time or full time)	Those with children working full time
Zero to 4 years	1992	14.8	9.3
	2002	18.1	10.7
5 to 9 years	1992	35.3	17.2
	2002	34.1	13.9
10 to 14 years	1992	51.7	20.6
	2002	55.5	15.5

Source: Data from NIPSSR 12th Basic Survey on Birth Trends for Married Couples, carried out in 2002, reported in Cabinet Office, *FY 2003 Annual Report on the State of Formation of a Gender-Equal Society—Outline*, 2004.

happen to a worker who insisted on signing onto a flextime program would be for him or her to be fired into a market where other work opportunities were available.

For much the same reasons labor market regulations were only marginally revised in the 1990s (see chapter 6), the abolition of the lifetime employment system was not even considered in the discussion of how to make employment compatible with child rearing. MOL officials, Nikkeiren, and the labor unions—which were the main actors in the policy process—were all too wedded to the existing order to consider rethinking the basic structure of the Japanese labor market. Though they attempted to make the existing system more family-friendly by adding provisions for childcare leave, sick-child leave, and flextime, the decision to leave the permanent employment system in place guaranteed that the impact on most workers' ability to secure more time for their families would be limited.

Child Allowances

While the government has at least attempted to lead social change in each of the three areas covered above, it has not even made a pretense of activism in the area of child allowances. Like many European countries, Japan provides child allowances as a way of providing income support to families. Though this program began with great fanfare in 1973, by the 1990s the value of this source of support had eroded to the point where it had little impact on the average family's finances: families with incomes in the bottom 60 percent received ¥5,000 ($42) each month for each child under three, with ¥10,000 ($84) provided if the child was the third or more in a family.[78] Given that men and women, when asked why they did not have more children, placed "the high cost of raising children" as the number-one reason in almost all surveys, one would have expected the government to raise this allowance as a way of combating the decline in fertility. Indeed, a number of political parties, including the DPJ and Kōmeitō (a moderate party backed by the Sōka Gakkai Bud-

TABLE 7.3.
Modifications in the child allowance program, 1999 and 2000

	Program prior to reforms	Kōmeitō demands	Program after 1999 and 2000 reforms
Size of allowance	¥5,000 for first and second child; ¥10,000 for third or more child	¥10,000 for first and second child; ¥20,000 for third or more child	¥5,000 for first and second child; ¥10,000 for third or more child
Age of children covered	under 3	through 16	under 6
Population of families eligible	bottom 60%	all	bottom 85%
Tax credit for children under sixteen	available	available	cancelled

dhist organization), pushed for an increase in this family benefit. Nevertheless, after two rounds of tinkering with the program in 1999 and 2000, it has been expanded barely at all.

The first decision point came in December 1999 when the second Angel Plan was being finalized and Kōmeitō was negotiating with the LDP and the Liberal Party over the first budget to be finalized under the three-party coalition. Kōmeitō argued for a major expansion in the program: doubling the per-child benefit, extending the program to children under sixteen, and ending means-testing in order to make it a universal benefit. The LDP and Liberals were not eager to spend so much on families, however, and they opposed the increase. So did the MHW, which argued that the cost of this program would make it difficult to increase spending on childcare services and other ministry priorities. If forced to choose, ministry officials argued, the money should go to childcare services instead of child allowances. As one official explained, "If you give cash to families, there's no guarantee it will go to the needs of the child. It might simply be spent on beer for dad. We prefer to provide services like childcare since we know these will go to children."[79]

When Kōmeitō did not get what it wanted the first year, it came back with the same demands a year later during budget deliberations in December 2000. Once again, however, it ran into opposition from its coalition partner, the LDP (the Liberals were out of the coalition by this time), and the MHW. After two rounds of pushing for a major expansion in the child allowance, Kōmeitō was forced to settle for a compromise that did little more than move money from one pot to another.[80] After two rounds of tinkering, the benefit has not been doubled; it has been extended to children under six; and it has been extended to 85 percent of families; but this expansion in spending on the child allowance has been funded almost entirely by eliminating a tax credit that had been available to families with children under sixteen (see table 7.3).[81] Parents of children under six are somewhat better off, but those with children of school age are worse off.

Tax Subsidies for Dependent Spouses

Taking a very different tack to the declining fertility problem from Kōmeitō, feminists have called on the government to eliminate the tax and benefit advantages provided to families with a "dependent spouse." As explained in chapter 3, wives of salaried employees who remain dependent on their husbands by virtue of low or no earnings are subsidized through rules that excuse them from having to pay pension premiums (they receive a basic pension even if they do not contribute to the program) and give them generous income tax exemptions. This system creates a situation in which a "dependent" woman faces a strong incentives to limit her earnings to a level below a threshold of about ¥1.3 million a year ($10,800), at which point she is required to begin paying pension premiums, loses two income tax deductions, and loses the dependent spouse allowance paid by her husband's employer. Because of these incentives, many women opt for part-time jobs and do not press for pay increases, since they find that any effort to increase their earnings above these thresholds results in little or no increase in their take-home pay.

Feminists argue that this system serves to perpetuate a gender-segregated labor market in which women are consigned to part-time work with low pay and few benefits. It leads them to limit their working hours, aggravating the looming labor shortage Japan faces because of demographic trends, and it leaves them dependent and vulnerable in a way that discourages them from having a larger number of children. At the same time, critics charge that the program is an inefficient and inequitable way of aiding families with children. Tax and benefit subsidies totaling ¥1.3 trillion ($10.8 billion) a year go to the nonworking or part-time–working wives of salaried workers. These couples, who tend to be among the higher-income families in Japan, receive these benefits even if their children are grown or they have no children at all. Families with children where wives work full time to make ends meet do not receive these tax breaks and benefits.[82] Critics propose that the sum of money devoted to subsidizing dependent spouses be transformed into a program of tax benefits or subsidies that go to all families with children.

During the 1990s, feminists made no progress at all in this reform campaign. In 2002, however, they were able to get one of the tax breaks eliminated, taking advantage of a tax reform initiative launched by Prime Minister Koizumi in an effort to "broaden the tax base." University of Tokyo professor Ōsawa Mari, who was serving on an advisory council in the Cabinet Office for Gender Equality, appeared before the government tax commission and argued for the elimination of both income tax deductions provided for dependent spouses. The sight of someone calling for a tax increase before a commission where most petitioners begged for tax breaks was so unusual that it was broadcast on TV.[83] The committee supported the elimination of one of the tax breaks, and this decision was ultimately ratified by the LDP tax commission and the coalition parties and went into effect in tax year 2003.[84]

This campaign to eliminate tax and benefit subsidies for dependent spouses may continue to make progress over the next several years. There is little sign, however, that the reformers will succeed in transforming these subsidies into an alternative program of support for families with children. The success Ōsawa had in 2002 was largely attributable to the tax commission's eagerness to raise government revenues in order to reduce the size of the budget deficit. While willing to boost pensions for the elderly at a rate surpassing the growth in GDP, the government has demonstrated that it is unwilling to extend more help to families with children, even under the pressure of a sharp decline in fertility rates.

Despite growing frustration on the part of Japanese women with their nation's gendered division of labor that asks them to give up their careers, time, and interests in order to care for children, Japan has moved slowly and unevenly to reform its male-breadwinner–based family policies. That slow pace of change, I have argued, is a product of exit dynamics that have allowed women who might have fought for change to escape, at least partially, from the difficulty of combining work and family. Particularly critical has been the loss of potential support from young Japanese women who grew up dreaming of fulfilling and challenging careers. Many of these women have avoided experiencing the challenges of balancing career with family by delaying or opting out of marriage and motherhood. As long as they remained single, the most capable of them could obtain and hold on to careers with all of the benefits and most of the protections afforded to men. Once they made this choice and passed their child-bearing years, however, they had little personal motivation to campaign for family policy reforms that would make it easier for others to combine work with motherhood. Similarly, as long as most married women had husbands who could earn enough money with enough security to provide for their family's economic needs, they could give up full-time work without assuming too much risk. Having done so, they too had little incentive to push for the degree of change that would be necessary to enable them to work full time while taking primary responsibility for child rearing.

As a result, Japanese women's frustrations with child-related family policies have taken the form of a "quiet rebellion." One by one, with no coordination and with little noise, women have been quitting their jobs or giving up on marriage—in the process losing the motivation to change the policies that pushed them into having to make these choices. It is possible that these marriage, birth, and work "strikes" will become widespread and serious enough that at some point society will be driven to reform. I discuss these possible future developments in the concluding chapter. In the period of time covered here, however, this quiet rebellion has actually hampered the reform process. Struggling to respond to the sharp decline in fertility rates and the looming labor shortage, bureaucrats have found it difficult to push through major reforms without the assistance of an active women's movement. Left to diagnose the problems, devise solutions, and generate support on their own, they have come up short of the level of change required.

Chapter 8

Exceptions That Prove the Rule

The preceding chapters have shown how one Japanese reform project after another has been abandoned or fallen far short of its goals: electricity market liberalization; Fiscal Investment and Loan Program reform; the privatization of the postal finance system and Japan Highway; the bad-loan cleanup; childcare leave; childcare services expansion; and labor market reforms of all kinds. The failure of hollowing out and declining fertility to motivate these reforms is evidence, I have argued, that limited exit has not proved sufficient to bring about needed changes in a Japanese system of social protection that has placed unsustainable burdens on women and firms—much less a comprehensive new system of social protection that works better in the nation's new socioeconomic context.

But Japanese social and economic policies have not stood completely still. Some areas have seen quite dramatic changes. In this chapter I examine two exceptions to the overall pattern of stasis, one affecting women and another affecting firms. In each case, I argue, the greater change seen in these policy areas has been produced by exit dynamics that are distinct from the limited exit pattern in which manufacturing firms exit through FDI in order to get around high costs and women "exit" from careers or children when faced with the difficulty of combining the two goals.

The first of these exceptions—the adoption of a long-term care insurance program for the frail elderly, explicitly designed to relieve women of the predominant burden of providing this care—is a case in which many women (and some men) found they had "no way out." Unlike young women with careers who had the option of falling back on one of two second-choice lifestyles, each providing a partial exit from the difficulty of combining work and family in the Japanese system, older women with established careers who suddenly found that they had to take on the responsibility of caring for frail relatives or in-laws had no way to escape. They couldn't choose not to have parents. The adoption of a progressive social insurance system guaranteeing access to a range of care services for aging seniors was possible, I argue, because the absence of exit options drove women to mobilize in the political arena to seek this change.

The second exceptional case is that of financial market reforms adopted during the 1980s and 1990s, culminating in the big bang reforms of 1996. Henry Laurence pointed to this case as an example of how exit could drive rapid change in public policy, even in a society like Japan where reforms threatened vested interests.[1] My account confirms the role of exit—the movement of financial transactions overseas—in driving change in this sector, but it emphasizes the exceptional nature of this sector. Once short-term capital flows were liberalized, it was quite easy for firms seeking lower cost financial services or new kinds of financial products unavailable in Japan to get around the remaining financial market regulations by taking business overseas. Unlike FDI, which required the slow buildup of overseas manufacturing and logistical facilities, financial transactions could be shifted with a few strokes of a computer keyboard and the help of a small overseas office in London, New York, or Singapore. This ease of movement generated much more abrupt exit flows in this sector, flows that were large enough and disconcerting enough that government officials had less difficulty making the case for reform. Reforms that were adopted often called for phase-in periods, but the direction of change has been sustained, and in aggregate, substantial. One can now purchase financial service products that were previously unavailable, and services cost much less. As we saw with the bad-loan problem, some banks and other financial institutions have even gone out of business. Reform in this sector is real, but the dynamics that brought it about are distinctive.

The consideration of these cases is critical to the argument of this book because they help highlight the importance of exit dynamics as a variable shaping public policy outcomes. The absence of change in policies affecting gender roles is a product of many things, including entrenched social norms that see caregiving as women's work. Similarly, the absence of change in the postal finance system and the electricity market reflects the political power of groups that benefit from status quo arrangements. Although I highlighted the role that limited exit played in sapping the strength of reform movements in these areas, entrenched norms and vested interests clearly contributed to the failure of these reforms as well. What we see when we focus on the two exceptional cases surveyed here is how gender-role norms and powerful vested interests have not been enough to forestall change when those who want reform have had either no way out or ample exit opportunities. Exit dynamics can trump politics.

Long-term Care Insurance

The contrast between the stories of policy stasis in earlier chapters and the story of eldercare policy innovation told here could not be greater. The government began dramatically increasing its spending on care services for the elderly under the Gold

Plans of 1990 and 1994, and later in that decade locked its commitment into place with the brand-new Long-term Care Insurance (LTCI: Kaigo Hoken) program, the first new social insurance program Japan had created since the 1960s. The program, approved by the Diet in December 1997 and put into operation in 2000, now guarantees care services, including short- and long-term care in nursing homes, daycare, and home visits, to all frail elderly citizens, regardless of income. Since it was implemented, the number of nursing homes providing care for elderly with dementia has grown from just 266 in 1999 to 1,312 in 2001. Over the same short time span, the volume of home visits providing help with bathing and nursing care has increased by 82 percent. As of March 2002, 2.3 million elderly citizens were receiving eldercare services of one kind or another (see table 8.1 for additional details on the growth in services planned).[2]

Also impressive is the sum of money dedicated to this new program. Services provided under LTCI were conservatively estimated to cost ¥4.7 trillion ($43 billion) in its first year, growing to more than ¥7 trillion ($70 billion) a decade later.[3] The program was funded in part through new social insurance premiums that are now being collected from all citizens over forty; but half of the funds for the program come from general tax revenues at the national and local levels. The willingness of the government to put general revenue into the Gold Plans and LTCI suggests that one cannot explain its decision to spend heavily on care services of this type while skimping on care services for children merely on the grounds that it was easier to fund this type of program through social insurance.

On the contrary, the scale and structure of this program clearly reflects the voices of politically engaged citizens. The initial Gold Plan, which paved the way for LTCI, was first pushed by LDP heavyweight Hashimoto Ryūtarō, who calculated that the popularity of expanded state-financed eldercare services would help the public forgive his party for pushing through a controversial new consumption tax in 1989. Having seen how popular these new programs were, the LDP then pushed through a second Gold Plan in 1994, with even more ambitious eldercare service goals, timed to help the party win upper and lower house elections held over the next two years.

The budget taps had already been running full force for almost a decade, when the government began deliberating whether to lock in its financial commitments in this area through a new social insurance program. In most countries in a similar situation, business groups and conservative politicians tend to raise objections to tax and social insurance commitments of this size and insist on building in budgeting and administrative means for controlling costs. In this case, however, eldercare services were so popular with the public that such objections were barely raised.[4] Consequently, the Japanese LTCI program, in contrast to similar programs in Sweden and Germany, has virtually no mechanisms for controlling costs. As John Campbell and Naoki Ikegami note, LTCI "is an entitlement program, and under present legislation, neither the national nor the municipal governments have any effective control over who will apply, whether they are eligible, the amount of entitlement, or

TABLE 8.1.
Planned growth in eldercare services, 1999–2004

Service Category	FY 1999	Goal for 2004 under New Gold Plan
Home help care	—	225 million hours
Home help workers	170,000 people	350,000 people
Home nursing care	—	44 million hours
Home nursing care stations	5,000 facilities	9,900 facilities
Day care visits for elderly	—	105 million visits
Day care centers	17,000 facilities	26,000 facilities
Short-term stays at care facilities	60,000 people	96,000 people
Welfare facilities for long-term care	290,000 people	360,000 people
Health facilities for long-term care	280,000 people	297,000 people
Group home for elderly with dementia	—	3,200 facilities
Low-cost home with care services	100,000 people	105,000 people
Center for the Life and Welfare of Elderly	400 facilities	1,800 facilities

Source: MHLW, *Long-term Care Insurance in Japan*, 2002.

what kind of services will be chosen."[5] Unlike urban childcare centers, where mothers sometimes have to wait many months before a spot opens up, the government is obliged to provide frail elderly with the care they need.

Why was the public so enthusiastic about this social insurance program when it was so disinterested in childcare services and other reforms designed to help mothers? In the latter case, one may recall, the MHW was so concerned about the absence of public enthusiasm for its initiatives that it went to work trying to *create* this support by sponsoring the People's Committee to Promote a Response to Declining Fertility. One reason the MHW never had to go to these lengths to build support for its eldercare initiatives was the inevitability of aging for all citizens, regardless of age or gender. With Japanese men and women looking forward to living to eighty-five or ninety, aging is something no one can expect to "exit" from (short of premature death or suicide). Eldercare is also an obligation that falls more evenly across genders than childcare. Retired husbands sometimes face the primary burden of caring for their ailing wives. An estimated 20 percent of those serving as primary caregivers to frail elderly are men.[6] This was therefore an issue that men could get concerned about.

Nevertheless, the policy debates over the Gold Plans and LTCI were of particular interest to women. This was because, though men sometimes end up caring for their aging relatives, in the vast majority of cases it remains the responsibility of women, in particular daughters and daughters-in-law. As John Campbell relates in his account of the process that led to the approval of LTCI legislation, media coverage of the long-term care problem most commonly featured the images of "the daughter-in-law trapped in a perpetual 'caregiving hell' (*kaigo jigoku*)."[7] In the archetypal story, this daughter-in-law was someone who had never cared much for her husband's parents, especially her meddling mother-in-law, but when her in-laws suddenly needed intensive in-home care, her husband simply assumed she would take on this burden, quitting her job if necessary. In some of the worst-case stories, women told of being forced to care single-handedly for a series of aging relatives: first her father-in-law, then her mother-in-law, and then her husband. By the end of this ordeal, the woman was inevitably exhausted and in need of care herself.[8]

What made this situation particularly intolerable for many women was their lack of any realistic exit options. As we have seen, Japanese women troubled by the difficulties of balancing work with child rearing at least have options: they can give up their careers to care for their children full time, they can ask their own mothers to help care for their children so they can continue working full time, they can work part-time, or they can avoid the balancing act by deciding not to marry and not to have children. With elderly relatives, in contrast, women have no way out. Divorcing their spouse to avoid caring for in-laws is technically possible, but something very few would consider. Avoiding their "responsibilities" to their own parents, or to their husband's, is difficult for most women, both because many feel caring for their elders is the "right thing to do" and because shirking such responsibilities is frowned upon by society.[9]

The problem was particularly great for women who had managed to continue working through their child-rearing years by relying on their mothers or mothers-in-law. When it came time to return the favor, these women found they had no one to rely on but themselves. Employment surveys show that the need to care for elderly relatives is one of the leading reasons women leave the workforce. Etō Mikiko describes the way this "no way out" situation drove women to become active participants in the policy process: "Faced with a situation where they were forced to resign from work and/or give up their lives outside the home entirely, women began to speak up."[10]

Motivated by the burden they faced and the lack of exit options, women stepped to the forefront of the movement supporting the expansion of eldercare services and the creation of LTCI. The initial push for eldercare services, in fact, came from a group of women who organized conference on "Women's Independence and the Aging Problem" in 1982 and began calling themselves the Women's Association for Improving an Aging Society.[11] Headed by Higuchi Keiko, the group's membership grew rapidly over the course of the 1980s and 1990s, drawing in full-time housewives as well as journalists, professors, and Diet members.

The group conducted surveys in the late 1980s that revealed the breadth of the need for social services to assist women who were caring for elderly relatives at home, and they used this data to back up their demand for a new LTCI system. The group's connections to the media helped generate sympathetic coverage, which tended to focus, as noted above, on the burden faced by women who were living in "care-giving hell." The group's high profile also led the MHW to invite Higuchi and two other Women's Association members to serve on a research committee set up to develop a proposal for a new social program for the elderly in 1989. The ministry then invited Higuchi and one other Women's Association member to sit on the advisory council that developed the detailed plan for LTCI in 1995.[12]

The Women's Association was by no means the only group that mobilized in response to concern about this issue. Other groups organized locally in order to directly assist women struggling to care for elderly relatives. The Kanagawa Club operating in the prefecture by that name in the Tokyo metropolitan area, for example, grew to involve 2,314 members in thirty-nine satellite groups providing "home-help services, day care services, meals on wheels, and transport services for the disabled elderly."[13] By taking on all of this work itself, the group dramatized the gaps in the system of public support and presented a model of what a system of socialized care for the elderly might look like. Their example was soon noticed by officials struggling to figure out how to respond to the policy challenge. Kanagawa Club members met regularly with MHW bureaucrats while the LTCI proposals were being developed, and one young MHW bureaucrat was even dispatched for a period of time to observe the group's operations.[14]

Women's groups thus played a critical role at the stage where the government was trying to understand the policy problem and to devise solutions. Women actively sought out government officials to communicate the nature of their burdens, and when the MHW began considering alternative ways of structuring the program in the 1990s, women's groups had representatives on the relevant advisory councils ready to recommend and critique various alternatives. Higuchi, in fact, is credited with helping to defeat efforts by some policymakers to structure the program so female relatives could be paid in cash to continue providing services they previously provided for free. Taking advantage of her position on the advisory council, she vigorously criticized that approach along feminist lines, arguing that paying cash to female relatives would simply perpetuate the gendered division of labor. Her strong opinion, and other similar opinions, helped keep this option off the table for most of the decadelong process of deliberations.[15] Although a system of payments to family members was introduced as a temporary measure at the very last minute when the program was initiated in 2000, sharp criticism from feminists led most localities to limit this option and rely mostly on professional service providers.

Finally, women played a critical role in generating the energy needed to push this expensive new program through the policy process. By 1996, a coherent LTCI proposal was on the table, but mayors and their contacts within the LDP were balking at the size of the price tag. Mayors worried in particular that local elderly would blame them if they couldn't expand and fund eldercare services fast enough after the government began to collect social insurance premiums. At this point, Higuchi joined with Hotta Tsutomu, the leader of a national organization of welfare volunteers, and Sugawara Hiroko, the editor of a journal for senior citizens, in gathering a variety of groups supporting LTCI under a high-profile group that went by the name Ten Thousand Citizens' Committee to Realize a Public Care of the Elderly System. The group held high-profile meetings in Tokyo, generated significant media attention, and publicized polls showing that a large majority of Japanese favored LTCI.[16] Their strong support was an important reason this large program was adopted in 1997 at a time when most of the Hashimoto cabinet's energies were being devoted to fiscal retrenchment.

The Big Bang Reforms in the Financial Sector

At about the same time that Hashimoto was pushing through the LTCI program, reducing (in this area at least) the burden of the Japanese system of social protection on women, he was simultaneously pushing through another far-reaching set of reforms addressing an area of high costs and inefficiency that burdened firms. Hashimoto's financial sector "big bang," adopted in 1996 and implemented over the next several years, was the culmination of a series of financial liberalization measures that the government had been implementing since the 1980s. Together, these reforms transformed a system that had been segmented and heavily regulated, with high, fixed prices for financial services and a myriad of regulations restricting the range of services provided, into one that was almost as freewheeling as financial markets in New York and London.

At the start of the process of liberalization in the early 1980s, financial markets were completely under the control of the Ministry of Finance and the cartels it oversaw. As described in chapter 3, under traditional arrangements MOF regulations confined each type of financial institution (trust banks, city banks, insurance firms, securities firms) to a narrow range of services. Many prices were set by the MOF while others were set by cartels of financial firms in each segment of the market. The rate of interest banks could offer to depositors was set by the MOF, as was the rate they could charge their borrowers. The bankers' cartel boosted the effective rate they charged on loans by requiring borrowers to maintain "compensating balances" (the requirement that a borrower keep a share of borrowed funds on deposit at a rate lower than the rate of interest on the loan).[17] Securities firms all charged the same regulated rates for their brokerage services. Auto insurance and life insurance provided the same terms at the same price.

This arrangement worked quite well for companies in the financial services sector since they were virtually guaranteed to earn profits and faced few surprises in their business environment, and it helped maintain macroeconomic stability for the economy as a whole, but it was not ideal from the point of view of financial service customers. The banks' practice of requiring compensating balances boosted the interest rates corporate borrowers had to pay for bank loans, and restrictions on raising funds via bonds kept most firms from gaining access to lower-cost funds through direct financing. Firms with pension assets to invest were restricted to low-return investment vehicles and deprived of the ability to invest in higher-return areas with the protection of sophisticated hedging strategies. Institutional investors allowed to invest in stocks were forced to pay high fixed fees to the securities firms that serviced their investment accounts and were forced to pay even more by unregulated "churning" tactics (purchases and sales of stock for the purpose of generating fees) that boosted the price investors had to pay their brokers.[18]

All of these manipulations added to the costs of doing business in Japan, in the same way that high labor prices and electricity prices and taxes did. Since some financial services were effectively unavailable inside Japan (e.g., only the largest and most stable corporations could issue unsecured bonds, and new innovations like warrant bonds and Nikkei-index futures were not allowed), it is hard to compare prices as we did for other business expenses in chapter 6. As late as 1995, after the MOF had liberalized laws restricting direct financing and authorized other products that were previously not allowed, government statistics estimated that it still cost Japanese firms 14 percent more to issue bonds in Japan than it did to do so in the United States.[19]

Faced with high costs for financial services, Japanese firms responded by seeking out lower costs overseas. Firms that could not raise capital through bonds in Tokyo, or faced higher costs there, issued bonds in London and New York. Henry Laurence documents the mushrooming exit trend that saw the volume and share of overseas bond listings by Japanese corporations spike from an average of ¥560 billion (19%) in 1975–79 to ¥3.2 trillion (50%) in 1985.[20] Similar trends characterized other financial service markets. Institutional investors seeking lower brokerage fees and opportunities to try out new investment products not available in Japan did business with foreign securities firms abroad. Derivative products were in particular demand by institutional investors who needed to hedge their positions in Japanese stocks and bonds. When exchange markets in Chicago, London, and Singapore opened Japanese Government Bond and Nikkei stock index futures markets, Japanese investors flocked to those cities. Laurence notes that by 1989 "over half of the euro-yen trading in Hong Kong and eurodollar trading in Singapore was being conducted by Japanese traders."[21]

Facing such rapid shifts in transactions, Japanese banks and securities firms both came to accept liberalization as inevitable—as something they would have to accept if they were going to hold onto the business they had and reclaim the transactions that were rapidly flowing overseas. First, the long-coddled banks, which had opposed measures designed to make it easier and cheaper for corporations to raise capital through bonds because they threatened their high-profit bank-loan business, accepted liberalization when they realized they were losing the business anyway to competitors operating overseas. Instead of seeking to block the liberalization of bond markets, banks decided to bargain in exchange for a piece of this action. Similarly, securities firms that relied heavily on fixed and high trading commissions for their earnings accepted reductions (and eventually liberalization) when they realized their clients were finding cheaper services through foreign brokerage firms.[22]

The other powerful actor that changed its position on liberalization was the Ministry of Finance. MOF officials long prioritized financial-system stability over other concerns such as service prices. To maintain the stability of markets, they believed, it was essential that their ministry retain discretionary power that they could use to intervene in case markets threatened to get out of control. For this reason, the MOF worked persistently through the 1980s to make the liberalization process as gradual and orderly as possible.[23] Nevertheless, concerns about the exit trends summarized above led MOF officials to make sure that all of its regulatory changes brought Japanese services and prices steadily closer to those available in overseas markets. As Laurence argues, MOF officials worried that unless Japan made financial services as available and attractively priced as those in overseas markets, Tokyo risked being relegated to the status of a second-class financial market.[24] As one MOF advisory council report put it in 1989, reforms "must aim to ensure that Tokyo can fulfill its responsibility as one of the big three financial centers alongside New York and London, and that it allows for easy operation by foreign institutions and users as well as Japanese."[25]

These shifts in position led the Japanese government to adopt a string of measures liberalizing financial service markets. Interest rates on large certificates of deposits were liberalized starting in 1979, culminating in complete liberalization of rates on all deposit accounts in 1992.[26] Brokerage fees on large transactions were reduced starting in 1980, falling by 58 percent by 1990. Fees on trades over ¥1 billion were deregulated in 1992.[27] Restrictions on bond markets were liberalized starting in 1984, making it possible for many more firms to issue straight unsecured bonds and convertible bonds.[28] Equally important were the breaches in the walls that had previously kept trust banks, city banks, and securities firms in their own narrow niches. In the mid-1980s, city banks were allowed to sell and trade Japanese government bonds, and starting in 1993 they were allowed (when authorized by MOF license) to set up securities subsidiaries and underwrite bonds.[29] Another wall fell in 1994 when Japanese regulators opened up the management of corporate pension assets to let in foreign investment banks.[30]

When Prime Minister Hashimoto endorsed the big bang in 1996 he was merely adding an exclamation point to a liberalization process that had been steadily opening up the financial sector to market competition for fifteen years. Once again Hashimoto and the MOF officials behind the plan were motivated by concerns that Japan's market was still not liberalized enough to stem the flow of financial transactions to overseas markets. The volume of shares being traded in Tokyo had fallen to one-fifth the volume in New York. Trading in the shares of Japanese companies on the London market grew to 18 percent of the level of trading taking place in Tokyo.[31] As one of the MOF officials involved in pushing for the plan put it, "High costs, a restrictive regulatory environment, and lack of dynamic players gradually eroded Japan's role as a major financial center. If a disproportionate amount of transactions of yen-based financial products were being conducted outside Japan, then clearly something had to be amiss."[32]

While the big bang reforms were phased in more gradually than the label suggests, by the end of the process very little of the traditional segmented, highly cartelized system remained.[33] One important step went into effect in 1998 at the start of the big bang reforms: rules requiring Japanese engaged in foreign exchange transactions to work through a Japanese bank (with high fees) were eliminated. This change was important because it meant Japanese investors could pay lower fees if they opened a foreign-currency savings or investment account. Now even small Japanese customers could afford to "exit" and seek higher returns (or less risk) in foreign-currency investments if Japanese financial firms failed to respond to market incentives or if the Japanese government dragged its feet on carrying out subsequent big bang reforms.

Despite concerns about whether Japanese financial firms were ready, most of the remaining big bang reforms were implemented on schedule. By the end of the phased implementation process in 2001, financial firms were free to set up holding companies to facilitate entry into all segments of the market. Banks no longer had to depend on MOF discretion before setting up securities subsidiaries. They could sell their own mutual funds, issue bonds, and sell insurance. Securities firms could manage pension fund assets. Life insurance companies could sell casualty insurance and vice versa. Brokerage fees on even the smallest stock trades were deregulated. Insurance firms could compete based on price and terms for the first time.

Despite all of these changes, some observers have questioned whether these steps have been sufficient to warrant being called "reform." The main charge has been that a final piece of the big bang, the increased stringency of accounting standards, has not been as meaningful as defenders of the reforms claim. The big bang legislation required Japanese corporations to adopt accounting rules closer to international standards. Assets that previously could be listed at book value, the value at which they were purchased, had to be listed at market value. This change meant that firms that had concealed losses by continuing to report high values for land and stocks purchased near the peak of the bubble now had to reveal to the world the extent of their losses. Corporations were also required to issue accounting reports on a consolidated basis, a change that was designed to make it more difficult for struggling firms to hide losses in subsidiaries. The problem, according to critics, is that chief financial officers, accountants, and auditors have not been subject to sanctions when they issue inaccurate financial reports. Even when the bankruptcy of a firm has revealed a statement by a financial officer or an auditor to be false, these individuals have not been subject to legal sanctions.

Mikuni Akio, the founder of Japan's leading independent bond-rating agency, and his coauthor, R. Taggart Murphy, charge that these enforcement failures have made the accounting reforms ineffective.[34] Investors still do not have accurate information on the financial health of firms listed on stock exchanges. Neither have they had an incentive to demand more accurate information as long as the government has been willing to protect investors from all or most of the risk of loss due to bank failure or corporate bankruptcy. The bending of accounting rules that has persisted under these conditions, by making weak Japanese corporations look more solvent than they are, has given banks an excuse to avoid having to push borrowers to restructure. The inaccurate financial reports, by making banks seem more solvent than they are, have also reduced pressure on banks to write off bad loans. As a result, Japan has yet to see banks emerge as effective agents for increasing the productivity of capital. The failure to enforce the advertised accounting standards has also delayed the emergence of a principal-agent model of capitalism in which stock- and bond-holders work to assure that capital is allocated productively.[35]

The critique of the big bang reforms by Mikuni and Murphy is consistent with my own criticism in chapter 6 of delays and insufficient conditionality in the Japanese government's handling of the bad-loan crisis. Both through its handling of bank bailouts and accounting rules, the government has attempted to prevent financial sector reforms from destroying the entire bank-centered system of social protection for firms and their workers. Nevertheless, the government's success (thus far) in preventing the big bang reforms from transforming the entire Japanese economy does not diminish the significance of the reform for the financial services sector. This sector has been transformed by liberalization. Firms are competing vigorously across what were once impenetrable segmental boundaries. A big reason Japanese banks and securities firms and insurance companies are in such trouble today is because competition has eliminated the excess profits they used to earn by operating as regulated cartels.[36] All of these firms now have to compete by offering lower prices and better service.

We will return in the final chapter to the question of whether the Japanese government can continue to protect the rest of the Japanese system of social protection from the challenges of the big bang reforms. The immediate question for us now is the question of why the government adopted these reforms in the first place, when reforms in so many other areas (labor markets, electricity markets, public sector reform) were being watered down? Henry Laurence, looking only at reforms in this sector, emphasizes the important role played by exit dynamics in causing financial service firms and the Ministry of Finance to change their positions. The rapid shift in financial transactions to overseas markets was apparent as soon as it began. These trends were noted in studies issued by both the bankers' association and MOF advisory councils. A 1986 survey of corporations by the bond underwriters' association showed that price and terms were the critical factors causing Japanese corporations to move business overseas.[37] Diagnosis and prescription were quite simple matters given this context. Even without Japanese corporations complaining to regulators about high costs, the banks and MOF could see that exit trends were creating a problem that had to be addressed, recognize exactly what was causing the exit, and diagnose how to go about reversing the trend.

The clarity with which exit trends were interpreted and digested in this issue area obviously contrasts starkly with what we observed in areas like labor markets and electricity. When firms began moving overseas to escape high costs in those sectors, bureaucrats were much slower to diagnose this type of hollowing out as a "problem." They found it much harder to say with certainty that prices for specific inputs like electricity or labor were the reason for specific cases of FDI. And they were not able to argue with any confidence that reforms designed to lower costs would bring much of this FDI home. A comparison of policymaking in a number of high-cost sectors, therefore, makes clear that the dynamics Laurence found to be at work in the financial services sector do not necessarily operate to generate a full range of economic reforms. The greater immediacy and clarity of the exit trend in the financial sector was a necessary condition that propelled the more significant reforms implemented in this sector.

The two cases of far-reaching reform examined in this chapter are important in their own right. The Long-term Care Insurance program is the first expensive new social insurance program created in Japan since the 1960s. With large numbers already benefiting from the program and many more having paid into the insurance program in the expectation of future benefits, it is likely to be an enduring element of Japan's system of social protection for years to come. What makes the story of its passage, and the Gold Plans that preceded it, all the more remarkable is the way these programs were structured to relieve family members, and especially women, of much of the burden of caring for aging relatives. Given how the willingness of families to care for aging relatives was extolled as recently as the 1980s as a virtue of the Japanese "welfare society," and how older Japanese still express a desire to be looked after by relatives rather than paid strangers, the creation of a large program that goes against the norms of relying on family caregivers to this degree is a striking policy development that calls for explication.

Similarly, the big bang reforms and the steps toward financial liberalization that preceded it stand out as an equally important break with the past pattern of regulation and cartels in this sector. As we have seen, banks played a vital role in making it possible for Japanese firms to play their outsized role in Japan's system of social protection. Because banks stood behind them, firms could afford to offer lifetime employment to their core workers and make long-term commitments to their suppliers and other business partners. By liberalizing this sector, the government risked collapse of this entire system—which it was stubbornly working to prop up in so many other ways—by exposing banks and other types of financial institutions to vigorous market competition.

While the two cases are important in their own right and have implications for the sustainability of the traditional Japanese system of social protection as a whole, in the remainder of this chapter I want to focus on what they have to teach us about the forces that shape economic and social reform in Japan and (by logic) in other countries as well. The cases are important because of how they contrast with the much larger number of partial and incomplete reforms that have emerged in Japan over the past twenty years in similar economic and social policy spheres.

The contrasting outcomes cannot be explained by differences in the political opportunity structure. Women who were frustrated with the absence of employment rules and childcare services conducive to balancing work and child rearing and those frustrated by their eldercare responsibilities both felt the need for reforms that challenged entrenched gender role norms. Liberal Democratic Party politicians spoke against "stranger care" of children as well as elders, calling on women and families to play the traditional role expected of them by society. The absence of women at senior levels in the bureaucracy and in the LDP worked against reforms in both areas. Nevertheless, we saw much more significant reforms, accompanied by infinitely greater expenditures of public funds, to relieve women of their eldercare burdens than we did in the area of childcare, where reforms have been limited and poorly funded.

Likewise, bankers and insurance company executives were just as eager to avoid liberalization and the uncertainties associated with having to compete in an open market as were the electric utilities, the postmasters, and the executives of Japan Highway. All of these industries had benefited from regulations that allowed them to avoid having to compete on price and had taken advantage of this protection to charge much higher prices, to pay more generous salaries, and to provide job guarantees and hefty benefit packages. To protect their cozy operating environments, all of them had developed close relations with the Liberal Democratic Party, complete with organizations designed to deliver money and votes to the long-ruling party. All of the political rules that made the Japanese political system responsive to demands from "vested interests" favored bankers just as much as they favored postmasters and electricity firms. Despite these similarities in the political context, we have seen that the government implemented far-reaching liberalization only in the financial services sector and not in any of the other sectors surveyed.[38] In terms of the political opportunity structure, reform of labor markets should have been *easier* than reform of the financial sector in that the unions that were the direct beneficiaries of regulations that preserved the lifetime employment system were not a core constituency of the LDP, while banks and other financial firms were for many years among the top financial donors to the party.

What explains the different outcomes across these similar cases is the contrast in *exit dynamics* that characterize each sphere. The pattern observed across the case studies is summarized in table 8.2. Most of the cases are ones characterized by "limited exit." Exit is not easy and takes time to cumulate in ways that create clear "problems" for society, and yet it is sufficient to provide an escape valve for those most frustrated with the status quo. In these situations, voices favoring reform fall silent while exit is insufficient to generate a policy response by bureaucrats, so we see little meaningful reform.

This pattern characterized all of the areas that generated exit through FDI (labor market reform, electricity market liberalization, and the various topics covered under public sector reform). When manufacturing FDI began growing in the 1980s, it was not initially regarded as a hollowing-out problem and was encouraged by state officials. Even though the inflexibility and costs of Japanese labor markets, the high costs of electricity, and rising tax rates all provided motivation in some instances of FDI, the connection between these policies and FDI were so murky as to make bureaucrats' work of diagnosing the problem and prescribing solutions diffi-

TABLE 8.2.
Exit, voice, and reform outcomes

	No Way Out	Limited Exit	Ample Exit
Exit/Voice patterns:	Reform driven by voice, when inability to exit drives those frustrated with the status quo to mobilize in the political arena	Little reform, when exit by those who might have mobilized in favor of change reduces pressure in the political arena but doesn't cause enough immediate and obvious pain to generate a meaningful response by bureaucrats	Reform driven by exit, when obvious problems created when large numbers of those frustrated with status quo seek to escape from the problem cause bureaucrats to craft meaningful solutions and push them through
Reform Outcomes:	Long-term care insurance	Labor market reforms; electricity liberalization; public works cutbacks; FILP and postal reform; highway privatization; badloan cleanup; childcare leave; childcare centers expansion	Big bang reforms in financial services sector

cult. Yet the availability of these exit opportunities enabled those Japanese manufacturers most sensitive to high costs to escape from their worst effects. Firms could subsidize high-cost, inflexible Japanese labor by taking advantage of low-cost, flexible Chinese labor, charting corporate survival strategies that did not require firms to challenge the lifetime employment system for core workers in Japan. In the absence of strong pressure from firms to reform labor laws, liberalize electricity markets, and accelerate public sector reform, reforms fell victim to the domestic political forces favoring the status quo.

We saw similar dynamics at work in the policy areas related to women with children. When some young women began putting off marriage in order to focus on careers, in part because they worried that work rules and social benefits would not allow them to continue in their chosen professions once they married and had children, officials were sure the resulting dip in fertility rates was temporary. It took officials many years before they concluded that the decline in fertility was likely to be deep and sustained and realized it would cause economic problems for the nation. Even then, they had difficulty showing that any specific reform would reverse this trend. For all of these reasons, neither this type of exit nor the exit of women from careers generated a sufficient response from officials.

But meanwhile these types of exit *were* sufficient to shrink the size of the constituency that should have been the vanguard of a strong young women's movement devoted to changing public policies and gender-role norms in Japan: working mothers struggling to hold onto careers in the face of the difficulties the system presented. Because many of these women did not have children, they never developed the motivation to demand changes in work rules that would be needed to enable future women like them to have successful careers *and* children. Those who gave up their careers and settled for full-time motherhood or part-time work also lost the motivation to challenge the gender-role segregation of the status quo. The "quiet rebellion" has yet to produce the "equality" some women hoped it would deliver.

The two cases that were the focus of this chapter show how exit dynamics that are distinct from the "limited exit" pattern helped produce more far-reaching changes in specific segments of Japan's system of social protection. The first case study, of the LTCI program, showed what could happen—even in a political opportunity structure as hostile to women as Japan's—when women had no way out. Stuck with care duties that placed them at severe economic risk and personal hardship and unable to choose not to have parents, Japanese women built women's groups from scratch and demanded action. They formed grassroots organizations to demand action and participated in all stages of the policy process. They defined the problem, participated in advisory councils that devised solutions, and pressured the government into approving a large new social insurance program.

The big bang case showed what happens at the opposite end of the exit spectrum when the affected groups (consumers of financial services) can easily escape, in this instance from the high costs of investing and borrowing in Japan. They didn't even have to mobilize in the political arena to demand reforms. Merely by taking advantage of the opportunities to raise funds and invest abroad, they transformed the politics surrounding financial market liberalization. The providers of financial services became advocates of reform, as a way of retaining the business that was flowing overseas, and the Ministry of Finance became the author of one liberalization step after another, culminating in the big bang reforms.

The story of economic and social reform in Japan is therefore more complex than can be captured in the "it's changing"—"no it's not" debate. Some aspects of the system are changing dramatically, while others are stubbornly resistant to reform. In the concluding chapter we will examine what this pattern of uneven policy change portends for the future of Japan's system of social protection, but here let us consider its implications for our understanding of how policy is made in Japan and in other nations.

First, the findings challenge the globalization literature that assumes exit by capital works in tandem with the voice of capital to put pressure on welfare states and systems of social protection more broadly defined. Although not all of this literature assumes these forces are destined to bring about a convergence of all national political economies on the liberal Anglo-American model, those that find evidence that some countries have resisted convergence put exclusive emphasis on political structures (electoral systems, constitutional design, political parties, union structure) that enable interests with a stake in social protection to resist change. Political scientists working to explain why Japan has been slow to reform have similarly emphasized domestic political variables such as the electoral system and the power of the bureaucracy.

What we have seen in this study is that exit *too* can work against reform. Capital moving overseas in the form of FDI does not move rapidly enough or send clear enough signals to motivate reform on its own. Yet by giving firms an escape valve, limited exit of this type takes these potential advocates of liberalization and lower prices out of the domestic reform debate. To understand how national political economies are responding to globalization, we need to look at both exit and voice and appreciate the ways they can work against each other.

Second, the findings challenge those who assume that the demographic and labor market effects of exit by women (declining fertility and labor shortages) will naturally work in tandem with the voices of women's movements to transform systems of social protections that are built on outdated gender norms. The slow pace of change in Japan in the face of record low fertility rates and projected labor shortages certainly should give pause to those who assume exit will bring about a transformation of gender norms in that country. Of course, not all analysts of the gender implications of welfare state structures assume that these are converging toward a single gender-neutral model, but those who find differences across countries continue to place primary emphasis on the political opportunity structures (electoral systems, parties, union structures, and cultural norms) that facilitate reform in some places while blocking it in others. Scholars who have studied policies affecting women in Japan have likewise focused exclusively on that political system's hostility to the women's movement.

We have seen in this study as well that exit can work against reform. Women who might have become the leading advocates of change (who demonstrated they could do so when they had no way out) lose their personal motivation to invest their energies in social action when they exit from the difficulty of combining careers with family by giving up one or the other of these goals. In order to understand how systems of social protections are responding to demographic and labor market trends, we need to appreciate how the individual choices women make about career and family shape their propensity to mobilize in favor of changes in the work-family system. As in the case of capital, we need to look at both exit and voice and appreciate how they can work against each other.

Chapter 9

Toward a New System of Social Protection in Japan

Is Japan changing . . . or not? Every author and commentator covering Japan's political economy has taken a stand on this question, and their answers have been all over the map. Some have pointed to the big bang in finance and the rash of mergers in the financial services sector and proclaimed that Japan has turned the corner. It has joined the liberal economic order and will soon see above-average growth and a recovery from its decade of stagnation.[1] Most, emphasizing persistent foot-dragging on bad-loan cleanup and labor market reform by a string of Japanese prime ministers and the fact that even "proreform" Koizumi has been forced to compromise repeatedly on his top priority of public sector reform, have argued the opposite point of view, that Japan is not changing much at all.[2]

The reality is a mix of the two views. What you "see" depends on which part of the elephant you're feeling. If you work in Japan's financial district and see Japanese financial institutions scrambling to survive and you find yourself repeatedly updating work addresses in your Palm Pilot because of all of the job-hopping in your formerly staid business, you are likely to conclude that Japan has come a long way. But if you cover Japanese budgets and follow Japanese politics, or if the industry you study is construction or electric utilities, you are likely to have a much more jaded view. Your evaluation of social policy reform may similarly depend on whether you just signed your mother-in-law up for Long-term Care Insurance services or just had a child and had to give up on your career ambitions.

What I've aimed to do in this book is to take in the whole picture and try to make sense of what is happening to Japan's convoy system of production and protection, the system that once worked synergistically to deliver both "miracle" growth rates and social security by relying heavily on women and firms. The system *is* changing. The big bang and the financial liberalization that preceded it are real. Financial regulators and the banks can no longer play the critical role they used to play in protecting large firms from market pressures and helping them live up to their lifetime employment commitments—at least not without large subsidies from the public treasury. Exactly because the financial sector is under so much pressure, beneficiaries of the traditional system have clung ever more desperately to the pieces of the system that are still afloat: labor market rules making it difficult to lay off core workers; regulations that protect sectors like electricity from competition; spending on public works; bank bailouts with few strings attached; and the structures of FILP and postal savings that allow the state to disguise subsidies to sectors of the economy that would otherwise have to shrink substantially. These elements of the old system have not changed much at all and have in fact become more important in the last decade and a half.

The way the system relies on women has changed as well. The LTCI program is huge and offers women with aging family members a rich menu of social services to relieve them of having to bear the burden of eldercare on their own. There have also been some new programs benefiting working women with children, such as childcare leave. Women in most full-time careers, however, find the child-related social benefits and work rules insufficient. About 80 percent are still leaving full-time work after having children.

Changed But Not Transformed

While Japan's convoy system is changing, it has not yet been transformed into a new system that synergistically provides both production and protection. Japan's GDP grew by a decent 2.7 percent in 2004, but growth was confined to the first quarter of the year and was concentrated in the sectors that have been the stalwarts of the old order, electronics and automobiles, riding the "China wave."[3] The largest firms in these sectors are charting survival strategies that rely on China-based production that will ultimately accelerate the hollowing out of Japanese manufacturing. During the transitional phase, however, they have increased exports to China of parts and equipment. One year of decent growth, the result at least in part of sales of the nation's "seed grain," is not enough to support the conclusion that Japan has turned the corner after twelve years in which growth averaged just 1.01 percent. That the boost provided by exports to China has not created sustained growth driven by domestic demand was confirmed by data released in June 2005 showing that the Japanese economy shrank during two of the final three quarters of 2004.[4]

Another reason for concern about whether reform has been sufficient to make the system more productive is the nation's continuing failure to create new growth industries and service sectors to eventually take the place of automobiles and electronics. Between 1982 and 2002, the list of the Top 30 firms in the United States (by stock market value) was transformed completely. Just six firms that were on the list in 1982 were still there in 2002.[5] Kodak, Xerox, RCA, and nineteen others had fallen off the list, but the United States had replaced them with twenty-four newcomers, many of which had not even existed in 1982. Japan's Top 30 list, in contrast, looked virtually the same in 2001 as it had in 1981. Just seven of those on the list were new private firms.[6] Economists have shown that only a small share of the increase in an economy's productivity comes from existing firms taking steps to make themselves more productive. Economies get a much larger boost from the process of "creative destruction" that sees new and more productive firms replace and take market share away from unproductive ones.[7] Japan is not tapping into this source of growth, and consequently it has been unable to significantly boost its productivity.[8] Its labor productivity has grown at a rate of only 1.4 percent a year since 1992, and despite the reforms adopted so far, this rate has accelerated only slightly in the most recent years (2002–04).[9]

One would expect that the effort Japan has made to keep its largest firms at the top of the list would mean, at least, that the modified convoy system is serving its *protective* purpose. On the contrary, large numbers of Japanese are falling through the cracks. The unemployment rate in 2004 remained near 5 percent. The proportion of adults who were not in the workforce was up from 35.8 percent in 1992 to 39.1 percent in 2003, suggesting that large numbers of discouraged workers had simply stopped looking for work.[10] A total of 19,458 businesses declared bankruptcy in 2002, more than in any year since 1984, and the Teikoku Databank continued to report high rates of bankruptcy in 2003 and 2004.[11] Suicides continued at near-record levels, with 32,325 killing themselves in 2004—many for financial reasons.[12]

More disturbing in terms of what it portends for the future of the current safety net is the fact that so many Japanese fell through the cracks even as the government was going deep into debt in an effort to patch the cracks as they were forming. When it became clear after the banking crisis took a turn for the worse in 1998 that the banks would not be able to carry many small and medium-sized businesses on their books, the government stepped in by offering to lend ¥12 trillion ($100 billion) to these firms through the Japan Finance Corporation for Small Business, part of the FILP system.[13] In effect, Japanese taxpayers had picked up the tab for a part of the convoy system that had once been handled by the banks.

By 2002 the government had used another ¥60 trillion to clean up after failing financial institutions and to inject capital into surviving banks. These funds were used in large part to keep money flowing to firms that were on the verge of insolvency. Rather than insisting that the banks write off their bad debt quickly in exchange for this money, the government allowed banks to burn through much of it without making a large dent in their bad-loan backlog. Financial authorities sometimes encouraged banks to throw good money after bad to keep struggling firms like Sogō afloat and to fulfill quotas of loans to small and medium-sized businesses.[14] In this way, too, taxpayers were now footing the bill where banks had once served this purpose.

These expenditures of public money were just a small part of the surge in deficit spending that the government has relied on to keep the economy from slipping into a deflationary spiral. Rather than using this fiscal stimulus as anesthesia—a temporary boost to the economy applied concurrently with the surgery of structural re-form—the Japanese government used it as a narcotic that would let it forget the structural problems for another day.[15] By 2001, when Koizumi took over as prime minister with a popular promise to bring wasteful public spending under control, the economy had become so dependent on annual fiscal deficits of 6 to 7 percent of GDP that he had to abandon his efforts to put a lid on public borrowing. Two years later, Japan's public debt had grown to 166 percent of GDP—a peacetime record for an industrialized nation—and was projected to reach 208 percent by 2008.[16] This effort to patch the cracks in the convoy system with public money is clearly unsustainable. The old system is unraveling, but a synergistic new system able to provide protection *and* production has yet to emerge.

Neither has the convoy system been transformed in terms of its reliance on un-paid caregiving by women, despite the addition of several social programs. While women responsible for the care of frail elderly relatives now have more support from social services, those with small children continue to bear most of the burden alone. Husbands are more overworked than ever and unable to help out much at home, especially since more of them now have to worry about the possibility of fu-ture layoffs. Some corporations have created leave and flextime programs to retain their most valued female workers after they have children, but firms that have ex-cess workers and employ women without valued skills continue to have ample room to push mothers into quitting by making use of the leeway afforded under work standards (e.g., by demanding overtime and transfers). Childcare leave and child-care services are being used by a small minority of women eager to hold on to career jobs, but in the absence of broader support from employers and husbands and ad-ditional social services, few women have the capability or the will to pull off the career-and-family balancing act.

The result is that most Japanese women are choosing family *or* career, even when they began their working life hoping to have both. The large number opting not to marry and have children pushed the fertility rate down to a record low of 1.289 in 2004. The rate for Tokyo fell below 1.00, suggesting that the national rate still had room to fall. Of those working women who have had children, over 80 per-cent are leaving the full-time workforce at least temporarily. If they return later, they tend to do so as poorly paid part-time workers.

These trends, too, are unsustainable. Japan's failure to make it easier for women to continue working with children has left it with a projected decline in the working-age population and in the worker-to-retiree ratio that are deeper and steeper than those facing any other industrialized nation. This decline has saddled future generations of Japanese with huge fiscal burdens—for pensions, for health care, and for Long-term Care Insurance—that will have to be borne through higher tax and social insurance contribution rates or more public debt. In this way too, Japan has purchased protection now, in the form of unpaid childcare by women, by selling its "seed grain," the population of workers it needs for future production.

Why Has Japan's Policy Response Been Inadequate?

Why have the Japanese put up with such an inadequate policy response? Why haven't they demanded that the government do something to revive the economy and head off national decline? Given the nation's record of revival and reinvention when faced with previous challenges, the arrival of the "black ships" and the devastation of World War II, one would have expected the Japanese to respond to this challenge too. What has happened this time? Where is the passion and energy that propelled Japan's earlier reform campaigns? The answer, I have argued, lies in the new mix of "exit" *and* "voice" strategies on the part of individuals and firms struggling to adapt to the changing socioeconomic environment.

Most of the literature analyzing Japan's recent economic difficulties has blamed politics, the structures of the political system that have given voice to the opponents of reform.[17] Scholars such as Mark Ramseyer and Frances Rosenbluth, Brian Woodall, and Kent Calder have pointed to the influence of the old lower house electoral system, which created incentives for LDP politicians to join factions and raise large sums of money to secure the "personal votes" they needed. Politicians' need for organized votes and money made them easy prey for opponents of reform who were willing to offer this help in exchange for the politicians' promises to block reform.[18] Others, such as Edward Lincoln, have argued that it comes down to simple political arithmetic. The number of voters benefiting from the status quo is greater than the number who might benefit from reform.[19]

Other political scientists writing about Japan, like Steven Vogel, have explained the delay in reform by pointing to the structures and norms of the bureaucracy and intermediary associations such as parties and big-business groups. The Ministry of Finance has long operated on the conviction that its regulatory power is vital to maintaining order in the financial system and the economy as a whole, making it a persistent opponent of liberalization. Keidanren includes both export-oriented firms like Toyota that would benefit from reform and sheltered sectors like cement and electricity that would be hurt by it. The leading political parties similarly have ties to a range of labor and business groups. As a result, no leading interest group or party has emerged to advocate bold economic reforms.[20]

Finally, scholars writing on gender policy, such as Susan Pharr, Frank Upham, and Mikanagi Yumiko, have likewise blamed the norms and structures of the political system.[21] Both the bureaucracy and the LDP have been dominated by men and by conservative norms that value the role women have traditionally played in the family over and above their potential to contribute through paid employment. Given this power structure, women's groups have had only limited opportunity to challenge public policies that push them to give up work and stay at home with their children.

The case studies of reform initiatives in this book include a great deal of evidence that politicians, interest groups, and norms have indeed blocked policy change. We saw how the traditional values of labor bureaucrats made them only halfhearted advocates of the "gender equal society" they were supposedly seeking to create. We saw how Ministry of Finance bureaucrats slowed down the pace of financial liberalization and sought to maintain their ability to protect the convoy system of banks. And in virtually every case of watered-down reform, in areas ranging from postal privatization to Japan Highway reform to work-rule changes, we saw LDP politicians playing a key role in blocking more far-reaching change.

Although the system's role in generating voices opposed to reform is an important part of the story, in this book I have focused on the absence of *countervailing* voices. It is true that many individuals, firms, and interest groups, as well as politicians and bureaucrats, benefit from the status quo, but many others do not. In particular, export-oriented firms and women have grown increasingly frustrated with the costs they bear under the convoy system of social protection. Why haven't they rebelled? If the structures of parties and interest groups are so constraining, why haven't they created new ones?

The answer, I have argued, lies in Japan's very success. For the first time in the country's history, individuals and firms have the wealth and freedom necessary to pursue private solutions to their economic problems—solutions that make perfect sense from an individual or corporate perspective but actually aggravate economic problems at the national level. Firms that were previously too poor and too regulated to pursue FDI as a strategy for getting around inefficiencies in Japan's home market now have ample resources and complete freedom to invest as much as they wish overseas. Likewise, women who were once too financially dependent to consider opting out of marriage and motherhood now have the resources to remain single. With the opening up of these exit opportunities, the passion and energy that women and firms might have devoted to political campaigns to transform the system of convoy capitalism have evaporated.

In the chapters that looked at Japan's response to industrial hollowing out and women's declining fertility, we saw how the decisions of firms and women to exit in these ways has taken them out of the policy process. Firms that had located facilities overseas to escape labor regulations in Japan had less motivation to seek controversial changes in the lifetime employment system at home. Once the firms with the highest electricity usage had relocated their most energy-intensive operations abroad or secured their own electricity through self-generation, they had less need to push Keidanren to take a proreform stand. Once women had opted not to have children, they had less motivation to join women's movements seeking expanded childcare services. To understand the predominance of voices opposed to reform in Japan, one has to understand how exit opportunities have drawn supporters of reform out of the political process.

In arguing that exit slows down reform in this way, I challenge another body of scholarship that sees globalization and demographic trends driving change in Japan, over the objections of political opponents. T. J. Pempel, in his book on "regime change," argues that recent progress in reform has been driven by financial and industrial globalization.[22] Henry Laurence similarly emphasizes how financial liberalization has been propelled forward by the decisions of large numbers of financial service customers to conduct transactions overseas.[23] The most optimistic of the recent crop of books may be the forthcoming volume by Yves Tiberghien, which sees foreign investors in the Japanese stock market scrutinizing a wide range of economic policies and business practices in Japan and accelerating structural reform by exiting, or threatening to exit, the market when reform does not move fast enough.[24]

While confirming the role of ample exit in driving the process of financial liberalization, I challenge the assumption that similar dynamics are propelling reform across the board. Exit does not speak for itself. Government officials watching exit trends have to diagnose the problem, sell solutions, and even mobilize support for reform in the Diet. We saw how all of these steps were more difficult when exit took women and firms out of the political process. It took years for officials to realize that industrial hollowing out and declining fertility were "problems" that required a government response, and even then they were uncertain what to do. Bureaucrats who were sure that high electricity prices were driving firms to relocate overseas could not prove that lower prices would bring any of this investment back home. It was one thing to show that high labor costs were pushing manufacturers to relocate factories in China, but quite another to show that any specific regulatory reform would put a dent in this trend. However well intentioned they might be, Health and Welfare officials have not been able to engineer a gender role revolution based on fears of declining fertility. Except when exit takes place quickly and with a magnitude that makes problems and solutions obvious, it is not a substitute for voice in propelling socioeconomic reform.

Equilibrium or Not

Are we there yet? The social scientists' version of this nagging refrain heard from the backseat on long car rides is the question: Are we at equilibrium yet? What readers familiar with the latest debates on institutional change in economics, sociology, and political science want to know is whether the forces of exit and voice I have described have given Japan a new set of institutions and policies that are likely to remain in place for some time. Does the mix of reforms in some areas and little change in others shown in table 8.2 represent a new stable equilibrium where the component parts reinforce each other as they did when convoy capitalism was humming along?

It is worth considering the possibility that the current system represents an equilibrium. Many Japanese firms are finding ways to survive by relocating operations overseas. They seem to have adjusted, for example, to high electricity prices. The industries that use large quantities have either moved abroad or built self-generating capacity, and those that remain don't use enough to complain. Japanese women too have started to embrace the childless lifestyles (single and DINK) as alternatives to the married-with-children norms that were prescribed in the past. Perhaps women of the future will simply divide themselves neatly into childless career women on the one hand and mothers on the other, the former supplying Japan with labor and the latter giving the nation its children. It is tempting to imagine that the number of jobs lost to hollowing out might equal the shrinkage in the workforce due to the decline in fertility rates, producing equilibrium in the job market. Posit a steady increase in Japanese labor productivity, brought on by the big bang regulatory reforms, add a few immigrants, and the current system appears almost functional. Indeed, these circumstances suggest that the half-reformed status quo could continue for several more years. Nevertheless, the insights we have gained into how exit and voice have combined to shape the transformation of Japan's system of convoy capitalism so far tell us enough to know that the transformation is destined to continue. The status quo is not a stable equilibrium because the limited exit trends I have described are cumulating and interacting in ways that promise to turn the current trickle of exit into *ample* exit unless something happens to shift the exit and voice dynamics in a new direction. In this final section, I consider what ample exit might look like before turning to two other scenarios based on alternative exit-and-voice dynamics that might emerge in the next decade.

Race for the Exits

Given Japan's demographics and its current fiscal situation, the only way the nation can steer itself onto a sustainable macroeconomic path is by adopting fundamental social and economic reforms designed to boost productivity, encourage the participation of women and immigrants in the workforce, and facilitate work-family balance so that families can choose to have more children.[25] If the limited exit trends described in this book continue and the policy process consequently fails to adopt these reforms, the demographic and fiscal noose will tighten until the exit trends grow into a true "race for the exits" crisis involving a steeper fall in fertility rates, high levels of emigration, a collapse of confidence in government bond markets, and capital flight.

Japan's fiscal situation is already precarious. As noted above, the trajectory of its fiscal policy is likely to push the nation's gross public debt past the 200 percent of GDP threshold in 2008. At about the same time, the nation will have to begin footing the bill for the retirement of the giant baby boom cohort, the first of whom turn sixty in 2007. Under these circumstances, every year of delay in changing a system that relies on public subsidies to keep inefficient segments of the economy afloat, that pushes the nation's most competitive firms to locate production overseas, and that discourages women from combining work and motherhood makes it more difficult for the nation to balance its books.

Delay tightens the noose, first, because both debt and demographics cumulate over time according to the mathematical rules of compounding. The deficits the government is running in an effort to prop up inefficient sectors and make up for the slack in private demand are adding every year to the sum of public debt, with interest. Unless the government can bring its accounts into primary balance soon, these interest payments will grow exponentially until they account for so much annual spending that they provoke a debt crisis. Similarly, low fertility rates compound over time as each generation of women that is small because their mothers had few children have few children themselves. The Japanese government's demographers have run the numbers and projected that the nation will shrink at an increasing rate over the course of the next century if fertility rates stabilize at 1.39 children per woman. In the first fifty years, the population will shrink by 21 percent, but in the second fifty years, it will shrink by 36 percent.[26]

The second reason delay tightens the noose is because the fiscal and demographic crises are interactive: the faster the population is projected to decline, the more difficult it is for the government to balance its books, and the more the government raises taxes and cuts spending in order to balance its books, the worse the demographics get. We saw the first of these relationships at work in the pension reform process discussed in chapter 6. This reform was forced on the government because demographers faced with falling fertility rates projected a faster pace of decline in the working-age population and consequently larger future shortfalls in pension revenues. Under the new rules adopted to address this shortfall in 2004, employers and employees have been asked to begin paying 0.35 percent more in premiums each year until 2017, taking the premium rate from 13.5 percent to 18.3 percent. The fact that the fertility rate has now fallen to 1.29 (far below the projected 1.39) means that the premium levels approved in 2004 are already inadequate and will have to be raised again in the next round of pension reform, along with rates for health insurance and Long-term Care Insurance, which have yet to be adjusted to take into account the latest demographic data. The steeper and more prolonged the decline in fertility rates, the higher premiums will have to go.

It is more difficult to project how this worsening budget, tax, and social insurance climate will affect individuals and firms, but it seems likely that they will aggravate the problems of hollowing out and declining fertility. Firms paying increasingly steep social insurance fees will have additional reason to move jobs overseas. Individuals faced with high taxes and shaky pension programs are likely to further shrink the number of children they choose to have and may even opt for emigration. If tax and social insurance contribution rates continue to rise and confidence in the fiscal sustainability of Japanese pension and health programs declines, some of the nation's most ambitious young people are likely to choose to seek their fortunes overseas, in places like Shanghai, Singapore, London, and Los Angeles.

The way debt and demographics cumulate and interact guarantees that, in the absence of the kinds of fundamental reforms summarized at the start of this section, Japan will eventually face a public debt crisis, accompanied by rapid inflation and capital flight. Today the flow of money out of Japan is roughly offset by the flow of money coming in. Japan remains a net external creditor, and it still has the world's largest foreign currency reserves to fight any attack on the value of its currency. In the short term, these circumstances mean no one is likely to begin a capital flight stampede out of fear that the value of the yen is about to collapse. If current fiscal deficit and public debt trends continue, however, at some point Japanese government bond markets will realize that there is no way for the government to service its debt other than through the deliberate acceleration of inflation. No one can predict when the bond markets will panic, but when the government's debt service burden reaches a certain point, the markets will conclude that it has no way to pay back that debt in real yen. Expecting the authorities to generate inflation to erode the purchasing power of the yen, markets will start to demand an inflation-risk premium. As this pushes up debt service costs, bond market investors will become even more concerned and demand an even larger inflation-risk premium. This dynamic could lead to very high inflation, surging interest rates, and a falling value of the yen that leads those holding yen to shift their money into other currencies (capital flight). While the Japanese government may be able to postpone this dynamic some years into the future due to the patience of Japanese investors, who own almost all Japanese government bonds, even domestic holders of government bonds will take flight at some point.[27]

What will this mean for Japan's system of production and protection? The kind of race for the exits described above will certainly make it obvious to all that Japan has a problem and has to act. Ample exit will lead to an exit-driven policy response. By this point, however, there won't be much leeway for those involved in the Japanese political process to craft a new system of social protection more suited to the times. As in the case of every other nation that has faced capital flight, Japan will be forced to modify its system to do whatever it takes to get the money to stop flowing out of the home currency. There will be little room to create new programs to aid women with children or the unemployed, since the markets will be calling for budget cuts. Convoy capitalism is therefore likely to be transformed into a new system that looks much more like the Anglo-American model, with all of the inequality and insecurity the U.S. and British systems have to offer.

Reform Driven by Voters with No Way Out

The preceding scenario began with the qualifier "if the limited exit trends described in this book continue and the policy process consequently fails to adopt reforms" and traced what could happen if the resulting deterioration in public finances leads exit trends to accelerate and take the form of emigration and capital flight. It is possible, however, that before this happens, the socioeconomic environment will shift in ways that lead a larger number of Japanese to feel they have no way out: that FDI and decisions not to marry or not to pursue full-time work are no longer viable exit options.

One reason so many Japanese women have been willing to accept the career-or-family choice up to this point is because most of them have felt financially comfortable giving up one or the other of these goals. Given Japan's relatively low divorce rate (especially for families with children) and the job security of most male breadwinners, wives giving up their own careers to stay at home with the children have not felt that vulnerable to these financial risks. If the divorce rate increases or if male workers face more job insecurity, however, women will no longer perceive full-time motherhood or part-time work as viable exit options. If they already have children and face this situation, their plight will resemble the "no way out" dynamic that led Japanese women to mobilize in favor of insurance for long-term care. It will also resemble the situation U.S. and British women found themselves in when divorce rates and unemployment rates rose abruptly in the 1970s. Under these circumstances, desperate Japanese mothers could become a political constituency for expanded midcareer job opportunities and childcare services. They might also become radicalized to the point of demanding that their husbands share more of the housework duties so that they can pursue careers they need as insurance against economic risks.

The situation faced by single women who choose not to marry could also become more desperate. Now, many of these women live with their parents or benefit from their parents' financial support in other ways.[28] Also, income and consumption tax rates remain relatively low. This combination of circumstances means that most can live quite comfortably on a single income, even though many do not earn high salaries. As tax rates rise in the future and as the fathers of these women retire, however, they are likely to see their disposable income shrink dramatically. Some of these women, with irregular work histories, will find that they qualify for only a small pension and have no savings. When young women see older single women caught in these circumstances, they may come to regard giving up on (two-income) marriage as an unacceptable choice and demand policy and gender-norm changes that make marriage a more attractive option to them.

Finally, the circumstances that make FDI a viable exit strategy for firms and their workers could change in ways that make one or the other feel they have no way out. The willingness of labor unions to support firms' FDI strategies has been contingent on firms' commitments to retain core workers. Some firms are already finding that they cannot afford to live up to the terms of this deal, and in the future more firms, especially those with large numbers of aging blue-collar workers, may find themselves in this position. When this happens, FDI along with lifetime employment for domestic workers will no longer be seen as a viable exit strategy. Firms will be put in the position where they need more flexibility under labor market regulations to lay off core employees, and unions will find that they need an alternative safety net arrangement to replace the old commitment from employers.

At this point, both sides will have a much greater incentive to mobilize in the political arena to revise the current system of social protection.

Rechanneling Frustrations from Exit into Voice

The above analysis suggests that at some point in the future large numbers of Japanese citizens with no way out are likely to demand changes in the nation's system of social protection. Unfortunately, by the time the circumstances confronting women, firms, and workers deteriorate to the point where they have no way out, the Japanese government may be so deeply in debt that it has little fiscal capacity to fund expanded unemployment insurance, retraining programs, or childcare services. Women and workers may find, with their backs to the wall, that they want the state to play a larger, social democratic role, but they may not reach this conclusion until the state has run out of money. By default, Japan will then end up with the same Anglo-American system anticipated in the first scenario.

Japan's best hope for transforming its convoy system into a new one that is protective as well as productive therefore lies in the emergence before that no-exit stage of a political entrepreneur who is able to take the frustrations that are leading women and firms to choose exit options and rechannel this energy into the political process. In 2001 when the LDP surprised most observers by choosing Koizumi to be party leader and prime minister, many hoped that the new maverick leader might play this role. He spoke eloquently of "structural reform with no sacred cows" and called for a long list of reforms ranging from postal privatization to childcare service expansion. Keidanren leaders as well as many women voters welcomed his leadership.

Over the next several years, however, Koizumi disappointed many of these hopes. He largely abandoned his efforts to reform Japan Highway and ended up doing little to help women balance work and family. Keidanren leaders, after watching the prime minister compromise on one public sector reform project after another, started treating him as a lame duck. Women voters, who had given Koizumi's LDP a disproportionate 41 percent of their proportional representation votes in 2001, gave him just 29 percent in the upper house election of 2004.[29]

In the summer and fall of 2005, Koizumi made another attempt to burnish his reputation as a reformer, gambling big with his decision to expel thirty-seven members of his party and call a snap election after the LDP "rebels" voted against his postal privatization plan. While the passage of this legislation and Koizumi's success in helping his party win forty additional single-member seats in urban areas have made it possible for Koizumi to claim that he has "changed the LDP" as he promised, his accomplishments to date make it premature to conclude that Koizumi is the political entrepreneur who can rechannel exit into voice and transform Japan's system of social protection. Even his vaunted postal privatization plan does not guarantee that postal savings will stop flowing to public corporations.

The reason Koizumi's entrepreneurship has fallen short of its potential is that the prime minister has never even attempted to sell the public on the transformation of convoy capitalism as a goal. His rhetoric refers to reform merely as a means, as a period of *pain* that the nation has to endure. Most of his agenda has involved plans for privatization, budget cuts, and bad loan write-offs, all promising to increase bankruptcies and unemployment. With such an unattractive product to sell, it is little wonder that Koizumi has only been able to win legislative victories when the victims of reform were confined to a narrow group (like postmasters and postal workers).

What Japan needs is a political entrepreneur who can sell the public on the attractions of an alternative system that can provide social protection as well as growth, one that is clearly *superior to a system of convoy capitalism that is headed toward collapse*. The new system will need to be liberal, in the sense that the state will no longer count on firms to offer lifetime employment and will no longer prop up banks and firms. But the system will not leave individuals to the vagaries of market forces. It will offer more generous unemployment insurance, extensive retraining opportunities, and work rules and benefits that enable women with children to work full time. Labor market flexibility means workers will face the possibility of being laid off, but it also means midcareer workers and women who take time off to care for their young children will have opportunities to go back into the workforce and seek out new careers.

The leader will also need to speak frankly to the country about demographics. The country faces such a steep fall in its working-age population that it needs to prepare immediately to welcome immigrants into the nation. Immigrants should be incorporated into the Japanese labor market as a vital component of the labor supply, but they must also be welcomed into Japanese society as a source of cosmopolitan culture, energy, and creativity. To make sure there are nurses able to care for aging Japanese baby boomers a decade from now, the government should set up training centers for nurses in the Philippines and other labor-rich nations and offer Japanese language instruction and job placement services along with traditional training in technical skills. But Japan should not restrict immigrants to low-paid service jobs. It should also work to convince software engineers from Bangalore and Shanghai to immigrate to Tokyo instead of the Silicon Valley.

I do not see any prominent figures in Japanese politics calling for a set of policies along these lines. Maehara Seiji, the new leader of the Democratic Party of Japan, favors "economic reform" but has yet to offer a coherent reform vision. The party supports expanded childcare services and greater spending on unemployment insurance, but it has not supported the kind of work-rule changes that would be needed to create a flexible labor market. An awkward union of old Socialists and neoliberals who broke away from the LDP in part because they found that party too corrupt, the DPJ has yet to decide whether it wants to be the party of Margaret Thatcher or the party of Tony Blair.[30]

In the end, the direction Japan takes will depend on whether those frustrated with the status quo can be induced to participate in the process of crafting a new system of social protection in the political arena or whether they will continue their attempts to escape from the system through individual exit strategies. Whatever choices they make, we can be sure Japan's social and economic system will continue to change, but whether those changes continue the unraveling of the convoy system or shape a new productive and protective system that works synergistically in an era of globalization and gender role change will depend on the combination of exit and voice strategies that they pursue.

Notes

1. Exit, Voice, and Japan's Economic Problems

1. Personal interview, December 10, 2002.

2. Data for the earlier periods is from the Penn World Tables; the average for the most recent period and other recent GDP data presented here is based on Cabinet Office figures for calendar years 1991–2003—online at http://www.esri.cao.go.jp/jp/sna/qe043–2/ritu-jcy0432.csv (accessed January 5, 2005).

3. The figure is for incomes after taxes and transfers, based on data drawn from the Statistics Bureau of the Management and Coordination Agency, *Kakei chōsa nenpō* (Family Income and Expenditure Survey—FIES).

4. Malcolm Sawyer, "Income Distribution in OECD Countries," *OECD Outlook*, 1976.

5. Tachibanaki Toshiaki, *Nihon no keizai kakusa: Shotoku to shisan kara kangaeru* (Tokyo: Iwanami Shinsho, 1998), 41–42.

6. Among those emphasizing the productive advantages of the system is Chalmers Johnson, who used the term "developmental state" to describe the distinctive features of Japan's political economy. I have chosen to use the term "convoy capitalism," popularized by Richard Katz, to describe the Japanese economic system rather than Johnson's or Ulrike Schaede's "cooperative capitalism," because I believe it best reflects the combination of private sector and state structures that make the Japanese system so distinctive. See Chalmers Johnson, *MITI and the Japanese Miracle: The Growth of Industrial Policy, 1925–1975* (Stanford: Stanford University Press, 1982); Ulrike Schaede, *Cooperative Capitalism: Self-Regulation, Trade Associations, and Antimonopoly Law in Japan* (Oxford: Oxford University Press, 2000); and Richard Katz, *Japanese Phoenix: The Long Road to Economic Revival* (Armonk, N.Y.: M. E. Sharpe, 2003).

7. For an account of how European welfare states developed mutually reinforcing productive and protective elements, see Philip Manow, "Comparative Institutional Advantages of Welfare State Regimes and New Coalitions in Welfare State Reforms," in *The New Politics of the Welfare State, ed.* Paul Pierson (Oxford: Oxford University Press, 2001), 146–64.

8. FIES data source cited in note 3. For a more complete evaluation of data on income inequality in Japan relative to other nations, see Leonard Schoppa, "Globalization and the Squeeze on the Middle Class: Does Any Version of the Postwar Social Contract Meet the Challenge?" in

Postwar Social Contracts under Stress: The Middle Classes of Japan, Europe, and America at the Century's End, ed. Olivier Zunz, Leonard Schoppa, and Nobuhiro Hiwatari (New York: Russell Sage, 2002), 319–44.

9. There were fifty-seven hundred homeless people in Tokyo in 2001, double the number five years earlier—David Drueger, "No Pain, No Gucci," *Far Eastern Economic Review* (July 12, 2001): 25.

10. Tachibanaki, *Nihon no keizai kakusa.*

11. See figure 6.3 in this volume.

12. This is the International Monetary Fund's figure for Japan's gross public debt in 2003—*World Economic Outlook* (April 2004): 12.

13. Richard Katz, *Japan—The System That Soured: The Rise and Fall of the Japanese Economic Miracle* (Armonk, N.Y.: M. E. Sharpe, 1998), 99–106.

14. Peter Hartcher, *The Ministry: How Japan's Most Powerful Institution Endangers World Markets* (Boston: Harvard Business School Press, 1998).

15. Jeffry A. Frieden and Ronald Rogowski, "The Impact of the International Economy on National Policies: An Analytical Overview," in *Internationalization and Domestic Politics,* ed. Robert O. Keohane and Helen Milner (Cambridge: Cambridge University Press, 1996), 25–47.

16. Two exceptions in the case of Japan are Ito Peng, "Social Care in Crisis: Gender, Demography, and Welfare State Restructuring in Japan," *Social Policy* (Fall 2002): 411–43; and Margarita Estevez-Abe, "Multiple Logics of the Welfare State: Skills, Protection, and Female Labor in Japan and Selected OECD Countries," *U.S.-Japan Program Occasional Papers* 99–02, 1999.

17. T. J. Pempel, *Regime Shift: Comparative Dynamics of the Japanese Political Economy* (Ithaca: Cornell University Press, 1998), 162–67.

18. Albert O. Hirschman, *Exit, Voice, and Loyalty: Responses to Decline in Firms, Organizations, and States* (Cambridge: Harvard University Press, 1970).

19. Theda Skocpol, "Bringing the State Back In: Strategies of Analysis in Current Research," in *Bringing the State Back In,* ed. Peter B. Evans, Dietrich Rueschemeyer, and Theda Skocpol (Cambridge: Cambridge University Press, 1985), 3–37.

20. Albert O. Hirschman, "Exit, Voice, and the Fate of the German Democratic Republic: An Essay in Conceptual History," *World Politics* 45, no. 2 (January 1993): 176.

21. Figure 1.2 and the systematic elaboration of how "exit dynamics" are likely to be related to reform outcomes are my own elaborations on Hirschman's logic. For a more formal treatment that derives some of the same implications emphasized here, see Scott Gehlbach, "A Political Model of Exit and Voice," unpublished manuscript, Department of Political Science, University of Wisconsin, 2004. Like Gehlbach, I subsume Hirshman's third term, "loyalty," in the calculation of exit costs. Hirschman argued that the responsiveness of a social organization would be better if its members were "loyal" and did not cut and run at the first sign of trouble. Some reviewers, including Brian Barry, "Review Article: 'Exit, Voice, and Loyalty,'" *British Journal of Political Science* 4, no. 1 (January 1974): 79–108, called his use of this term an "ad hoc equation filler." The predictions based on the logic summarized here do not depend on the existence of "loyalty," but such sentiments could be seen as part of the cost of exit that is distinct from more quantifiable costs such as the cost of buying a more expensive home in a different school district. Barry also faulted Hirschman's model for suggesting that exit and voice are either-or alternatives when in fact individuals can choose "silent non-exit" or "exit plus voice." Indeed, low-cost exit gives those threatening to leave significant bargaining leverage, allowing them to combine threats of exit with voice to gain maximum concessions. My model recognizes that "exit plus voice" is a possible outcome when exit costs are very low, treating this as one mechanism through which low-cost exit can drive reform at the right end of figure 1.2. While recognizing this possibility, my model emphasizes what Gehlbach calls the "dynamic effects of exit" in the medium range, where exit is too

costly to allow voice to be amplified by credible threats of exit but too low to generate voice via the "no way out" dynamic. Within this range, exit reduces the motivation to use voice by "increasing the relative attractiveness of silence."

22. This is, of course, the aim of the "school voucher" reform movement. See John E. Chubb and Terry M. Moe, *Politics, Markets, and America's Schools* (Washington, D.C.: Brookings Institution, 1990).

23. See Ronald Dore, *Flexible Rigidities: Industrial Policy and Structural Adjustment in the Japanese Economy, 1970–1980* (Stanford: Stanford University Press, 1986), and Ronald Dore, *Stock Market Capitalism: Welfare Capitalism: Japan and Germany versus the Anglo-Saxons* (Oxford: Oxford University Press, 2000).

24. Anthony Downs, *An Economic Theory of Democracy* (New York: Harper, 1957); Mancur Olson, *The Logic of Collective Action: Public Goods and the Theory of Groups* (Cambridge: Harvard University Press, 1965); and Mancur Olson, *The Rise and Decline of Nations: Economic Growth, Stagflation, and Economic Rigidities* (New Haven: Yale University Press, 1982).

2. Taking Exit and Voice Seriously

1. Frieden and Rogowski, "The Impact of the International Economy on National Policies: An Analytical Overview," in *Internationalization and Domestic Politics,* ed. Robert O. Keohane and Helen V. Milner (Cambridge: Cambridge University Press, 1996), 25–47.

2. Richard Clayton and Jonas Pontusson, "Welfare-State Retrenchment Revisited: Entitlement Cuts, Public Sector Restructuring, and Inegalitarian Trends in Advanced Capitalist Societies," *World Politics* 51 (October 1998): 67–98.

3. See various contributions to Paul Pierson, ed., *The New Politics of the Welfare State* (Oxford: Oxford University Press, 2001), but especially his introduction and conclusion. See also Cathie Jo Martin, "Corporatism from the Firm Perspective: Employers and Social Policy in Denmark and Britain," *British Journal of Political Science* 34 (2004): 1–21. The reference to social democratic and Christian Democratic welfare regimes comes from Gøsta Esping-Andersen's *Three Worlds of Welfare Capitalism* (Princeton: Princeton University Press, 1990). The third "regime" is the liberal one.

4. Geoffrey Garrett and Peter Lange, "Internationalization, Institutions, and Political Change," in *Internationalization and Domestic Politics,* ed. Keohane and Milner, 48–75; and Geoffrey Garrett, *Partisan Politics in the Global Economy* (Cambridge: Cambridge University Press, 1998). The institutional features listed here are just some of those identified as important in the literature. See also the chapters by Giuliano Bonoli and Herbert Kitschelt in *New Politics of the Welfare State,* ed. Pierson, 238–302.

5. Garrett and Lange, "Internationalization, Institutions, and Political Change," 73.

6. Frances M. Rosenbluth, "Internationalization and Electoral Politics in Japan," in *Internationalization and Domestic Politics,* ed. Keohane and Milner, 137–56. See also Frances Rosenbluth and Michael F. Thies, "The Electoral Foundations of Japan's Banking Regulation," *Policy Studies Journal* 29, no. 1 (2001): 23–37.

7. Steven Vogel, "Can Japan Disengage? Winners and Losers in Japan's Political Economy, and the Ties That Bind Them," *Social Science Japan Journal* 2, no. 1 (April 1999): 3–21. See also Vogel, "The Crisis of German and Japanese Capitalism: Stalled on the Road to the Liberal Market Model?" *Comparative Political Studies* 34, no. 10 (December 2001): 1103–33; Vogel, "When Interests Are Not Preferences: The Cautionary Tale of Japanese Consumers," *Comparative Politics* 31, no. 2 (January 1999): 187–207; and Lonny E. Carlile and Mark C. Tilton, eds., *Is Japan Really Changing Its Ways?* (Washington, D.C.: Brookings Institution, 1998).

8. T. J. Pempel, *Regime Shift: Comparative Dynamics of the Japanese Political Economy* (Ithaca: Cornell University Press, 1998).

9. Philip G. Cerny, "Globalization and the Changing Logic of Collective Action," *International Organization* 49, no. 4 (Autumn 1995): 595–625; Paulette Kurzer, *Business and Banking: Political Change and Economic Integration in Western Europe* (Ithaca: Cornell University Press, 1993); William Greider, *One World, Ready or Not: The Manic Logic of Global Capitalism* (New York: Simon and Schuster, 1997); Jeffrey A. Winter, *Power in Motion: Capital Mobility and the Indonesian State* (Ithaca: Cornell University Press, 1996).

10. Helen V. Milner and Robert O. Keohane, "Internationalization and Domestic Politics: An Introduction," in *Internationalization and Domestic Politics*, ed. Keohane and Milner, 19.

11. Robert H. Bates and Da-Hsiang Donald Lien, "A Note on Taxation, Development, and Representative Government," *Politics and Society* 14, no. 1 (1985): 53–70.

12. Their model is based on the assumption the state is a single actor (the king) and mobile asset holders have control over critical resources that the king needs to be able to tax in order to win wars. They argue that in this situation the king will be much more responsive to the demands of those who are exiting (or threatening to exit) than those who remain in the country because he realizes that unless he shares power with mobile asset holders, they will take their assets elsewhere and cause him to lose wars.

13. Geoffrey Garrett, "Capital Mobility, Trade, and the Domestic Politics of Economic Policy," *International Organization* 49, no. 4 (Autumn 1995): 657–87; Garrett, "Global Markets and National Politics: Collision Course or Virtuous Circle?" *International Organization* 52, no. 4 (Autumn 1998): 787–824; Garrett, *Partisan Politics in the Global Economy.*

14. Henry Laurence, *Money Rules: The New Politics of Finance in Britain and Japan* (Ithaca: Cornell University Press, 2001).

15. Pempel, *Regime Shift*, 163.

16. T. J. Pempel, "Structural *Gaiatsu:* International Finance and Political Change in Japan," *Comparative Political Studies* 32, no. 8 (December 1999): 928.

17. Layna Mosley, "Room to Move: International Financial Markets and National Welfare States," *International Organization* 54, no. 4 (Autumn 2000): 737–73.

18. *Financial Times*, March 5, 2004, p. 1.

19. For an overview of how these market dynamics affected many states with heavily regulated financial markets, see Michael Loriaux, "The End of Credit Activism in Interventionist States," in Loriaux et al., *Capital Ungoverned: Liberalizing Finance in Interventionist States* (Ithaca: Cornell University Press, 1997): 1–16. For a discussion of how these forces played out in Japan, see Frances M. Rosenbluth, *Financial Politics in Contemporary Japan* (Ithaca: Cornell University Press, 1989); and Laurence, *Money Rules.*

20. Laurence, *Money Rules*, 193–94. Laurence emphasizes that the shift in bargaining power toward large consumers of financial services will not lead to liberalization in all areas of financial regulation, stressing that it will lead to more liberal rules governing product diversity and prices and stricter rules providing consumer protection. He lists several additional causal pathways through which shifts in bargaining power will bring about the latter, stricter regulations in the area of consumer protection.

21. Chiara Saraceno, "Family Change, Family Policies and the Restructuring of Welfare," in *Family, Market, and Community: Equity and Efficiency in Social Policy*, ed. OECD (Paris: OECD, 1997), 81–100; Ōawa Mari, "Twelve Million Full-time Housewives: The Gender Consequences of Japan's Postwar Social Contract," in *Social Contracts under Stress: The Middle Classes of America, Europe, and Japan at the Turn of the Century*, ed. Olivier Zunz, Leonard Schoppa, and Nobuhiro Hiwatari (New York: Russell Sage, 2002), 255–77.

22. Joyce Gelb, *Feminism and Politics: A Comparative Perspective* (Berkeley: University of California Press, 1989).

23. Julia S. O'Connor, Ann Shola Orloff, and Sheila Shaver, *States, Markets, Families: Gender, Liberalism and Social Policy in Australia, Canada, Great Britain, and the United States* (Cambridge: Cambridge University Press, 1999); Susan Pedersen, *Family Dependence and the Welfare State* (Cambridge: Cambridge University Press, 1993); Diane Sainsbury, *Gender, Equality and Welfare States* (Cambridge: Cambridge University Press, 1996); Anne Helene Gauthier, *The State and the Family: A Comparative Analysis of Family Policies in Industrialized Countries* (Oxford: Clarendon Press, 1996).

24. Gelb, *Feminism and Politics*. Her work builds on the approach to social movements pioneered by Sydney Tarrow. See his *Power in Movement: Social Movements, Collective Action and Politics* (Cambridge: Cambridge University Press, 1994).

25. O'Connor, Orloff, and Shaver, *States, Markets, and Families*.

26. Susan Pharr, *Losing Face: Status Politics in Japan* (Berkeley: University of California Press, 1990).

27. Frank Upham, *Law and Social Change in Postwar Japan* (Cambridge: Harvard University Press, 1987), 124–65.

28. Mikanagi Yumiko, *Josei to Seiji* (Tokyo: Shinhyōron, 1999), 140–41. See also Joyce Gelb, who focuses on the contrast between American and Japanese political structures to explain much of the divergence in policy outcomes in areas affecting women in her most recent work, *Gender Policies in Japan and the United States: Comparing Women's Movements, Rights, and Politics* (New York: Palgrave, 2003).

29. The Swedish case is discussed below. On France in the 1960s, see Kimberly J. Morgan, "The Politics of Mothers' Employment: France in Comparative Perspective," *World Politics* 55 (January 2003), especially 279–82.

30. I do not mean to imply in any way that a decision not to marry and have children or a decision to give up a career constitutes a "sacrifice" for all women. I use the term exit only to refer to cases in which women give up on one or the other when they would ideally have preferred a life course in which they combined having a family with pursuing a full-time career.

31. Gauthier, *The State and the Family*, 17.

32. Ibid.

33. According to the labor economists' dynamic model of the labor market, these are among the strategies firms can use to expand the supply of labor when faced with a shortage of workers. See Malcolm S. Cohen, *Labor Shortages as America Approaches the Twenty-first Century* (Ann Arbor: University of Michigan Press, 1995), 6–7.

34. Yashiro Naohiro, *Shōshi kōreika no keizaigaku: Shijō jūshi no kōzō kaikaku* (Tokyo: Tōyō Keizai Shimpōsha, 1999).

35. Ministry of Health and Welfare, *Kōsei hakusho—Heisei 10–nen-han: Shōshi shakai wo kangaeru*, 1998.

36. Ito Peng, "Social Care in Crisis: Gender, Demography, and Welfare State Restructuring in Japan," *Social Policy* (Fall 2002): 411–43. See also Patricia Boling, "Family Policy in Japan," *Journal of Social Policy* 27, no. 2 (1998): 173–90; and Glenda Roberts, "Pinning Hopes on Angels: Reflections from an Aging Japan's Urban Landscape," in *Family and Social Policy in Japan: Anthropological Approaches*, ed. Roger Goodman (Cambridge: Cambridge University Press, 2002), 54–91.

37. Gauthier, *The State and the Family*, 127.

38. Ibid., 128.

39. Ibid., 140.

40. Ibid., 201.

41. Ibid., 48–57; Sainsbury, *Gender, Equality and Welfare States;* Kees van Kersbergen, *Social Capitalism: A Study of Christian Democracy and the Welfare State* (London: Routledge, 1995).

42. Ellis S. Krauss and Robert Pekkanen, "Explaining Party Adaptation to Electoral Reform: The Discreet Charm of the LDP?" *Journal of Japanese Studies* 30, no. 1 (Winter 2004): 1–34.

3. Productive and Protective Elements of Convoy Capitalism

1. OECD, *Social Expenditures Database* (Paris: OECD, 2000).

2. Nakagawa Yatsuhiro, "Japan, the Welfare Super-Power," *Journal of Japanese Studies* 5, no. 1 (Winter 1979): 5–51. Nakagawa also called Japan a "paradise for the worker" (39).

3. Ibid., 29.

4. Ezra Vogel, *Japan as Number One: Lessons for America* (Cambridge: Harvard University Press, 1979).

5. See, for example, T. J. Pempel, *Policy and Politics in Japan: Creative Conservatism* (Philadelphia: Temple University Press, 1982); Ronald Dore, *Flexible Rigidities: Industrial Policy and Structural Adjustment in the Japanese Economy, 1970–1980* (Stanford: Stanford University Press, 1986).

6. Gøsta Esping-Andersen, *Three Worlds of Welfare Capitalism* (Cambridge: Polity Press, 1990).

7. Gøsta Esping-Andersen, "Hybrid or Unique? The Japanese Welfare State between Europe and America," *Journal of European Social Policy* 7, no. 3 (1997): 179–89.

8. John C. Campbell, "Japanese Long-term Care Insurance and Welfare State Comparisons," paper presented at the annual meeting of the Association for Asian Studies in Boston, March 11–14, 1999.

9. Müge Kökten, "Schizophrenic Social Policy: Explaining Discrepancies in Levels of Social Support for the Elderly and the Unemployed in Japan," PhD diss., University of Virginia, 2002.

10. Toshimitsu Shinkawa and T. J. Pempel, "Occupational Welfare and the Japanese Experience," in *The Privatization of Social Policy: Occupational Welfare and the Welfare State in America, Scandinavia, and Japan,* ed. Michael Shalev (London: Macmillan, 1996), 281.

11. Ibid. According to one study, Japan's large firms devote more expenditures to nonstatutory benefits (those that are not required by law) than they do to statutory programs—a pattern that he finds to be in sharp contrast to the system in Europe where statutory programs account for the bulk of social expenditures. See Young-Hoon Cho, "The Growth of Enterprise Welfare in Japan," *Economic and Industrial Democracy* 17 (1996): 283.

12. Sheldon Garon, *The State and Labor in Modern Japan* (Berkeley: University of California Press, 1987), 198 and 204.

13. Shinkawa and Pempel, "Occupational Welfare," 291.

14. John C. Campbell, *How Policies Change: The Japanese Government and the Aging Society* (Princeton: Princeton University Press, 1992), 58–60.

15. Ibid., 62–88.

16. Ten million people were receiving pension benefits under these programs. This and other data in the paragraph is drawn from the Ministry of Health and Welfare, *Annual Report on Health and Welfare 1998–1999: Social Security and National Life* (Tokyo: MHW, 1999), 453–55. The pension system offers generous coverage to a broader segment of the working population (60 percent) than do other social programs. Unemployment insurance, discussed below, covers a much smaller proportion; and the "lifetime" employment rules do not apply to employees of small firms. My estimate that just one-third of Japanese employees enjoy European levels of social protection is based on the share that enjoys the *complete package* of benefits and protections.

17. Japan Institute of Labor (JIL) data available on the web at http://www.jil.go.jp/kisya/daijin/981023_02_d/981023_02_d_kekka.html (accessed February 25, 2002).

18. MHW, *Annual Report on Health and Welfare 1998–1999*, 452.

19. The proportion of employees receiving pension fund benefits such as lump-sum payments was actually quite high, even for medium-sized firms with thirty to ninety-nine workers (86% of such firms in 1998). Also notable is the fact that even nonmanagerial employees with only a junior high school degree qualified for lump-sum payments under these programs, averaging ¥11.5 million ($96,000)—JIL website cited in endnote 17.

20. Garon, *State and Labor in Modern Japan*, 205.

21. The program uses general tax revenues to cover the co-payments of patients over seventy—see Campbell, *How Policies Change*, 144–53.

22. Ibid., 306.

23. Margaret Lock, "Ideology, Female Midlife, and the Greying of Japan," *Journal of Japanese Studies* 19, no. 1 (Winter 1993): 49–50.

24. Figures are for public and mandatory private expenditures on unemployment insurance and active labor market policies in 1995, calculated based on the System of National Accounts, 1968—OECD, *OECD Social Expenditure Database*.

25. Kökten, "Schizophrenic Social Policy," chap. 3.

26. Data from Japan's special labor force survey in February 1998, cited in Douglas Ostrom, "Unemployment in Japan: How Serious Is the Problem?" *JEI Report* 2A (January 15, 1999), 4.

27. Nomura Research Institute estimate based on the historical relationship among labor, capital, and output—cited in ibid, 5.

28. According to one comparative analysis, Japan's unemployment insurance system was stingier even than that in the United States, replacing just 9.9% percent of a worker's previous earnings (on average) in 1995 because so many workers qualify for few or no payments. The United States, in the same year, replaced 11.8% of workers' wages whereas Britain replaced 18.1%, Italy 19.7%, and Denmark 32.8%. See Douglas Ostrom, "Prospects for Economic Reform in Japan: Where Is the Safety Net?" *JEI Report* 37A (October 3, 1997), 10.

29. The 270 days benefit was available only to those forty-five to sixty years old who had been employed over ten years and were "involuntarily" laid off. In contrast, a similar worker "voluntarily" agreeing to retire early would get only 150 days. A younger worker, aged forty-four and laid off involuntarily after having worked over ten years, would get only 180 days. See data reported in Kökten, "Schizophrenic Social Policy," chap. 4.

30. OECD, *Social Expenditures Database*.

31. Fukuda Motoo, *Shakai hoshō no kōzō kaikaku: Kosodate shien jūshi gata shisutemu e no tenkan* (Tokyo: Chūō Hōki Shuppan, 1999), 5.

32. In comparison, in the same year (1996) parents of a child born in Germany could expect a monthly payment of 220 marks from birth through age eighteen, for a total child-rearing subsidy of 47,520 marks (worth $31,680 at an exchange rate of $1 = 1.5 marks)—see Fukuda, *Shakai hoshō no kōzō kaikaku*, 9.

33. The figure cited is for the "standard amount" of public assistance provided in 1999 to the type of family described, according to the Ministry of Health and Welfare, *Annual Report on Health and Welfare 1998–1999*, 405.

34. Child support by ex-husbands to custodial mothers is relatively rare in Japan, with one study showing that only 10–20% of divorced mothers receive support payments from their ex-husbands—Harald Fuess, *Divorce in Japan: Family, Gender, and the State, 1600–2000* (Stanford: Stanford University Press, 2004), 158. As a result the "family" that bears the burden of supporting divorced single mothers is not that of the ex-husband but the wife's own parents and other relatives.

35. In 1996, the vast majority of single mothers lived with their parents, including 84% of single mothers aged twenty to twenty-four, 80% of those twenty five to twenty-nine, and 70% of those thirty to thirty-four—Kōseishō, *Kōsei hakusho—Heisei 10–nen-han*, 1998, 105.

36. Ibid., 406 and 440.

37. Ministry of Internal Affairs and Communications, Statistics Bureau, *Jūtaku tochi tokei chōsa—Heisei 10–nen*.

38. About half the *kōei* units had at least one household member over sixty-five in 1998—based on data from the Ministry of Internal Affairs and Communications (MIAC), Statistics Bureau, *Jūtaku tochi tokei chōsa—Heisei 10–nen.*

39. Ministry of Education, *Kodomo no gakushūhi chōsa—Heisei 12–nen-han* (Tokyo: MOE, 2000).

40. Just 22% of firms with over thirty employees granted childcare leave benefits to women in 1992, prior to the implementation of the new law mandating such benefits (discussed in chapter 7). See Suzuki Kazue, "Women Rebuff the Call for More Babies," *Japan Quarterly* 42, no. 1 (January–March 1995): 19.

41. See section on childcare in chapter 7.

42. Zenkoku Hoiku Dantai Renrakukai Hoiku Kenkyūjo, *Hoiku hakusho 2000* (Tokyo: Sōdo Bunka, 2000), 50. The government's attempts to increase childcare slots during the 1990s are discussed in chapter 7.

43. OECD, *Society at a Glance: OECD Social Indicators* (Paris: OECD, 2001), 53. A large portion of the latter group of Japanese children, aged three to six, is enrolled in public or private kindergartens. Most of these institutions, however, provide instruction for just three to four hours a day, hardly sufficient to allow their mothers to maintain careers. Most also require extensive involvement on a day-to-day basis by mothers. See Anne Allison, "Producing Mothers," in *Re-Imaging Japanese Women*, ed. Anne E. Imamura (Berkeley: University of California Press, 1996), 135–55.

44. OECD, *Society at a Glance*, 53. See also Janet C. Gornick and Marcia K. Meyers, *Families That Work: Policies for Reconciling Parenthood and Employment* (New York: Russell Sage Foundation, 2004).

45. The total number of children waiting for spots in childcare centers stood at 28,481 in 1995, with most of these in the large metropolitan areas—see Ministry of Health and Welfare (MHW), *Hoiku saabisu no jukyū—tokki no jōkyō* (April 1, 2000), p. 1.

46. Ōsawa Machiko, *Atarashii kazoku no tame no keizaigaku Kawariyuku kigyō shakai no naka no josei* (Tokyo: Chūkō Shinsho, 1998), 103.

47. Mary Brinton, *Women and the Economic Miracle: Gender and Work in Postwar Japan* (Berkeley: University of California Press, 1993).

48. See Julia S. O'Connor, Ann Shola Orloff, and Sheila Shaver, *States, Markets, and Families: Gender, Liberalism and Social Policy in Australia, Canada, Great Britain and the United States* (Cambridge: Cambridge University Press, 1999)

49. Machiko Ōsawa and Jeff Kingston, "Flexibility and Inspiration: Restructuring and the Japanese Labor Market," *Japan Labor Bulletin*, 35, no. 1 (January 1, 1996): 4.

50. Dore, *Flexible Rigidities;* James C. Abegglen and George Stalk Jr., *Kaisha: The Japanese Corporation* (New York: Basic Books, 1985); Michael Gerlach, *Alliance Capitalism: The Social Organization of Japanese Business* (Berkeley: University of California Press, 1992); Masahiko Aoki and Ronald Dore, eds., *The Japanese Firm: The Sources of Competitive Strength* (Oxford: Oxford University Press, 1994); W. Carl Kester, "American and Japanese Corporate Governance: Convergence to Best Practice," in *National Diversity and Global Capitalism*, ed. Suzanne Berger and Ronald Dore (Ithaca: Cornell University Press, 1996), 107–37.

51. Dore, *Flexible Rigidities*, 71; Paul Sheard, "Interlocking Shareholding and Corporate Governance," in Aoki and Dore, *Japanese Firm*, 310.

52. This account is based on Richard Pascale and Thomas P. Rohlen, "The Mazda Turnaround," *Journal of Japanese Studies* 9, no. 2 (Summer 1983): 219–63.

53. Dore, *Flexible Rigidities*, 77.

54. Ibid, 1–2.

55. Henry Laurence, *Money Rules: The New Politics of Finance in Britain and Japan* (Ithaca: Cornell University Press, 2001); Steven K. Vogel, *Freer Markets, More Rules: Regulatory Reform in Advanced Industrial Countries* (Ithaca: Cornell University Press, 1996).

56. Ulrike Schaede, "The Japanese Financial System: From Postwar to the New Millennium," *Harvard Business School Case 9–700–049* (January 5, 2000), 2.

57. This system of segmented financial markets was revised starting in 1993 with the adoption of the Financial System Reform Act and again with the adoption of the "big bang" reforms in 1996. For details, see chapter 8.

58. Horiuchi Akiyoshi, "Financial Fragility and Recent Developments in the Japanese Safety Net," *Social Science Japan Journal* 2, no. 1 (1999): 27.

59. Schaede, "Japanese Financial System," 5.

60. Steven Vogel, *Freer Markets, More Rules*.

61. Leonard Schoppa, *Bargaining with Japan: What American Pressure Can and Cannot Do* (New York: Columbia University Press, 1997), 146–80; Frank Upham, "Privatizing Regulation: The Implementation of the Large-Scale Retail Stores Law," in *Political Dynamics in Contemporary Japan*, ed. Gary D. Allinson and Yasunori Sone (Ithaca: Cornell University Press, 1993), 264–94; and Jean Heilman Grier, "Japan's Regulation of Large Retail Stores: Political Demands versus Economic Interests," *University of Pennsylvania Journal of International Economic Law* 22, no. 1 (Spring 2001): 1–60.

62. Brian Woodall, *Japan under Construction: Corruption, Politics, and Public Works* (Berkeley: University of California Press, 1996), especially 36–50; and John McMillan, "Dangō Japan's Price-Fixing Conspiracies," *Politics and Economics* 3 (1991): 201–18.

63. Woodall, *Japan under Construction*, 49.

64. The figure for the share of the labor force in construction is for 1992, from Woodall, *Japan under Construction*, 29.

65. Mark Tilton, *Restrained Trade: Cartels in Japan's Basic Materials Industries* (Ithaca: Cornell University Press, 1996).

66. Chalmers Johnson, *MITI and the Japanese Miracle: The Growth of Industrial Policy, 1925–1975* (Stanford: Stanford University Press, 1982).

67. Coal mining is generally treated as another "basic material industry." This sector faced structural adjustment pressures sooner and more severely. It also included a large number of small-scale operators. Consequently, many firms in this sector did have to lay off workers, and some went bankrupt. See Suzanne Culter, *Managing Decline: Japan's Coal Industry; Restructuring and Community Response* (Honolulu: University of Hawaii Press, 1999); and Robert M. Uriu, *Troubled Industries: Confronting Economic Change in Japan* (Ithaca: Cornell University Press, 1996), 95–102.

68. Genda Yūji summarizes the case law on the doctrine of abusive dismissal in "Youth Employment and Parasite Singles," *Japan Labor Bulletin* 39, no. 3 (March 2000). See also Yashiro Naohiro, *Koyō kaikaku no jidai: Hatarakikata wa dō kawaruka* (Tokyo: Chūkō shinsho, 1999), 85–86; and Curtis Milhaupt, J. Mark Ramseyer, and Michael K. Young, *Japanese Law in Context: Readings in Society, the Economy, and Politics* (Cambridge: Harvard University Press, 2001), 384–98.

69. Noguchi gave the system this name because it took shape during World War II, around 1940—see Noguchi Yukio, *1940–nen taisei: Saraba 'senji keizai'* (Tokyo: Tōyō Keizai Shimpōsha, 1995), 19–29.

70. The provisions of the Labor Standards Act providing these protections for women were revised in 1985 and again in 1999. See discussion in chapter 7.

71. Brinton, *Women and the Economic Miracle,* 132–33, 168–72; Frank K. Upham, *Law and Social Change in Japan* (Cambridge: Harvard University Press, 1987), 127–32.

72. Upham, *Law and Social Change in Japan,* 153.

73. Mari Ōsawa, "Twelve Million Full-time Housewives: The Gender Consequences of Japan's Postwar Social Contract," in *Social Contracts Under Stress: The Middle Classes of America, Europe, and Japan at the Turn of the Century,* ed. Olivier Zunz, Leonard Schoppa, and Nobuhiro Hiwatari (New York: Russell Sage, 2002), 255–77.

74. Hiroki Satō, "Labour Policies for Part-time Workers in Japan," a conference paper prepared for the OECD conference on "Changing Labour Markets and Gender Equality: The Role of Policy," October 12–13, 1998.

75. Ōsawa, *Atarashii kazoku no tame no keizaigaku,* 213–14.

76. Some of these women chose to work part-time not so much because of the policy incentives but because this was the lifestyle they preferred. Others did not "choose" it so much as they were unable to find full-time work even though they wanted to work longer hours. The net effect of these choices, however, is quite clear. In 1998, 57% of those returning to work after a period without a job were hired as "part-time" workers. This contrasted with a very different pattern for women hired straight out of school, only 15% of whom chose to work part time. See MOL, Women's Bureau, *Josei rōdō hakusho—Heisei 11–nen-han,* 2000, appendix, 41.

77. Satō, "Labour Policies for Part-time Workers in Japan," 7.

78. Ōsawa, *Atarashii kazoku no tame no keizaigaku,* 102.

79. For a full analysis of this poll data, see analysis in chapter 4.

80. Iwao Sumiko, "Working Women and Housewives," *Japan Echo* 28, no. 2 (April 2001): 53.

81. Robin LeBlanc, *Bicycle Citizens: The Political World of the Japanese Housewife* (Berkeley: University of California Press, 1999), 26. See also a similar point by Sheldon Garon, *Molding Japanese Minds: The State in Everyday Life* (Princeton: Princeton University Press, 1997), 180.

82. Allison, "Producing Mothers," 135–55.

83. Susan Orpett Long, "Nurturing and Femininity: The Ideal of Caregiving in Postwar Japan," in *Re-Imaging Japanese Women,* ed. Imamura, 156–76; Lock, "Ideology, Female Midlife, and the Greying of Japan."

84. Noriko O. Tsuya, Larry Bumpass, and Minja Kim Choe, "Gender, Employment, and Housework in Japan, South Korea, and the United States," *Review of Population and Social Policy* 9 (2000): 210. The data showed that in 1987–88 American husbands spent 7.8 hours and their wives 32.4 on household chores, with the figure rising to 11 hours for husbands whose wives worked 49 or more hours.

85. Maeda Masako, "Shōshika no naka no shakai hoshō seido," *Sekai* 659 (March 1999): 89.

86. Brinton, *Women and the Economic Miracle;* Dore, *Flexible Rigidities,* 96–97.

87. Richard Samuels, *The Business of the Japanese State: Energy Markets in Comparative and Historical Perspective* (Ithaca: Cornell University Press, 1987).

88. Ibid., 261. The transition away from coal nevertheless took three decades, a point that is emphasized even more strongly than in Samuels's book by Robert Uriu in *Troubled Industries,* 95–102.

89. Samuels, *Business of the Japanese State,* 131.

90. Ibid., 2.

91. National Institute of Population and Social Security Research, *Population Projections for Japan, 2001–2050* (Tokyo: NIPSSR, 2002).

92. Survey from 1988, cited by Long, "Nurturing and Femininity," 165. See chapter 4 for more detailed data and trends over time.

93. Ibid., 162. See also Lock, "Ideology, Female Midlife, and the Greying of Japan."

94. Maeda, "Shōshika no naka no shakai hoshō seido," 86. See also the comments of Ōsawa Machiko, another feminist labor economist, who writes that the gender-based two-track employment system used to be efficient when young male workers were plentiful—in *Atarashii kazoku no tame no keizaigaku,* 117.

95. Ronald Dore, "Equality-Efficiency Trade-offs: Japanese Perceptions and Choices," in *The Japanese Firm,* ed. Aoki and Dore, 379–91. Dore has continued to defend the Japanese model in the face of Anglo-American triumphalism in the 1990s, but his more recent publications have admitted that the Japanese system *has* sacrificed some efficiency, but for the noble purpose of protecting stakeholders and not just stockholders. See his *Stock Market Capitalism : Welfare Capitalism : Japan and Germany versus the Anglo-Saxons* (Oxford: Oxford University Press, 2000).

4. The Race for the Exits Begins

1. Mireya Solis, *Banking on Multinationals: Public Credit and the Export of Japanese Sunset Industries* (Stanford: Stanford University Press, 2004), 55–73.

2. Mark Mason, *American Multinationals and Japan: The Political Economy of Japanese Capital Controls, 1899–1980* (Cambridge: Harvard University Press, 1992), 154.

3. Chalmers Johnson, *MITI and the Japanese Miracle: The Growth of Industrial Policy, 1925–1975* (Stanford: Stanford University Press, 1982), 278–79.

4. Ministry of Finance, *Zaisei kinyū tokei geppō,* various issues—online at http:www.mof.go.jp/kankou/hyou/g596/596_02_01.xls (accessed September 17, 2002).

5. Robert Angel, *Explaining Economic Policy Failure: Japan in the 1969–1971 International Monetary Crisis* (New York: Columbia University Press, 1991), 119.

6. Ministry of Finance data.

7. Frances M. Rosenbluth, *Financial Politics in Contemporary Japan* (Ithaca: Cornell University Press, 1989), 78–95.

8. Bela Balassa and Marcus Noland, *Japan in the World Economy* (Washington, D.C.: Institute for International Economics, 1988), 49–50.

9. Leonard Schoppa, *Bargaining with Japan: What American Pressure Can and Cannot Do* (New York: Columbia University Press, 1997), 49–85; John H. Kunkel, *Demanding Results: U.S. Market Access Policies toward Japan* (Cambridge: Cambridge University Press, 2003).

10. David Weinstein, "Historical, Structural, and Macroeconomic Perspectives on the Japanese Economic Crisis," in *Japan's New Economy: Continuity and Change in the Twenty-first Century,* ed. Magnus Blomström, Byron Gangnes, and Sumner La Croix (Oxford: Oxford University Press, 2001), 37–43.

11. Exchange rate figures given are averages for the calendar years specified—University of British Columbia, Sauder School of Business, Pacific Exchange Rate Service—online at http://fx.sauder.ubc.ca/ (accessed February 25, 2005).

12. Between 1970 and 1995, the Japanese yen appreciated by 383% against the dollar. The only other currencies rivaling the yen during these years were the German mark (up 256%) and the Swiss franc (up 370%).

13. For a more thorough comparison of how the American, European, and Japanese approaches to social protection fared when faced with the challenge of globalization, see Leonard

Schoppa, "Globalization and the Squeeze on the Middle Class: Does Any Version of the Postwar Social Contract Meet the Challenge?" in *Postwar Social Contracts under Stress: The Middle Classes of Japan, Europe, and America at the Century's End,* ed. Olivier Zunz, Leonard Schoppa, and Nobuhiro Hiwatari (New York: Russell Sage, 2002), 319–44.

14. T. J. Pempel, *Regime Shift: Comparative Dynamics of the Japanese Political Economy* (Ithaca: Cornell University Press, 1998), 163–67.

15. NIPSSR, *Population Projections for Japan, 2001–2050,* 2002, 6. These figures were actually a few percentage points lower than those for Japanese women earlier this century, when women married at rates as high as 97–98%! For comparative reference, consider that of American women in the same cohort (aged forty to forty-four in 1990), 92% had married and 84% had at least one child. U.S. rates too were higher earlier in the century (e.g., women born in the 1930s), when American women married and had children at similar rates to Japanese women born in 1950.

16. This metaphor was one I often heard mentioned in conversations with young Japanese women my age (I was twenty-two and living in Japan in 1985).

17. Ministry of Justice data for 1998, cited by Karen Kelsky, *Women on the Verge: Japanese Women, Western Dreams* (Durham: Duke University Press, 2001), 103.

18. Ministry of Justice website: www.moj.go.jp/TOUKEI/t_n01.html (accessed January 6, 2005).

19. A majority of women married as recently as the late 1950s reported that their marriages were arranged through introductions (*miai kekkon*), and this figure stood at 30% in the late 1970s. By 2002, however, it had fallen to 7.4%. Of those married between 2000 and 2002, 88.6% reported they had married for love (*ren'ai kekkon*)—see NIPSSR, *Dai-12–kai shusshō dōkō kihon chōsa: Fūfu chōsa no kekka gaiyō,* 2004, 4.

20. Ōsawa Machiko, *Atarashii kazoku no tame no keizaigaku: Kawariyuku kigyō shakai no naka no josei* (Tokyo: Chūkō shinsho, 1998), 225.

21. Fuke Shigeko, *Kaisha o yamete, ryūgaku shimasu* (Tokyo: Daiyamondosha, 1990), 281, cited in Kelsky, *Women on the Verge,* 90.

22. See Yashiro Naohiro, *Shōshi kōreika no keizaigaku* (Tokyo: Tōyō Keizai Shimpōsha, 1999), 13–29; Ōsawa, *Atarashii kazoku no tame no keizaigaku.*

23. Prime Minister's Office, *Danjo kyōdō sankaku hakusho—Heisei 12–nen-han,* 2000, 54.

24. Ōsawa, *Atarashii kazoku no tame no keizaigaku,* 31.

25. Prime Minister's Office, *Danjo kyōdō sankaku hakusho—Heisei 12–nen-han,* 2000, 54.

26. By 1980, the proportion of women employed in family businesses had fallen to just 10%—Ōsawa, *Atarashii kazoku no tame no keizaigaku,* 31.

27. See Yamada Masahiro, *Parasaito shinguru no jidai* (Tokyo: Chikuma Shinsho, 1999).

28. Yamada, *Parasaito shinguru no jidai;* for an account in the U.S. press, see Peggy Orenstein, "Parasites in Pret-a-Porter," *New York Times Magazine,* July 1, 2001, 31–36.

29. Others put more stress on stagnant wage growth for young people than does Yamada. See Yūji Genda, "Youth Employment and Parasite Singles," *Japan Labor Bulletin* 39, no. 3 (March 1, 2000).

30. Yamada Masahiro, "Parasite Singles Feed on Family System," *Japan Quarterly* 48, no. 1 (January–March 2001): 13.

31. Kelsky, *Women on the Verge,* 15–16.

32. Noriko O. Tsuya and Karen Oppenheim Mason, "Changing Gender Roles and Below-Replacement Fertility in Japan," in *Gender and Family Change in Industrialized Countries,* ed. K. O. Mason and An-Magritt Jensen (Oxford: Clarendon Press, 1995), 154, updated with 1997 data from the same series published by the Prime Minister's Office, Public Information Section, "Danjo kyōdō sankaku shakai ni kansuru yoron chōsa," September 1997—online at http://www1

.ipss.go.jp/tohkei/Data/Relation/2_Factor/1_kekkon/1–2–A07.htm (accessed September 17, 2002).

33. Ibid., 155, updated with data from the same series published by the Cabinet Office, Public Information Section, "Danjo kyōdō sankaku shakai ni kansuru yoron chōsa," November 2004—online at http://www8.cao.go.jp/survey/h16/h16–danjo/images/z14.gif (accessed February 10, 2005).

34. Morita Akio, "'Nihon-gata keiei' ga ayaui," *Bungei shunju* 70, no. 2 (February 1992): 94–103; "Shin-jiyū keizai e no teigen," *Bungei shunju* 71, no. 2 (February 1993): 94–103.

35. John H. Dunning and Robert D. Pearce, *The World's Largest Industrial Enterprises: 1962–1983* (New York: St. Martin's Press, 1985), 149–50.

36. METI, *Dai 33–kai wagakuni kigyō no kaigai jigyō katsudō kekka gaiyō*, March 31, 2004, figure 5.1—online at http://www.meti.go.jp/statistics/downloadfiles/h2c402fj.pdf (accessed February 10, 2005).

37. John Nathan, *Sony* (Boston: Mariner Books, 1999), 103.

38. Sony, "Global Localization"—online at http://www.sony.net/Fun/SH/1–29/h1.html (accessed May 21, 2004).

39. Historical data supplied by the company.

40. Honda, "Glocalization"—online at http://www.hondacorporate.com/worldwide/index.html?subsection=glocalization (accessed May 21, 2004).

41. Toyota, "Domestic Production and Sales Up in FY 2003"—online at http://www.toyota.co.jp/en/news/04/0426.html (accessed May 21, 2004).

42. 2001 data for Canon's overseas production ratio, supplied by the company.

43. Sony, "Global Localization"—online at http://www.sony.net/Fun/SH/1–29/h1.html (accessed May 21, 2004).

44. UNCTAD, *World Investment Report 2001* (New York), 95.

45. Sony does not report data on the foreign share of all assets but reported in 1999 that 62% of its "long-lived" assets (plants and equipment) were located abroad. See Keith Cowling and Philip R. Tomlinson, "The Japanese Crisis—A Case of Strategic Failure?" *Economic Journal* 110 (June 2000): 369.

46. Thanks to Edward Lincoln for this point.

47. METI, *Dai-33–kai kaigai jigyō katsudō kihon chōsa kekka gaiyō*, March 31, 2004, figure 11.1—available online at http://www.meti.go.jp/statistics/downloadfiles/h2c402fj.pdf (accessed February 11, 2005).

48. Cowling and Tomlinson, "Japanese Crisis," 373.

49. METI, *Structural Reform Issues and Economic and Industrial Policy* (Tokyo: METI, 2002).

50. Mark Magnier, "'Chic Cheap' Retailer Explodes on the Japanese Clothing Scene," *Los Angeles Times*, December 28, 2000, p. C1.

51. Kent Calder, "Assault on the Bankers' Kingdom: Politics, Markets, and the Liberalization of Japanese Industrial Finance," in *Capital Ungoverned: Liberalizing Finance in Interventionist States*, ed. Michael Loriaux et al. (Ithaca: Cornell University Press, 1997), 24–25.

52. Henry Laurence, *Money Rules: The New Politics of Finance in Britain and Japan* (Ithaca: Cornell University Press, 2001), 180.

53. MITI, *Biggu ban kōsō* (Tokyo: Tsūshō Sangyō Chōsakai Shuppanbu, 1997), 4–5.

54. The total fertility rate is a demographic statistic that is calculated by taking the actual number of children born to all women between fifteen and forty and then adding to this an extrapolated number of children younger women between these ages can be expected to have if they give birth at the rates of those above them in age. Thus, for example, if women aged twenty-seven give birth to an average of 0.12 children in a given year, the total fertility rate is calculated by as-

suming all women between fifteen and twenty-six will go on and have 0.12 children during the year when they are twenty-seven.

55. Calculated based on survey data presented in Iwasawa Miho, "Dare ga 'ryōritsu' wo dannen shiteirunoka," *Jinkō mondai kenkyū* 55, no. 4 (December 1999): 23. Iwasawa's data analysis was based on the 1997 survey.

56. I am quite aware that my use of terms like "decisions" and "opt" suggests a degree of choice some women may not have. Indeed, the argument I am developing is that women have been constrained in their ability to choose the life course they want. They *would* marry and have children if society gave them opportunities to have the kind of marriage, motherhood, and work experiences they desire, but it doesn't.

57. The completed fertility rate for married women (calculated by asking women married fifteen to nineteen years how many children they gave birth to) has remained steady at around 2.2 since 1972. In 2002, the number of births stood at 2.23—see data in NIPSSR, *Dai-12-kai shusshō dōkō kihon chōsa,* 2004, 5.

58. Ibid., 18; for a more complete quantitative analysis linking the decline in fertility in Japan to the delay in marriage, see Tsuya and Mason, "Changing Gender Roles and Below-Replacement Fertility in Japan," 147–48.

59. Iwasawa Miho, "Kekkon shinai henjintachi: Hikongata kappuru wo mitomeru shakai e," *Chūō kōron* 115, no. 13 (December 2000): 93.

60. In 2000, just 1.6% of births took place outside of marriage, compared to an EU average of 20% (with national rates ranging from 6% in Greece to 50% in Denmark)—Harald Fuess, *Divorce in Japan: Family, Gender, and the State, 1600–2000* (Stanford: Stanford University Press, 2004), 154.

61. On the other hand, we cannot assume that all women who can't find an appropriate partner are hoping for one who will help with the housework and childcare and support their career aspirations. Some are no doubt frustrated by the opposite concern: they want to stay home as full-time housewives but can't find a partner with the income to support this lifestyle. Feminist Ueno Chizuko suggests that this latter problem is a significant part of the reason for the delay and decline in marriage—see her "Women and the Family in Transition in Postindustrial Japan," in Joyce Gelb and Marian Lief Palley, eds., *Women of Japan and Korea: Continuity and Change* (Philadelphia: Temple University Press, 1994), 33.

62. Marjorie Coeyman, "In Japan, Life without Children is Savored with Guilt," *Christian Science Monitor,* March 27, 2002. Government surveys show that the general population continues to feel strongly that "if a couple marry, they should have children," with 85% of respondents agreeing with this statement in a 2000 poll—Prime Minister's Office, "Shōshika ni kansuru yoron chōsa," February 2000.

63. NIPSSR, *Dai-11-kai shusshō dōkō kihon chōsa: Nihonjin no kekkon to shussan,* 1997, 39.

64. Quoted in Orenstein, "Parasites in Pret-a-Porter," 34.

65. Another 447,000 quit work to provide nursing care for frail family members—see Ministry of Internal Affairs and Communications (MIAC), Statistics Bureau, "Shūgyō kōzō kihon chōsa," available online at http://www.stat.go.jp/data/shugyou/2002/kakuhou/zuhyou/z115 .xls (accessed June 15, 2005).

66. These figures are for 2000 when these work-with-children rates were actually up slightly from the situation that prevailed before childcare leave and other reforms were introduced. Data on work-with-children rates are from MIAC, Statistics Bureau, "Rōdōryoku chōsa tokubetsu chōsa"; data on unmarried women's work rate are from MIAC, Statistics Bureau, "Rōdōryoku chōsa—Heisei 12-nen," available online at http://www.stat.go.jp/data/roudou/2000n/zuhyou/ 200400.xls (accessed September 23, 2002).

67. Kelsky, *Women on the Verge,* 2.

68. These patterns are averages for the years 1995–2000. Contrary to the popular view that it is women who are leaving Japan, statistics show that *men* are the ones leaving and staying abroad (Japanese men saw net outflows for all ages from twenty-two to sixty-two). For all of these statistics, see NIPSSR, *Population Projections for Japan, 2001–2050*, 2002, 20. Note that the tendency of women to return to Japan is in part a result of immigration policies of Western nations such as the United States that make it difficult for Japanese women who arrive on student visas to stay unless they marry or have an employer-sponsor.

69. The proportion of marriages recorded in Japan that included a Japanese woman and a foreign groom grew from 0.4% in 1980 to 1.0% in 2001, but meanwhile the proportion of marriages involving a Japanese man and a foreign bride grew from 0.6% to 4.0% over the same period. Interestingly, of "international marriages" involving Japanese men, fully 91% were to women from Korea, China, the Philippines, and Thailand—statistics calculated based on data published by the Ministry of Health, Labor and Welfare (MHLW), Statistics and Information Section, online at http://www.mhlw.go.jp/toukei/saikin/hw/jinkou/suii01/marr2.html (accessed September 17, 2002).

70. Karen Kelsky, "Flirting with the Foreign: Interracial Sex in Japan's 'International' Age," in Rob Wilson and Wimal Dissanayake, eds., *Global-Local: Cultural Production and the Transnational Imaginary* (Durham: Duke University Press, 1996), 173–92; see also her *Women on the Verge.*

71. Nakamae International Economic Research, *Scenarios for the Future of Japan: Research Material* (Tokyo, 1999), 73–83.

72. Nakamae International Economic Research, *Scenarios for the Future of Japan*, 47.

73. METI, *Kyōsōryoku aru tasankaku shakai: 21-seiki keizai sangyō seisaku no bijon* (Tokyo: METI, 2000), 126.

5. The Policy Impact of Hollowing Out

1. Henry Laurence, *Money Rules: The New Politics of Finance in Britain and Japan* (Ithaca: Cornell University Press, 2001), 193.

2. See, for example, Jeffrey A. Winters, *Power in Motion: Capital Mobility and the Indonesian State* (Ithaca: Cornell University Press, 1996); Robert O. Keohane and Helen Milner, *Internationalization and Domestic Politics* (Cambridge: Cambridge University Press, 1996).

3. Even before this date, selected industries (especially coal and textiles) had faced adjustment pressures of the kind described here, but it was only in the 1980s that a broader cross-section of Japanese firms began to face these challenges. For a discussion of how the textile and coal industries dealt with adjustment pressures, see Ronald Dore, *Flexible Rigidities: Industrial Policy and Structural Adjustment in the Japanese Economy, 1970–80* (Stanford: Stanford University Press, 1986); and Robert M. Uriu, *Troubled Industries: Confronting Economic Change in Japan* (Ithaca: Cornell University Press, 1996).

4. Ikuo Kume, *Disparaged Success: Labor Politics in Postwar Japan* (Ithaca: Cornell University Press, 1998), 229–30.

5. Mark Tilton discussed both the cement and steel industries' strategies, along with those of several other impacted industries—all of which supported convoy capitalism rather than seeking to escape from its constraints or reform it. See his book *Restrained Trade: Cartels in Japan's Basic Materials Industries* (Ithaca: Cornell University Press, 1996).

6. Mireya Solis, *Banking on Multinationals: Public Credit and the Export of Japanese Sunset Industries* (Stanford: Stanford University Press, 2004), 148–49.

7. Tilton, *Restrained Trade*, 53. Japanese electricity prices were pushed up faster than those in

other nations by the oil crises because Japanese electricity producers relied on oil for a much larger share of their production. U.S., Canadian, and Latin American producers were able to keep costs lower by using lower-priced hydroelectric power.

8. Tilton, *Restrained Trade*, 52; and Solis, *Banking on Multinationals*, 152.

9. For background on structural adjustment in this industry see Dore, *Flexible Rigidities;* Uriu, *Troubled Industries;* and Dennis McNamara, *Textiles and Industrial Transition in Japan* (Ithaca: Cornell University Press, 1995).

10. Solis, *Banking on Multinationals*, 128.

11. Ministry of Finance, *Zaisei kinyū tōkei geppō*, various issues.

12. Richard Katz, *Japanese Phoenix: The Long Road to Economic Revival* (Armonk, N.Y.: M. E. Sharpe, 2003), 45.

13. Solis, *Banking on Multinationals*, 141.

14. Uriu, in *Troubled Industries*, emphasizes how slowly the Japanese textile industry consolidated during the 1970s and 1980s, but relative to textile industries in other advanced industrialized countries, and especially given the rapid consolidation in the 1990s (after Uriu's data was compiled), the case can fairly be described as relatively speedy structural adjustment.

15. Tilton, *Restrained Trade*, 57.

16. Tilton, *Restrained Trade*, 57–60; Solis, *Banking on Multinationals*, 168–69; and Paul Sheard, "Corporate Organization and Industrial Adjustment in the Japanese Aluminum Industry," in *International Adjustment and the Japanese Firm*, ed. Paul Sheard (St. Leonards, Australia: Allen and Unwin, 1992), 125–39.

17. Solis, *Banking on Multinationals*, 135, focuses on support for these firms' FDI strategies; Dore, *Flexible Rigidities*, looks primarily at the ability of the firms to take advantage of aspects of the Japanese system to consolidate production at home.

18. Uriu, *Troubled Industries*, 47–95.

19. Solis, *Banking on Multinationals*, 136.

20. Ibid., 142.

21. Ministry of Finance, *Zaisei kinyū tōkei geppō*, various issues.

22. Hidetaka Yoshimatsu, "Economic Interdependence and the Making of Trade Policy: Industrial Demand for an Open Market in Japan," *Pacific Review* 11, no. 1 (1998): 34–35.

23. Interview by the author with an executive in strategic planning division of a Japanese electronics firm, December 2002.

24. Walter Hatch and Kozo Yamamura, *Asia in Japan's Embrace: Building a Regional Production Alliance* (Cambridge: Cambridge University Press, 1996), 29.

25. Christina Davis, *Food Fights over Free Trade* (Princeton: Princeton University Press, 2003), 129.

26. Yoshimatsu, "Economic Interdependence," 36.

27. Terutomo Ozawa, "Japan in a New Phase of Multinationalism and Industrial Upgrading: Functional Integration of Trade, Growth, and FDI," *Journal of World Trade* 25 (1991): 51. See also Terutomo Ozawa, *Multinationalism, Japanese Style: The Political Economy of Outward Dependency* (Princeton: Princeton University Press, 1979).

28. Ibid., 60.

29. This "flying geese" theory is discussed critically in Hatch and Yamamura, *Asia in Japan's Embrace*, 27–28.

30. Quoted in Yoshiaki Nakamura and Minoru Shibuya, *The Hollowing Out Phenomenon in the Japanese Industry* (Tokyo: Research Institute of International Trade and Industry, 1995), 11–12.

31. Ibid, 12.

32. MITI, Industrial Policy Bureau, *Action Plan for Economic Structure Reform*, March 1998, 11.

33. Ōki Kazunori, *Sangyō kūdōka ni dō tachimukaunoka* (Tokyo: Shin Nihon Shuppansha, 1996); and Nihon Gakujitsu Kyōryoku Zaidan, *Sangyō kūdōka mondai wo kangaeru* (Tokyo: Nihon Gakujitsu Kyōryoku Zaidan Kokuritsu Insatsu Kyoku, 1995).

34. Nakamura Yoshiaki, "What Are the Issues Surrounding Hollowing Out of Industry?" January 15, 2002—online at http://www.rieti.go.jp/en/columns/a01_0028.html (accessed February 4, 2004).

35. NEC, "Haado disuku sōchi no kaigai seisan kyoten chakkō ni tsuite"—online at http://www.nec.co.jp/press/ja/9807/2001.html (accessed May 19, 2004).

36. Mitsui Chemicals, "Mitsui Chemicals Boosting Overseas PET Bottle Resin Capacity"—online at http://www.mitsui-chem.co.jp/e/new/001113.eb.htm (accessed May 19, 2004).

37. Solis, *Banking on Multinationals*, 178.

38. Interview with Watanabe Kunio, December 16, 2002.

39. David Bailey, "Explaining Japan's *Kūdōka* (Hollowing Out): A Case of Government and Strategic Failure?" *Asia Pacific Business Review* 10, no. 1 (October 2003): 2.

40. Ibid., 4, citing Fukushima H., "Introduction," in Fukushima H., ed., *Changes in Agglomeration Structure of Small and Medium-Sized Enterprises in the Machinery and Metal Industries: A Survey of the Actual State in Ohta Ward, Tokyo* (Tokyo: Nihon University, Research Institute of Economic Science, 2001).

41. Michael Moore, *Roger & Me*, Warner Brothers, 1989; Barry Bluestone and Bennett Harrison, *Deindustrialization of America: Plant Closings, Community Abandonment, and the Dismantling of Basic Industry* (New York: Basic Books, 1982).

42. Rengō, *Seisaku, seido: Yōkyū to teigen, 2004–2005* (Tokyo: Rengō, 2003), 14.

43. Ibid, 31–32.

44. MITI Industrial Policy Bureau, *Action Plan for Economic Structure Reform*.

45. Nakamura, "What Are the Issues Surrounding Hollowing Out of Industry?"

46. Ronald Dore, "Japan's Reform Debate: Patriotic Concern or Class Interest? Or Both?" *Journal of Japanese Studies* 25, no. 1 (Winter 1999): 74.

6. Case Studies in Economic Reform

1. In the Bureau of Labor Statistics study cited here, compensation costs include "pay for time worked, other direct pay (including holiday and vacation pay, bonuses, other direct payments, and the cost of pay in kind), employer expenditures for legally required insurance programs and contractual and private benefit plans, and, for some countries, other labor taxes. . . . The compensation measures are computed in national currency units and are converted into U.S. dollars at prevailing commercial market currency exchange rates. They are appropriate measures for comparing levels of employer labor costs, but they do not indicate relative living standards of workers or the purchasing power of their incomes."

2. *Daily Yomiuri*, November 6, 2001, p. 9.

3. See the discussion of the lifetime employment system in chapter 3.

4. "Distribution of National Income and National Disposable Income (1990–2001)," *Japan Statistical Yearbook 2004*, online at http://www.stat.go.jp/english/data/nenkan/zuhyou/y0310000.xls (accessed June 15, 2004).

5. Interview with Watanabe Kunio, December 16, 2002.

6. *Financial Times*, January 7, 2003, p. 15.

7. Miura Mari, "From Welfare through Work to Lean Work: The Politics of Labor Market Reform in Japan," PhD diss., University of California at Berkeley, 2002, 104.

8. Okuda speech, "Management beyond National Frameworks," for the Nikkei Global Management Forum in Tokyo, October 7, 1999.

9. Miki Shimogori, "Toyota Chief Sounds Alarm on Restructuring Spree," Reuters, May 13, 1999.

10. Miura, "From Welfare through Work to Lean Work," 150–51.

11. The phasing in of later pension eligibility begins with male employees, who will see their eligibility for the basic portion of the pension extended from sixty to sixty-five between 2001 and 2013. Male employees are currently entitled to the earnings-related portion (tier two) at age sixty, but this too is due to be extended in stages between 2013 and 2025. The age at which women can receive the basic pension is being extended to sixty-five in stages between 2006 and 2018. Female employees will see their earnings-related pension age extended to sixty-five in stages between 2018 and 2030.

12. Miura, "From Welfare through Work to Lean Work," 152.

13. Tetsuo Kukawa and Katsuya Yamamoto, "Japanese Employees' Pension Insurance: Issues for Reform," *Japanese Journal of Social Security Policy* 2, no. 1 (June 2003): 9.

14. In 2001, Nikkeiren merged with Keidanren to form a single, united big-business federation known as Nippon Keidanren (Japan Business Federation).

15. Keidanren was involved throughout deliberations on pension policy from 2002 to 2004, and its policy evolved over time in response to positions taken by the MHLW and the LDP. This summary of what business wanted reflects reporting on what Okuda tried to get in negotiations prior to the announcement of the government's policy and his public championing of a consumption tax increase from 5% to 16% to cover social insurance costs after he failed to convince the LDP to reduce pension benefits and premiums in the first round. See *Asahi Shimbun*, January 26, 2004.

16. *Daily Yomiuri*, December 19, 2002, p. 18.

17. *Daily Yomiuri*, January 10, 2003, p. 12.

18. Miura offers a detailed chronology of the policymaking in this case in her dissertation, "From Welfare through Work to Lean Work," 160–71.

19. MITI, *Action Plan for Economic Structure Reform*, March 1998, 9.

20. Economic Strategy Council, *Strategies for Reviving the Japanese Economy*, February 26, 1999, 29–30.

21. Miura, "From Welfare through Work to Lean Work," 200.

22. Ibid, 202–3.

23. Takashi Araki, "Characteristics of Regulations on Dispatched Work (Temporary Work) in Japan," *Japan Labor Bulletin* 33, no. 8 (August 1, 1994).

24. Data shown in figure 6.1.

25. For details, see Miura, "From Welfare through Work to Lean Work," 214–48; Takashi Araki, "1999 Revisions of Employment Security Law and Worker Dispatching Law: Drastic Reforms of Japanese Labor Market Regulations," *Japan Labor Bulletin* 38, no. 9 (September 1, 1999); and Charles Weathers, "Temporary Workers, Women, and Labor Policymaking in Japan" (manuscript, Economics faculty, Osaka City University).

26. Yūji Genda, "Youth Employment and Parasite Singles," *Japan Labor Bulletin* 39, no. 3 (March 1, 2000).

27. Ronald Dore, "Japan's Reform Debate: Patriotic Concern or Class Interest? Or Both?" *Journal of Japanese Studies* 25, no. 1 (Winter 1999): 80.

28. Miura, "From Welfare through Work to Lean Work," 4.

29. 1997 IEA data from *Energy Prices and Taxes* cited in OECD, *The OECD Review of Regulatory Reform in Japan*, 1999, 73.

30. Martha Harris, "Electric Power Restructuring in the UK, United States, and Japan: Markets, Politics, and Public Goods," in *Energy Market Restructuring and the Environment: Governance and Public Goods in Globally Integrated Markets*, ed. Martha Harris (Lanham, Md.: University Press of America), 54.

31. Georg Erdmann, "Transformation in the German Electricity Sector," *IAEE Newsletter*, February 2000.

32. METI, *White Paper on International Trade 2000: Key Points*, May 16, 2000, 51.

33. Electricity purchase figure is for 2001 from METI, "Revised Report on the 2001 Structural Survey of Energy Consumption," 2002, 8; the dollar figure was computed by multiplying this total by the per kilowatt hour figure for Japanese industrial electricity costs (in dollars) reported in IEA, *Key World Energy Statistics*, 2003, 43.

34. OECD, *OECD Review of Regulatory Reform in Japan*, 74.

35. Keidanren, *Sangyō kyōsōryoku kyoka ni muketa teigen*, December 15, 1998, 6.

36. Interview with Kinbara Kazuyuki, deputy director of the International Economic Affairs Bureau of Keidanren, December 10, 2002. His comments echo the diagnosis of Steven Vogel, who has noted that Keidanren as a whole is hamstrung in its ability to advocate reform by its cross-industry structure. See Steven Vogel, "Can Japan Disengage? Winners and Losers in Japan's Political Economy, and the Ties That Bind Them," *Social Science Japan Journal* 2, no. 1 (April 1999): 3–21.

37. Interview with Kawamoto Akira, director of the Electricity Market Division within METI, December 11, 2002.

38. Paul Scalise and Chris Rowland, "Electricity Deregulation in Japan Round 3: METI's Subcommittee Reconvenes," Dresdner Kleinwort Wasserstein Online Research, 17 January 2002, 5.

39. Interview with Kawamoto, December 11, 2002.

40. According to Paul Scalise, the DKW analyst covering the electric industry, Toyota was paying an estimated ¥11.9 per kWh for its electricity, about two yen higher than the ¥9.9 paid on average by industrial users nationwide. Toyota was very interested in seeing a cut in the price it had to pay. E-mail communication dated October 19, 2001.

41. METI, *Dai-33–kai kaigai jigyō katsudō kihon chōsa kekka gaiyō*, March 31, 2004, figure 5.1—available online at http://www.meti.go.jp/statistics/downloadfiles/h2c402fj.pdf (accessed February 11, 2005).

42. Ibid.

43. As long as the utilities were the monopoly supplier, users did not have much bargaining leverage in these negotiations, but firms could negotiate for lower prices based on promises to help utilities deal with high peak demand, pleas of poverty, or reciprocal favors.

44. The energy-intensive sectors were iron and steel, chemicals, ceramics, and pulp/paper. See METI, *Revised Report on the 2001 Structural Survey of Energy Consumption*, 13.

45. METI, *White Paper on International Trade 2000: Key Points*, May 16, 2000, 51.

46. Interview with Kawamoto, December 11, 2002.

47. Ibid.

48. International Energy Agency, *Energy Policies of IEA Countries: Japan 1999 Review* (Paris: OECD/IEA, 1999), 2.

49. For details on these incidents, see International Energy Agency, *Energy Policies of IEA Countries: Japan 2003 Review* (Paris: OECD/IEA, 2003), 105–7.

50. *Economist*, July 17, 2003.

51. *Daily Yomiuri*, March 21, 2001, p. 7.

52. Interview with Kawamoto, December 11, 2002.

53. METI, *Wagakuni denki jigyō wo meguru genjō ni tuite*, 2002.

54. IEA, *Energy Policies of IEA Countries: Japan 2003 Review*, 9, 125.

55. Interview with Kawamoto, December 11, 2002.

56. IEA, *Energy Policies of IEA Countries: Japan 2003 Review*, 139.

57. For a summary of the 2003 changes, see IEA, *Energy Policies of IEA Countries: Japan 2003 Review*, 132–35.

58. Ibid., 123.

59. SourceOECD Revenue Statistics, *Tax Revenue as Percent of GDP—Three Year Moving Average*, vol. 2004, release 01. Note that Britain, which had a government that spent about the same proportion of GDP, took in 37.1% of GDP in revenue that year.

60. International Monetary Fund, *World Economic Outlook*, April 2004, 12. There is a heated debate as to whether *gross* public debt or *net* debt is the more appropriate measure of the precariousness of Japan's public finances. Christian Broda and David E. Weinstein argue that net debt is the more appropriate measure. According to their calculations, Japan's net debt stood at 62% of GDP at the end of 2002, not too different from the level in the United States and other advanced industrialized states—see "Happy News from the Dismal Science: Reassessing Japanese Fiscal Policy and Sustainability," *NBER Working Paper* 10988, December 2004; Robert Madsen argues that many of the debts the Japanese state owes itself, such as the government bonds held by the pension system, require the state to pay interest and cannot be netted away in any real sense since any attempt by the state to renege on its bonds would spark a public outcry. He also argues that the authors overstate the state's assets and ignore hidden liabilities, especially its underfunded public pension liabilities and its liability as a guarantor of last resort for underfunded private pensions, insurance firms, and banks. These considerations, he argues, make it appropriate to use gross public debt as a "crude, ballpark means of estimating Japan's future financial position"—see "What Went Wrong? Aggregate Demand, Structural Reform, and the Politics of 1990s Japan," *MIT Working Paper* 04–01, 65–66.

61. Lonny E. Carlile, "The Politics of Administrative Reform," in *Is Japan Really Changing Its Ways?* ed. Lonnie E. Carlile and Mark C. Tilton (Washington, D.C.: Brookings Institution, 1998), 76–110.

62. Leonard Schoppa, *Bargaining with Japan: What American Pressure Can and Cannot Do* (New York: Columbia University Press, 1997), 122 and 141.

63. Adam Posen, *Restoring Japan's Economic Growth* (Washington, D.C.: Institute for International Economics, 1998).

64. The data for public works spending in figure 6.4 is for the "general government" portion of what the OECD National Accounts refers to as "gross fixed capital formation." The proportions of GDP reported here using this categorization are lower than those cited earlier in the discussion of Dokō's Rinchō campaign because the latter included infrastructure investment by public corporations.

65. Sakakibara Eisuke, "Moving beyond the Public Works State," *Japan Echo* 25, no. 1 (February 1998); Brian Woodall, *Japan under Construction: Corruption, Politics, and Public Works* (Berkeley: University of California Press, 1996); Alex Kerr, *Dogs and Demons: Tales from the Dark Side of Japan* (New York: Hill and Wang, 2001).

66. Posen, *Restoring Japan's Economic Growth*, 118–19.

67. Ibid, 44.

68. *JEI Report* 45B, December 3, 1999.

69. Economic Strategy Council of Japan, *Strategies for Reviving the Japanese Economy*, February 26, 1999, 21–23.

70. Takero Doi and Takeo Hoshi, "Paying for the FILP," National Bureau of Economic Research Working Paper 9385, December 2002, 2.

71. For background on this system, see Thomas F. Cargill and Naoyuki Yoshino, *Postal Savings and Fiscal Investment in Japan* (Oxford: Oxford University Press, 2003); Chalmers Johnson, *Japan's Public Policy Companies* (Washington, D.C.: American Enterprise Institute, 1978); and Kent E. Calder, *Strategic Capitalism* (Princeton: Princeton University Press, 1995).

72. Doi and Hoshi, "Paying for the FILP," 2.

73. Cargill and Yoshino, *Postal Savings and Fiscal Investment in Japan,* 12.

74. Doi and Hoshi, "Paying for the FILP," 4.

75. Ibid, 14.

76. Yoshisuke Iinuma, "Massive Government Debt: The Next Challenge," *Oriental Economist Report* 72, no. 7 (July 2004): 10.

77. Cargill and Yoshino, *Postal Savings and Fiscal Investment in Japan,* 8.

78. Ibid., 150–53.

79. Keidanren, "First Phase Proposal Regarding Reforms of Special-Purpose Corporations and Other Such Entities," March 28, 2000.

80. Edward J. Lincoln, *Arthritic Japan: The Slow Pace of Economic Reform* (Washington, D.C.: Brookings Institute, 2001), 178.

81. Doi and Hoshi, "Paying for the FILP," 17–18.

82. MOF, *FILP Report 2003,* online at http://www.mof.go.jp/zaito/English/Zaito2003.html (accessed July 21, 2004).

83. Doi and Hoshi, "Paying for the FILP"; Masahiro Kikkawa, Takeshi Sakai, and Hiroyuki Miyagawa, "Soundness of the Fiscal Investment and Loan Program," in *Structural Problems of Japanese Financial System,* ed. Mitsuhiro Fukao (Tokyo: Japan Center for Economic Research, 2000).

84. Doi and Hoshi, "Paying for the FILP," 16.

85. Cargill and Yoshino, *Postal Savings and Fiscal Investment in Japan,* 145–46; Patricia Maclachlan, "Post Office Politics in Modern Japan: The Postmasters, Iron Triangles, and the Limits of Reform," *Journal of Japanese Studies* 30, no. 2 (Summer 2004): 281–313.

86. Imai Takashi, "Imakoso nihon keizai no kōzō kaikaku no dankō wo," speech delivered at the conclusion of the sixty-third general meeting of Keidanren, May 25, 2001.

87. Kobayashi Keiichiro, "The Points of Contention Surrounding Postal Services Reform," RIETI Policy Debate, Round 12, online at http://www.rieti.go.jp/en/special/policy-debate/12.html (accessed July 7, 2004).

88. *Financial Times,* July 4, 2002, p. 9; Maclachlan, "Post Office Politics," 310.

89. *Japan Times,* March 5, 2005.

90. Richard Katz, *Japanese Phoenix: The Long Road to Economic Revival* (Armonk, N.Y.: M. E. Sharpe, 2003), 271–72.

91. The ¥100 trillion figure was cited as an estimate of total bad loans by a wide variety of analysts in the late 1990s but was much higher than was ever reported by the banks themselves or official bank regulators in Japan. See Richard Katz, *Japanese Phoenix,* 82–86.

92. Ryoichi Mikitani, "The Facts of the Japanese Financial Crisis," in *Japan's Financial Crisis and Its Parallels to U.S. Experience,* ed. Ryoichi Mikitani and Adam S. Posen (Washington, D.C.: Institute for International Economics, 2000), 32.

93. Financial Services Agency data cited in Katz, *Japanese Phoenix,* 87.

94. Katz, *Japanese Phoenix,* 86.

95. Peter Hatcher, *The Ministry: How Japan's Most Powerful Institution Endangers World Markets* (Boston: Harvard Business School Press, 1998), 130.

96. Jennifer Amyx, *Japan's Financial Crisis: Institutional Rigidity and Reluctant Change* (Princeton: Princeton University Press, 2004), 165.

97. Ibid, 168–69.

98. See the lecture by Keidanren chairman Shōichirō Toyoda, of Toyota, on December 1, 1995, titled "The Japanese Economy and Europe-Japan Relations"—online at http://www.keidanren.or.jp/english/speech/spe006.htm (accessed July 26, 2004).

99. Keidanren, "Toward Stabilizing Financial Systems," July 23, 1998—online at http://www.keidanren.or.jp/english/policy/pol081.html (accessed July 26, 2004).

100. Amyx, *Japan's Financial Crisis,* 218.

101. The financial regulatory structure changed several times during this period. Much of the work done by the Financial *Services* Agency after the most recent reorganization in 2001 was done earlier by the Financial *Supervisory* Agency. Both were known by the acronym FSA. See Amyx, *Japan's Financial Crisis,* for background, especially 231.

102. Katz, *Japanese Phoenix,* 96–98; Lincoln, *Arthritic Japan,* 180.

103. Okuda Hiroshi press conference, October 7, 2002—online at http://www.keidanren.or.jp/english/speech/press/2002/1007.html (accessed July 27, 2004).

104. Richard Katz, "Coming Up Short: PM Koizumi Goes AWOL on Takenaka, Bank Reform," *Oriental Economist Report* 70, no. 11 (November 2002): 1–3.

105. FSA, "The Status of Non-Performing Loans as of end-March 2004," July 30, 2004, table 2, online at http://www.fsa.go.jp/refer/refer.html (accessed March 16, 2005).

7. The Policy Impact of Exit by Women

1. Shimomura Mitsuko quoted by Peggy Orenstein, "Parasites in Pret-a-Porter," *New York Times Magazine,* July 1, 2001, 35.

2. See endnote 54 in chapter 4.

3. NIPSSR, *Population Projections for Japan, 2001–2050* (Tokyo: NIPSSR, 2002), 6.

4. The NIPSSR predicts the working-age population of Japan will fall from 86.4 million in 2000 to 57.8 million by 2044 and to 43.2 million in 2072.

5. The year of the fire-horse arrives once every sixty years—see Chizuko Ueno, "The Declining Birthrate: Whose Problem?" *Review of Population and Social Policy* 7 (1998): 103.

6. Quoted by Suzuki Kazue, "Women Rebuff the Call for More Babies," *Japan Quarterly* 42, no. 1 (January–March 1995): 14.

7. Ueno, "Declining Birthrate," 106 and 115.

8. Quoted in Suzuki, "Women Rebuff the Call for More Babies," 16.

9. Interviews with MHLW officials, April and May 2001.

10. Interview with Asada Chihoko, May 9, 2001.

11. Interview with Kamohara Motomichi, May 10, 2001.

12. Jinkō Mondai Shingikai, "Shōshika ni kan suru kihonteki kangaekata ni tsuite," October 1997, http://www1.mhlw.go.jp/shingi/s1027-1.html (accessed April 19, 2001); and MHW, *Kōsei hakusho—Heisei 10–nen-han: Shōshi shakai wo kangaeru,* 1998. These two reports are discussed below in the section on childcare services and the Angel Plans.

13. Yamada Masahiro, *Parasaito shinguru no jidai* (Tokyo: Chikuma Shinsho, 1999).

14. Interview with Yashiro, December 20, 2002.

15. See detailed discussion below.

16. This claim is based on the author's conversations, over a period of several years in the 1990s, with officials in six ministries about their personal work and family situations and the situations of their colleagues. These officials were not randomly selected and number only thirty. No official statistics on the family and work status of bureaucrats are maintained by the government, and I have not been able to locate a survey of government officials on this topic.

17. Interview with MHLW official, May 10, 2001.

18. On the origins of these two strands of the women's movement in the 1950s, see Sandra Buckley, "A Short History of the Feminist Movement in Japan," in *Women of Japan and Korea: Continuity and Change,* ed. Joyce Gelb and Marian Leaf Palley (Philadelphia: Temple University Press, 1994), 153–55.

19. See Patricia Maclachlan, *Consumer Politics in Postwar Japan* (New York: Columbia University Press, 2002).

20. Robin M. LeBlanc, *Bicycle Citizens: The Political World of the Japanese Housewife* (Berkeley: University of California Press, 1999), 121–63.

21. Chizuko Ueno, "Women and the Family in Transition in Postindustrial Japan," in *Women of Japan and Korea,* ed. Gelb and Palley, 30–31.

22. Ueno, in an interview conducted by Sandra Buckley, quoted in her book *Broken Silence* (Berkeley: University of California Press, 1996), 276–77.

23. For a critique of the EEOL along these lines, see Mari Ōsawa, "Twelve Million Full-time Housewives: The Gender Consequences of Japan's Postwar Social Contract," in *Social Contracts under Stress,* ed. Olivier Zunz, Leonard Schoppa, and Nobuhiro Hiwatari (New York: Russell Sage, 2002), 255–77.

24. Frank K. Upham, *Law and Social Change in Japan* (Cambridge: Harvard University Press, 1987), 149.

25. Ueno writes: "The sole survivors on the career track, the women middle managers who are promoted, have no family responsibilities. Some are single and some get help from their mothers or their mothers-in-law."—in Ueno, "Women and the Family in Transition in Postindustrial Japan," 37. Ministry of Labor data confirms that a disproportionate share of women in the workforce live in three-generation households where grandmothers are available to help with childcare: 41.4% of mothers of young children in these types of households work, whereas just 25.2% of those in nuclear families work—data cited in Ito Peng, "Social Care in Crisis: Gender, Demography, and Welfare State Restructuring in Japan," *Social Politics* (Fall 2002): 418.

26. For example, Higuchi Keiko, who was a leading force behind the campaign for long-term care insurance in Japan; and Kawamoto Yūko, a mother of two boys who has maintained a career as a McKinsey and Company consultant and member of government advisory panels, featured on the cover of *Aera,* April 5, 2004.

27. The movement of that period was most vividly exemplified by the activism of the Pink Helmet Brigade (Chūpiren). See Buckley, "Short History of the Feminist Movement in Japan," 170–71.

28. Ueno, in interview with Sandra Buckley, *Broken Silence,* 284.

29. Data from the Akarui Senkyo Suishin Kyōkai, cited by Gill Steel, "Gender and Political Behaviour in Japan," *Social Science Japan Journal* 7, no. 2 (October 2004): 229; and by Sherry Martin, "Alienated, Independent, and Female: Lessons from the Japanese Electorate," *Social Science Japan Journal* 7, no. 1 (April 2004): 9.

30. Peng, "Social Care in Crisis," 424.

31. Yumiko Mikanagi, "Japan's Gender-Biased Social Security Policy," *Japan Forum* 10, no. 2 (1998): 192.

32. Nakamae International Economic Research, *Scenarios for the Future of Japan: Research Material* (Tokyo: Nakamae International Economic Research, 1999), 46.

33. Interview with Kamohara, May 10, 2001.

34. Ibid.

35. Takahashi Sakutarō, *Shōsetsu ikuji kyūgyōra ni kansuru hōritsu* (Tokyo: Rōmu Gyōsei Kenkyūjo, 1991). Takahashi was the MOL bureau chief who managed the drafting and passage of the legislation.

36. Interview with Kumagai Takeshi, the director of the MHLW Work and Family Division, May 10, 2001.

37. Interview with Kumagai.

38. Katsura Maruyama, "The Cost Sharing of Child and Family Care Leave," *Review of Population and Social Policy* 8 (1999): 55.

39. Interview with Kumagai.

40. Takahashi, *Shōsetsu ikuji kyūgyōra ni kansuru hōritsu.*

41. Maruyama, "Cost Sharing of Child and Family Care Leave," 56–57; also interview with Kumagai.

42. Parents on leave were also exempted under the new program from having to pay health insurance and pension premiums during the period they were on leave.

43. Ministry of Internal Affairs and Communications, Statistics Bureau, "Rōdōryoku chōsa tokubetsu chōsa," 2001.

44. MIAC, Statistics Bureau, "Shūgyōkōzō kihon chōsa," 2001.

45. Information in this section based on interview with MOL official Kumagai.

46. The calculation came down to the following: the 40% leave pay plus the 13% benefit premium new parents on leave did not have to pay brought their total benefits to 53%, which was safely below the 60% salary replacement provided to the "real unemployed."

47. Maeda Masako, "Shōshika no naka no shakai hoshō seido," *Sekai* 659 (March 1999): 88; Takahashi Yuri and Yoshida Masayuki, "Kaisha wa ikuji wo wakarō to shinai," *Shūkan tōyō keizai*, October 23, 1999, 94–96.

48. MHLW data cited in interview with Ishikawa Kenji, December 12, 2002. On men's attitudes toward taking leave, see Takashi Koyama, "Men Wary of Taking Leave for Childcare," *Daily Yomiuri*, May 26, 2000; and J. Sean Curtin, "The Declining Birthrate in Japan: Part I—Numerical Targets for Childcare Leave," Glocom Platform website http://www.glocom.org/special_topics/social_trends/20021118_trends_s17/ (accessed July 22, 2003).

49. Ryūichi Yamakawa, "Recent Developments Regarding Child and Elder Care Leave in Japan," *Japan Labor Bulletin* 33, no. 1 (October 1, 1994).

50. Interview with Ishikawa Kenji, December 12, 2002. The MHLW report presenting the Plus One Plan pictured a layered birthday cake, with the most recent plan standing atop two layers representing the earlier Angel Plans.

51. The MHLW drew up guidelines along the lines summarized here, required large employers to set leave take-up rate targets, and required them to meet these targets within two to five years, but the legislation gave the ministry no enforcement powers, making the entire enterprise essentially voluntary—see *Japan Labor Bulletin* 42, no. 8 (August 1, 2003), p. 5.

52. Japan Institute of Labor, *The Japan Labor Flash* (e-mail journal) No. 26 (November 1, 2004), online at http://www.jil.go.jp/foreign/emm/bi/26.htm (accessed February 21, 2005).

53. Toyota's own translation of the group name is "Diversity Group"—interview with Katō Yoshirō, December 9, 2002.

54. For an analysis of the choice of name, see Glenda S. Roberts, "Pinning Hopes on Angels: Reflections from an Aging Japan's Urban Landscape," in *Family and Social Policy in Japan: Anthropological Approaches*, ed. Roger Goodman (Cambridge: Cambridge University Press, 2002), 57.

55. Margarita Estevez-Abe, "Multiple Logics of the Welfare State: Skills, Protection, and Female Labor in Japan and Selected OECD Countries," *U.S.-Japan Program Occasional Paper* 99–02 (1999), 32–33.

56. Patricia Boling, "Family Policy in Japan," *Journal of Social Policy* 27, no. 2 (1998): 176.

57. MHW, *Annual Report on Health and Welfare, 1998–1999* (Tokyo: Japan International Corporation of Welfare Services, 1998), 437.

58. Interview with MHLW official Kamohara Motomichi, May 10, 2001.

59. A number of analysts have observed that the two needs mentioned here, childcare and eldercare, have been in direct competition for funds, particularly at the local level, with childcare losing out. This result reflects localities' obligation to contribute a significant portion of funds to the building and operation of both types of centers and localities' *obligation* under the Long-term Care Insurance program to provide eldercare services to all those in need. Parents were not able to secure a similar guarantee for their services, and so they lost out. See Maeda, "Shōshika no naka no shakai hoshō seido," 88.

60. The problem is concentrated in urban areas. In 2000, 83% percent of centers had no waiting lists. At the same time, however, twenty thousand children were waiting for spots to come open in the urban prefectures of Saitama, Tokyo, Kanagawa, Osaka, and Hyōgo—MHW, *Hoiku saabisu no jukyū—tokki no jōkyō,* April 1, 2000, 5.

61. These figures are based on data from the *Hoiku hakusho* (Childcare White Paper) for the number of children served on November 1, 1989, and October 1, 2000. The ratios were calculated by using census records for live births in the preceding years for the denominator. The last age group was defined as 4 to 6.5 because the cutoff date for elementary school is April 1, meaning half of the six-year-olds were still too young for elementary school and eligible for childcare instead.

62. MHW, *Hoiku saabisu no jukyū—tokki no jōkyō,* April 1, 2000, 1. The data show that two-thirds of those on waiting lists in 2000 were two or younger (4).

63. *Japan Labor Bulletin,* February 1, 2003, 5.

64. Baby hotels have a tarnished reputation because a number of infants have died there. Unlike the United States, where cheap home-based daycare is widely available, baby-sitting services in Japan are very costly, with many charging over $150 a day—Roberts, "Pinning Hopes on Angels," 58.

65. Jinkō Mondai Shingikai, *Shōshika ni kansuru kihonteki kangaekata ni tsuite,* October 1997.

66. Mukuno is quoted in Kabashima Hideyoshi, "Seifu wa musaku dattanoka," *Chūō kōron* 115, no. 13 (December 2000): 99.

67. MHW, Children and Families Bureau, *Shōshika taisaku suishin kihon hōshin to shin enzeru puran,* 1999, 20.

68. This section draws heavily on Takashi Araki, "Recent Legislative Developments in Equal Employment and Harmonization of Work and Family Life in Japan," *Japan Labor Bulletin* 37, no. 4 (April 1998).

69. Law Concerning the Welfare of Workers Who Take Care of Children or Other Family Members Including Childcare and Family Care Leave—referred to in short as the Childcare and Family Care Leave Law.

70. Hamada Fujio, "Kaisei danjo koyō kintō hō no kadai," *Nihon rōdō kinkyū zasshi* 27 (1997).

71. Firms are prohibited from requiring voluntary overtime and have been forced to pay back wages when their practices have been challenged, but a recent survey by the Japanese trade union confederation (Rengō) suggests that enforcement is clearly inadequate. Its survey revealed that half of all workers put in voluntary overtime, with the average unpaid hours coming to thirty hours a month—*Japan Labor Bulletin,* February 1, 2003, 2.

72. *Japan Labor Bulletin,* December 1, 2002, 6.

73. *Japan Labor Bulletin,* January 1, 2002, 2.

74. DPJ, "Policies for the 19th House of Councilors Elections: A Fair Deal for All," April 17, 2001—online at http://www.dpj.or.jp/english/policy/19hc-elec.html (accessed October 10, 2001).

75. Cited in Howard French, "Japan's Neglected Resource: Female Workers," *New York Times,* July 25, 2003, p. 3.

76. Interview with Ishikawa Kenji, December 12, 2002.

77. MHLW, *Josei rōdō hakusho—Heisei 14–nen-han*, 2002, 5.

78. See chapter 3 for background on the program.

79. Interview with Kamohara, May 10, 2001.

80. *Yomiuri Shimbun*, December 20, 2000.

81. The extension of the child allowance from those under three to those under elementary school age and the expansion of coverage from the bottom 60% to the bottom 72% (both agreed to in December 1999) was funded entirely by shrinking the tax exemption for children under sixteen. Similarly, the slight expansion in the program to cover the bottom 85% of income earners, in the reform agreed to in December 2000, was funded by shrinking other MHLW programs, most of them for children—see *Yomiuri Shimbun*, December 20, 2000.

82. Sechiyama Kaku, "Shifting Family Support from Wives to Children," *Japan Echo* 28, no. 1 (February 2001): 35–42.

83. Interview with Ōsawa Mari, December 17, 2002.

84. Before this reform, all dependent spouses were entitled to deduct ¥380,000 ($3,166) from the family's taxable income under a "basic dependent spouse" deduction. In addition, dependent spouses from families below an income ceiling of ¥10 million were allowed to deduct up to ¥380,000 more (with the exact amount depending on the dependent spouse's income) under a "special dependent spouse" deduction. It was this second deduction that was eliminated—see *Asahi Shimbun*, December 11, 2002, for background.

8. Exceptions That Prove the Rule

1. Henry Laurence, *Money Rules: The New Politics of Finance in Britain and Japan* (Ithaca: Cornell University Press, 2001).

2. The MHLW estimates that three million are eligible for benefits. All figures come from Ministry of Health, Labor and Welfare. *Long-term Care Insurance in Japan*, July 2002—online at http://www.mhlw.go.jp/english/topics/elderly/care/ (accessed July 10, 2003).

3. John C. Campbell and Naoki Ikegami, "Long-term Care Insurance Comes to Japan," *Health Affairs* 19, no. 3 (2000): 27.

4. John C. Campbell, "How Policies Differ: Long-Term Care Insurance in Japan and Germany," in *Aging and Social Policy—A German-Japanese Comparison*, ed. Harald Conrad and Ralph Lutzeler (Munich: Iudicium, 2002), 157–88.

5. Campbell and Ikegami, "Long-term Care Insurance Comes to Japan," 37.

6. A survey of those providing care to the frail elderly in Tokyo found that 19% were men—Margaret Lock, "Ideology, Female Midlife, and the Greying of Japan," *Journal of Japanese Studies* 19, no. 1 (Winter 1993): 53. Another survey of caregivers in Shiga found that 14% were men—Susan Orpett Long, "Nurturing and Femininity: The Ideal of Caregiving in Postwar Japan," in *Re-Imaging Japanese Women*, ed. Anne E. Imamura (Berkeley: University of California Press, 1996), 167.

7. Campbell, "How Policies Differ," 181.

8. The fifty to seventy-year-olds caring for aging relatives tend to come from large families, which means that with daughters-in-law taking primary responsibility, daughters frequently avoid having to care for their own parents, as do the women married to the second and third sons. The generation that will care for the baby boomers, however, will be from much smaller families, increasing the likelihood that one woman will face the burden of caring not only for her in-laws but also her own parents.

9. For a discussion of the social and psychological pressures facing women caring for elderly relatives, see Long, 167–70.

10. Mikiko Etō, "Public Involvement in Social Policy Reform: Seen from the Perspective of Japan's Elderly-Care Insurance Scheme," *Journal of Social Policy* 1 (2001): 20.

11. Ibid., 20–21: Ito Peng, "Social Care in Crisis: Gender, Demography, and Welfare State Restructuring in Japan," *Social Politics* (Fall 2002): 420.

12. Mikiko Etō, "Women's Leverage on Social Policymaking in Japan," *PS: Political Science and Politics* 34, no. 2 (June 2001): 244; Peng, "Social Care in Crisis," 423.

13. Ibid., 242.

14. Ibid., 244.

15. Campbell, "How Policies Differ," 182.

16. Etō, "Public Involvement in Social Policy Reform," 26–27; Peng, "Social Care in Crisis," 424.

17. The cartels operated freely because the financial services sector was exempted from the antimonopoly law's anticartel provisions. See Frances Rosenbluth, *Financial Politics in Contemporary Japan* (Ithaca: Cornell University Press, 1989), 38–42.

18. For background on how the prereform system worked against the interests of financial service customers, see Laurence, *Money Rules*, 106–17.

19. MITI Industrial Policy Bureau, *Action Plan for Economic Structure Reform*, March 1998, 4.

20. Laurence, *Money Rules*, 123.

21. Ibid., 135.

22. Ibid., 132 and 135.

23. Steven Vogel, *Freer Markets, More Rules: Regulatory Reform in Advanced Industrial Countries* (Ithaca: Cornell University Press, 1996), 192.

24. Ibid., 126–28.

25. Second Financial System Subcommittee of the Financial System Research Council, *On a New Japanese Financial System*, Interim Report, May 1989, cited by Laurence in *Money Rules*, 128.

26. Vogel, *Freer Markets, More Rules*, 179.

27. Laurence, *Money Rules*, 132.

28. Rosenbluth, *Financial Politics in Contemporary Japan*, 81.

29. Vogel, *Freer Markets, More Rules*, 184; Laurence, *Money Rules*, 139.

30. Laurence, *Money Rules*, 179–80.

31. Ibid., 180.

32. MOF official Ariyoshi Akira, quoted in Laurence, *Money Rules*, 180.

33. For details on what the big bang entailed, see Ernest T. Patrikis, "Japan's Big Bang Financial Reforms," *Brooklyn Journal of International Law* 24, no. 2 (1998): 577–92; and Edward Lincoln, *Arthritic Japan: The Slow Pace of Economic Reform* (Washington, D.C.: Brookings Institution, 2001), 160–64.

34. Akio Mikuni and R. Taggart Murphy, *Japan's Policy Trap: Dollars, Deflation, and the Crisis of Japanese Finance* (Washington, D.C.: Brookings Institution, 2002), 207–13.

35. Ibid.; Lincoln, *Arthritic Japan*, 162.

36. For a discussion of banks' adjustment problems, see Anil K. Kashyap, "Sorting Out Japan's Financial Crisis," *National Bureau of Economic Research Working Paper* 9384 (December 2002), 3–6.

37. Laurence, *Money Rules*, 124.

38. I am not claiming that no other Japanese sectors have seen meaningful liberalization. Telecommunications is another area where the last several years have seen real erosion in the dom-

inance of Nippon Telegraph and Telephone and the ability of this firm to protect and nurture suppliers. Whereas its long-distance telephone charges and Internet access costs were once among the highest in the industrialized world, regulatory actions that facilitated access to the NTT's "last-mile" network by upstart rivals such as Softbank have led to real competition in all telecom service markets, precipitating sharp reductions in all of these costs. By 2003, broadband access to the Internet was cheaper in Japan than in the United States. One reason I did not add a case study of this sector is because I was struck by the distinctive role played by foreign pressure (*gaiatsu*) in accelerating change in this sector. As I have argued elsewhere, foreign pressure can make it easier for domestic political actors who favor change to win internal political debates in Japan—see Leonard Schoppa, *Bargaining with Japan: What American Pressure Can and Cannot Do* (New York: Columbia University Press, 1997). Foreign pressure was also a factor in the debates over electricity liberalization, bank reform, and financial liberalization, but because it was a factor across reform and limited reform cases, I do not believe it played a systematic role in shaping the pattern of outcomes surveyed here. Had I considered the telecom case, it could easily have bolstered the book's argument on exit dynamics. One reason the government felt pressure to allow Softbank to gain access to NTT's last mile was because broadband customers and Internet start-up firms, frustrated by Japan's high Internet access charges and their inability to find a way around this barrier (you couldn't get to the Internet without some cooperation from NTT), mobilized in the political arena. Internet entrepreneurs lobbied METI officials and Internet users organized online petition drives.

9. Toward a New System of Social Protection in Japan

1. Fred Bergsten and Adam Posen of the Institute for International Economics are on record with the view that "Japanese potential output has risen to 2.5% per year, on the basis of the reforms and restructuring accomplished to date, and could rise even further if liberalization continues"—see C. Fred Bergsten, "The Resurgent Japanese Economy and a Japan–United States Free Trade Agreement," paper presented to the Foreign Correspondents Club of Japan, May 12, 2004.

2. Richard Katz, *Japanese Phoenix: The Long Road to Economic Revival* (Armonk, N.Y.: M. E. Sharpe, 2003); Edward Lincoln, *Arthritic Japan: The Slow Pace of Economic Reform* (Washington, D.C.: Brookings Institution, 2001); Akio Mikuni and R. Taggart Murphy, *Japan's Policy Trap: Dollars, Deflation, and the Crisis of Japanese Finance* (Washington, D.C.: Brookings Institution, 2002).

3. Data for GDP growth during calendar year 2004, reported by the Cabinet Office online at http://www.esri.cao.go.jp/jp/sna/qe051-2/rnen.html (accessed June 21, 2005).

4. The government estimated that the economy shrank by 0.2% in the second quarter and another 0.2% in the third quarter before managing positive growth of 0.1% in the fourth quarter—Cabinet Office data reported online at http://www.esri.cao.go.jp/jp/sna/qe051-2/rshihanki .html (accessed June 21, 2005).

5. The six were IBM, Texas Instruments, AT&T, Hewlett-Packard, Honeywell, and Motorola. Data from Yasunobe Shin, "Top 30 Firms in Japan and the United States," PowerPoint slide from Stanford University presentation, December 2002.

6. The pattern for Japanese firms in general is similar to that of the top thirty. Japanese firms had an average annual turnover rate of 6% during the 1990s, much lower than the OECD average of 20%. See Katz, *Japanese Phoenix*, 223.

7. OECD, *OECD Economic Outlook* (Paris: OECD, 2001).

8. Katz, *Japanese Phoenix*, 223–27. Robert Madsen makes a similar point in his "What Went

Wrong? Aggregate Demand, Structural Reform, and the Politics of 1990s Japan," *MIT Working Paper* 04–01 (2004).

9. "Reform Not Yet Lifting Potential Growth," *Oriental Economist Report*, January 2005, 9.

10. Employment statistics are from the *Japan Statistical Yearbook 2005*—online at http://www.stat.go.jp/data/nenkan/zuhyou/y1601000.xls (accessed January 11, 2005).

11. The number of firms declaring bankruptcy in 2003 and 2004 were 16,624 and 13, 837, respectively—Teikoku Databank figures reported online at http://www.tdb.co.jp/english/news_reports/backnumber2004.html (accessed June 21, 2005).

12. National Police Agency figures reported in "Suicides Top 30,000 for Seventh Year," *Daily Yomiuri*, June 3, 2005, p. 1.

13. Richard Katz, *Japan—The System That Soured: The Rise and Fall of the Japanese Economic Miracle* (Armonk, N.Y.: M. E. Sharpe, 1999), 222–23.

14. See Madsen, "What Went Wrong?" 45–48.

15. Richard Katz employs this metaphor in "Japan's Phoenix Economy," *Foreign Affairs* 82, no. 1 (January–February 2003).

16. The IMF pegged Japan's gross public debt in 2003 at 166% of GDP—*World Economic Outlook*, April 2004, 12. The Economist Intelligence Unit estimated that this figure would grow to 208% by 2008—see Madsen, "What Went Wrong?" 66–67.

17. The summary of the literature here emphasizes the work of political scientists, but economists too have been quick to blame "politics" for Japan's economic difficulties. See, in particular, Katz, *Japanese Phoenix*, and Lincoln, *Arthritic Japan*.

18. J. Mark Ramseyer and Frances M. Rosenbluth, *Japan's Political Marketplace* (Cambridge: Harvard University Press, 1993), 16–37; Brian Woodall, *Japan under Construction: Corruption, Politics, and Public Works* (Berkeley: University of California Press, 1996), 103–23; Kent E. Calder, *Crisis and Compensation: Public Policy and Political Stability in Japan, 1949–1986* (Princeton: Princeton University Press, 1988), 61–66.

19. Lincoln, *Arthritic Japan*, 97.

20. Steven Vogel, "Can Japan Disengage? Winners and Losers in Japan's Political Economy, and the Ties That Bind Them," *Social Science Japan Journal* 2, no. 1 (April 1999): 3–21; and Steven Vogel, "When Interests Are Not Preferences: The Cautionary Tale of Japanese Consumers," *Comparative Politics* 31, no. 2 (January 1999): 187–207.

21. Susan Pharr, *Losing Face: Status Politics in Japan* (Berkeley: University of California Press, 1990); Frank Upham, *Law and Social Change in Postwar Japan* (Cambridge: Harvard University Press, 1987), 124–65; Mikanagi Yumiko, *Josei to Seiji* (Tokyo: Shinhyōron, 1999).

22. T. J. Pempel, *Regime Shift: Comparative Dynamics of the Japanese Political Economy* (Ithaca: Cornell University Press, 1998).

23. Henry Laurence, *Money Rules: The New Politics of Finance in Britain and Japan* (Ithaca: Cornell University Press, 2001).

24. Yves Tiberghien, *Global Capital Flows and the Erosion of the Social Contract: The Politics of Corporate Restructuring in Japan, France, and South Korea* (forthcoming).

25. This is essentially the conclusion of METI's recent studies of the economy, including *Kyōsōryoku aru tasankaku shakai* (Tokyo: Tsūshō Sangyō Chōsakai, 2000). See also Michael Smitka, "Japanese Macroeconomic Dilemmas: The Implications of Demographics for Growth and Stability," paper presented to the Japan Economic Seminar in Washington, D.C., April 8, 2004.

26. NIPSSR, *Population Projections for Japan: 2001–2050 (with Long-Range Population Projections for 2051–2100)*, January 2002.

27. Ministry of Finance officials have insisted that a public debt crisis is impossible to imagine

in Japan because almost all of this debt is held by Japanese citizens. Because Japanese holders of debt instruments know their money will have to be in yen in order for them to spend it, the theory goes, they won't convert their yen into foreign currencies at the first sign of inflation. If Japan can run a moderate inflation rate that is slightly above the interest rate the government is paying on its debt (some of which is locked in at low rates for ten to twenty years) the government should be able to reduce the real size of its debt without having to default. The problem with this theory is that it assumes Japanese will watch complacently while their savings are eroded by inflation when they have exit options. They can buy gold. They don't even have to wire their money overseas to convert it into dollars, much less load it in suitcases, since Japan-based banks offer dollar savings accounts that earn dollar interest rates. They might decide to convert their money into dollars and retire in Hawaii or Australia. While the government might try to stop Japanese from fleeing to foreign currencies by imposing capital controls, the mere possibility that this might happen is likely to provoke the kind of stampede Japanese officials argue is impossible to imagine.

28. For an analysis of the financial circumstances of households in which single adult children live with their parents, see NIPSSR, *Setainai tanshinsha ni kansuru jittai chōsa,* 2001.

29. *Asahi Shimbun* exit poll data—online at http://www2.asahi.com/2004senkyo/topics/deguchi_04.html (accessed July 19, 2004).

30. Gerald L. Curtis, *The Logic of Japanese Politics: Leaders, Institutions, and the Limits of Change* (New York: Columbia University Press, 1999), 194; Leonard Schoppa, "Neoliberal Economic Policy Preferences of the 'New Left': Home-Grown or Anglo-American Import?" in *The Left in the Shaping of Japanese Democracy: Studies in Honour of J. A. A. Stockwin,* ed. Rikki Kersten and David Williams (London: Routledge, 2005).

Index